Movie Comedians

To my beloved wife Diana;
the one who believes,
the one who cares . . .

To my brother John;
who insists that he "saw 'em all" . . .

and to Jesus Christ;
without whom . . .

Movie Comedians

The Complete Guide

by

James L. Neibaur

McFarland & Company, Inc., Publishers
Jefferson, North Carolina, and London

Library of Congress Cataloging-in-Publication Data

Neibaur, James L., 1958–
  Movie comedians.

  Bibliography: p.
  Includes filmographies and index.
  1. Moving-picture actors and actresses—Biography.
2. Comedians—Biography. 3. Comedy films—History and
criticism. 4. Comedy films—Catalogs. I. Title.
PN1998.A2N45 1986   791.43′028′0922 [B]   84-43204

ISBN 0-89950-163-X (acid-free natural paper) ∞

Printed in the United States of America.

McFarland Box 611 Jefferson NC 28640

Acknowledgments

I'd like to express my deepest appreciation to the following special people who were kind enough to help me in the preparation and construction of this book.

For granting me interviews: Morey Amsterdam, Edward Bernds, Joe Besser, Gabriel Dell, George "Spanky" McFarland, Emil Sitka, and the late Buster Crabbe, Clyde Cook, Phil Silvers, and Jules White.

For providing me with much-needed photographs: Ron Antrim, Joe Besser, Steve Cox, Ted Ewing, Donald Key, Greg Lenburg, Gary L. Schneeberger, Emil Sitka, Joe Stabile, and Pat Triggiano; *The Big Reel*, Blackhawk Films, and Jerry Lewis Productions; and a special nod to the studios who produced the films from which these stills came, Columbia Pictures, MGM, Paramount Pictures, RKO, Hal Roach Studios, Mack Sennett Studios, United Artists, Universal, Warner Brothers, and Monogram/Allied Artists.

For allowing me to borrow freely from their film and video tape libraries: Bruce D. Bennett, Frank Cairo, Don Kapla, Mike Mahnke, Steve Morelli, John Neibaur, Ted Okuda, Henry "Hank" Trudrung, Brian Weiher.

And finally, my thanks to those who helped in other significant ways: Peter Jackel, Ron G. Penzkowski, Bob Quinty, David Shepard, David Schultheiss, University of Wisconsin–Parkside, *Variety*, my wife and my family.

The following ratings are used in the filmographies

*****	Superlative
****	Excellent
***	Worthwhile
**	Average
*	Weak
°	Dreadful

Table of Contents

Introduction

Is there anyone in popular culture more beloved than a comedian? No other film genre — be it western, melodrama, musical, or horror film — is as well loved as comedy. And the comedians who make those films worth loving are thought of as cult heroes, great artists, even role models.

Comedy has developed in motion pictures into an art form which has the power to help us forget about our troubles, even if only for a short time, and escape into a fantasy world of humor created by the almighty movie comedian.

Movie comedians have evolved from the turn of the century onward into major creators of joy, happiness, expressions of human merriment.

We cannot define screen comedy, for the genre is too new and experiments are forever being conducted to find something innovative. But the importance and popularity of screen comedy warrant a book on those who helped shape it into the essential part of world culture it has already become. The individuals whose profound creative brilliance in discovering and developing various ways of making people laugh deserve to be acknowledged for their contributions.

John Bunny, the first movie comedian, found as far back as the turn of the century that an individual's embarrassment when caught in an uncomfortable situation would make audiences laugh. Because the audience could relate the situation to some problem in their past, they were actually laughing at themselves. This basic thesis was pushed even further by the Mack Sennett studios when physical discomfort or slapstick proved to be a very valid form of comedy.

Charlie Chaplin made profound advances in screen comedy when he transformed the clown from faceless buffoon to a substantial person with a heart and soul — one whose cleverness we laughed at and whose situation we sympathized with. Chaplin taught us to love the comedian.

Buster Keaton found humor in man's relationship with inanimate objects, personifying implements which seemed to outsmart the individual. Harold Lloyd gave underdogs a never-say-die attitude, teaching, through humor, that if you do your best and never give up you'll eventually succeed.

Laurel and Hardy found humor within human relationships. The Marx Brothers brought a humor of teasing to the screen, taken one step further by W.C. Fields, who made groundbreaking discoveries in the humor of human inadequacies and stereotypes without being downright cruel.

Comedians must rely on skills as well as creativity. While not creative

1

filmmakers like their celluloid predecessors, Abbott and Costello deserve recognition for their impeccable timing and delivery in executing the immortal "Who's on First" routine, as well as several other burlesque sketches which may have been lost forever if Bud and Lou hadn't preserved them on film.

Screen comedy was at its creative peak in the twenties and thirties when the most innovative of clowns flourished, but the forties saw a wave of brash personalities invading the star ranks of movie comedians. And when television seemed to spell the end of the movie comedian in the fifties and sixties, Jerry Lewis came along to show us that the genre was still alive and capable of creativity.

Experiments within the movie industry got so out of hand during the sixties that even Lewis left motion pictures in 1970, not to return for another decade, but his departure left the field open for the innovative Woody Allen and satirical Mel Brooks comedies.

By 1980, many new styles and techniques in screen comedy had developed. But because it takes many years to properly appreciate and assess screen comedy it is difficult to say whether the movie comedian has reached his full maturity.

The films of the early masters can be judged upon each individual's entire filmed output and how important his work is to the realm of screen comedy. Present-day stars must be judged on what they have accomplished thus far.

It is unlikely that the obnoxious Steve Martin character will last like the characters of Groucho Marx or W.C. Fields have lasted, but one can never accurately foresee the future in screen comedy appreciation. The Marx Brothers' *Duck Soup* is today considered an American screen classic, but was a box office flop when released in 1933. Laurel and Hardy are now regarded as the finest of comedy teams, but critics dismissed them as insignificant when their product was initially released. Abbott and Costello's comedies were huge hits with both moviegoers and critics in their day, but now the films just seem quaint and dated.

This book will take us from the turn of the century, through the silent era, the talkies, right up to today's stars. The entire evolution of the movie comedian will be examined, with each of the important links acknowledged for their contributions. Their styles, techniques, creations, discoveries, experiments, and films will be analyzed in order to show their merits as contributors to the most important and most popular of all forms of communication.

As writer-director Preston Sturges showed with his classic *Sullivan's Travels*, a poet or a scholar can reach some of us, but comedy can reach all of us. Comedy is all that some people have.

So let us now escape into a world where laughter is the key to open all doors. Those doors will enable us to look beyond the gags and see the fascinating, profound, brilliant individuals responsible for so much happiness, for so many people, for such a long time.

1

The First Movie Comedians

Where did it all begin? When did movies first get funny? Not long after they were created, actually.

As early as 1896, French film pioneers Auguste and Louis Lumière were responsible for thirty-second comedy films in which silly things happen to people (a boy putting a wet washcloth on a sleeping man's face) for comic effect.

The first internationally famous comedian, however, was a Frenchman by the name of Max Linder. This dapper gentleman created well over three hundred comedies, only a handful of which exist today, especially in this country.

Linder's first work, filmed in France from 1905 to 1915, is very basic. Predictable situations, such as Linder trying to ice skate but falling down repeatedly, actually were symbolic of his attempt to use the film medium properly.

Linder didn't really begin to make full use of film's scope and potential for his comic creativity until moving to America in 1917. By that time, Chaplin and others had already defined comedy to its present-day limitations. Linder's few remaining works show a great potential for creativity, especially those films which he did in this country, but he never managed to develop a distinct style of comic characterization or cinematic technique. He had the talent; he just never quite found himself.

By the late teens and early twenties, Max Linder was left far behind by Chaplin, Keaton, and Lloyd, all of whom managed to define their technique in a way which Linder could not accomplish. His early work is notable as primitive screen comedy, but he has been so overshadowed in the field that many film historians remember him only as the bizarre comic who committed suicide with his wife, leaving a baby daughter behind, in 1923.

The daughter, Maude, took notice of her father's screen work, and for a while crusaded to restore his films and put his name among the greats of movie comedy where she felt it belonged. Sadly, however Max Linder never utilized his talents or the film medium well enough to attain prominence. His early contributions can be acknowledged only in passing.

John Bunny, however, did manage to make some definite progress in the development of screen comedy as early as 1910. The British-born Bunny was the

John Bunny is the first important movie comedian.

first American movie star, and was a comedian of enough innovation to make his worth more substantial than Linder's.

Bunny developed a comedy of situation, the same which is used today in television. Playing a henpecked husband opposite nagging wife Flora Finch, the short, rotund Bunny would place his Everyman character in situations which have been called upon literally hundreds of times over the years. Little of Bunny's screen work has survived, but the existing examples show a structure now considered basic in situation comedy.

The Troublesome Secretaries (1911) finds Bunny in need of a secretary, interviewing several pretty young things while his wife fumes. *A Cure for Pokeritis* (1912) has Bunny sneaking off to a poker game behind Flora's back. Flora then stages an elaborate hoax to play on her errant husband by enlisting friends and relatives to pose as cops for a mock raid. These two examples show the basic marital comedy structure created by Bunny nearly a century ago. That structure is still used today, after countless revisions by W.C. Fields, Laurel and Hardy, Edgar Kennedy, Leon Errol, and by television's "I Love Lucy," "The Honeymooners," and even the animated "Flintstones."

These later treatments, of course, were enhanced by dialogue, while Bunny's original renditions were silent. Bunny's acting was pantomime—an excellent use of body movement and facial expressions, exaggerated only slightly for comic effect.

Bunny was also a profound man in what he foresaw. A highly successful and extremely well-paid stage actor, Bunny gladly took a large cut in salary when he made the transition from legitimate theater to the then-scoffed-at "flickers," because he could foresee their development, knowing they would soon become a popular art form. He was the first to adapt books to the screen, the initial example being Dickens' classic *Pickwick Papers*, shot on location in England in May 1912. He also foresaw the coming of talking pictures and color films, although neither of these practices was even attempted in his lifetime.

And finally, John Bunny was the original movie star, mobbed by fans wherever he went, and looked up to as a popular cult figure. When he died on April 26, 1915, newspapers across the country carried front-page eulogies for the beloved star who today is recognized only by comedy film historians and students as the original screen clown.

While nobody seriously rivaled Bunny in these very early days of screen comedy (and it wouldn't be until Chaplin's rise that a comic equaled or surpassed Bunny's innovation in the field), there were other popular comics around during the period.

Augustus Carney is important for paving the way toward a continuing comedy series featuring a continuing cast in a rural locale. As Alkali Ike, Carney romanced Sophie Clutts and was rivaled by Mustang Pete.

The films were popular, especially with rural audiences, and this popularity was said to have gone to Carney's head. Playing ornery Ike slowly transformed the once likeable Carney into a difficult actor to work with.

Leaving Essanay, his home studio, for a bigger salary at Universal, Carney, then known as Universal Ike, clashed with Director Harry Edwards and studio head Carl Laemmle once too often and was discharged. Word spread quickly that he was impossible to work with, and his career never regained composure. His failure represents one of the first instances of a vindictive studio.

Carney's heyday was between 1909 and 1914. Few people who lived during that period are alive today, and Carney's name did not last over the years.

Another of the many sad stories from this period involves a comic named Billy "Muggsy" Quirk. While the situation comedy would someday override the slapstick comedy of silent pictures, Quirk's troubles involved an opposite trend, which occurred years earlier.

Billy began in bit parts around 1907 and soon showed enough promise in the "flickers" that he landed his own starring series at the old Biograph studios in 1910. Quirk's films were popular and considered good in comparison to the few films of the day (there were so few this far back that little criticism occurred). Billy went to Universal in 1913, and while his Biographs were praised, his Universal efforts were not. He went to Vitagraph the following year, but then success of John Bunny at this studio overshadowed Billy's, along the fact that slapstick was beginning to surpass situation comedy in films.

By the end of the teens he was doing small parts at cheap studios. In 1920 he attempted suicide, despondent over losing his career before it could take off.

His suicide attempt was no more successful than his career. Quirk soon faded into obscurity, and died in 1926 at the age of 53.

One comic who did succeed in situation comedies at Vitagraph despite Bunny and despite the rise of slapstick was Sidney Drew. He and wife Lucille McVey wrote, directed, and appeared in a series of early silent sitcoms for Vitagraph, and later the newly formed Metro, throughout the teens.

Period critics predicted big things for Sidney and Lucille, but when their son was killed in action during World War I, Drew was so devastated that he died six months later. Had he lived to see the resurgence of quiet comedy in the twenties, he surely would have reigned supreme. Lucille remained active as a writer for the screen until her death in 1926.

The situations of early screen comedy were overtaken completely by the slapstick of the Sennett studios and the rise of Chaplin from the mid-teens onward, but the changing tastes reverted to the original styles by the twenties. While the Hal Roach studios were on hand to present us with such new faces as Charley Chase, Harold Lloyd, and Laurel and Hardy, none of the screen's original comics lived or lasted professionally long enough to make a comeback when their kind of comedy returned to the silent screen.

2

Early Comedy Studios

Mack Sennett Productions

Slapstick's rise in the mid-teens was due almost completely to the Mack Sennett–produced comedies of this period. Slapstick was experimented with and ultimately transformed into a veritable science by Sennett and his players.

Sennett began with D.W. Griffith. It was while in charge of Griffith's comedy productions that Mack first learned his craft. When he began producing his own films, he borrowed from the farce of the French cinema and added what are now considered very basic raw materials to this style of comedy, including the pie in the face.

Charlie Chaplin worked at Sennett's Keystone studios for a year, making his first films there, developing the genesis of his tramp character and his supreme knowledge of comedy.

Another of the most important names at this studio was Roscoe "Fatty" Arbuckle, an obese, baby-faced man who was very graceful for his girth, and who possessed a boyishness that attracted audiences.

Mabel Normand, a cute, impish girl, played opposite Fatty (and Chaplin, among others) in several of his best films. Transcending the woman's usual limitations in film at this time, Mabel also co-wrote, directed and created many important gags in the Sennett-produced pictures.

The Keystones were wild affairs with little subtlety. Melodrama was played for slapstick, with innocent female victims in the clutches of an evil Sennett "heavy" (Kewpie Morgan, among others). The victims would be rescued by a group of daffy, acrobatic policemen generally known as the Keystone Cops. The Cops consisted of Sennett character players, among them Ford Sterling, Chester Conklin, Hank Mann, Edgar Kennedy, Tom Kennedy, Al St. John, Andy Clyde, Slim Summerville, and Charley Murray.

A wild chase with genuine excitement and a huge, well-timed slapstick melee would ensue, and right would triumph. Although this premise was used in virtually every Keystone picture, it never really grew stale, with the talent and charisma of the performers and production staff giving it a new twist each time so as not to make it a redundant practice.

7

This was during the teens. Sennett chose a milder, tamer approach in the next decade, due mostly to audiences complaining that they were tired of the knockabout stuff and desired something with more finesse. The films of the Hal Roach studios, featuring such comics as Charley Chase, Harold Lloyd, and Laurel and Hardy, followed this practice of less wild physical comedy and more finesse, making Hal Roach a serious rival for Sennett at this time.

Arbuckle and Normand, Sennett's two major players (other than Chaplin, of course, who was there only a year) had left the studio by the late teens. Fatty remained a highly successful comedy performer in the Joe Schneck-produced Paramount releases between 1917–1921, with newcomer Buster Keaton appearing in a handful of the earlier ones before going off on his own.

The bottom dropped out for Arbuckle in 1921 when he was accused of raping and murdering actress Virginia Rappe. Newspapers painted ugly accounts of this big monster taking sexual advantage of the meek, hapless virgin. Circumstances later proved Arbuckle innocent of the charges, while Miss Rappe was revealed to be not the wide-eyed virgin the press had created.

Although acquitted, Arbuckle did no screen work other than directing under an assumed name (William Goodrich, based on Keaton's suggestion that he call himself Will B. Goode) throughout the twenties, when the public was still disposed to consider him a monster.

It wasn't until 1933 that Fatty made another film, a handful of two-reelers for Warner Brothers' Vitaphone company. Arbuckle's death later that year—many say of a broken heart—halted whatever success he may have been able to achieve in this comeback.

Mabel Normand was not getting enough substantial work in features at Sennett's (despite proving herself as the star of Mack's feature *Mickey* in 1916), so she left for Samuel Goldwyn's more prestigious studios in 1918. Unfortunately, none of her Goldwyn-produced films are known to survive today, but period reviews lead one to believe that she was well received.

Normand's poor work habits caused Goldwyn to fire her in 1921, after which she returned to do three more films at Sennett's and five featurettes for Hal Roach in 1926 and 1927. In failing health during the last half of the decade, Mabel contracted tuberculosis and died in January 1930.

During the twenties, Sennett, in an attempt to battle rival Hal Roach, initiated a series of "star" vehicles, featuring the major performers on his lot. More subtle than the early Keystones, these films held their own for a while, but did not have the strength to compete with the Roach product, which boasted better names than Sennett's did at this time.

The most important star at Sennett's during the twenties was undoubtedly Harry Langdon. Audiences found the wistful, naive child-man so endearing that Langdon was a serious rival for Chaplin's coveted crown.

While his early films for Sennett—*Smile Please, All Night Long, Feet Of Mud, Soldier Man*, and *Picking Peaches*—were pretty standard slapstick endeavors, Langdon's character was put to full use in the Sennett featurette *Satur-*

Fatty Arbuckle (center) and Mabel Normand (right) were among Sennett's most important players of the teens. (Left: Alice Davenport.)

Harry Langdon was at one time considered as great a comic as Chaplin.

day Afternoon, which set the foundation for the character found in his best vehicles, made after leaving Sennett and producing his own comedies in 1927.

Three features Langdon made in collaboration with Frank Capra (who later went on to direct such screen classics as *It Happened One Night, Mr. Deeds Goes to Town, Mr. Smith Goes to Washington*, and *It's a Wonderful Life*), remain among the most engaging comedies of the silent screen. While *The Strong Man, Tramp Tramp Tramp*, and *Long Pants* (all 1927) aren't up to the standards of Chaplin's *City Lights* or Keaton's *The General*, they did prove Langdon to be a skilled and inventive comedian, not to be taken lightly.

Unfortunately, Harry Langdon became a victim of the ever-powerful human ego, firing Capra and believing that he, like Chaplin or Keaton, could play all the parts in production as well as acting.

Langdon inserted more and more pathos into his films. While pathos emerged naturally from his character in earlier works, it seemed forced in films like *The Chaser* (1928).

When talkies came in, Harry had some limited success as a character player in cheap features, star of cheaper shorts, and as advisor on some Laurel and Hardy vehicles, but for the most part his talent was being wasted.

A has-been clown prince, relegated to pale imitations of his best work which lay so far behind him, Harry sank into a deep depression and began to look much older than his actual age. Harry Langdon died broke, unhappy, and forgotten in 1944 at the age of 60. Had he been able to discipline himself, he might be better remembered today.

Two other comedians who made names for themselves in Sennett-produced films during the twenties were Ben Turpin and Billy Bevan.

Turpin was a bizarre, funny-looking, cross-eyed man who got laughs simply due to his freaky appearance and not for any strong comic creativity. Turpin's films, particularly *The Daredevil* and *Idle Eyes*, were usually very funny, with great gags performed well by the comic, but his forte seemed to be playing straight in romantic scenes and relying on his bizarre appearance for laughs.

Bevan was a lot like Harry "Snub" Pollard at the Hal Roach studios in that he had the skills to perform the comedy well. He was not a creator in the sense that Chaplin, Keaton, or even Harry Langdon was, and like Pollard (or Turpin), had no substantial screen personality.

Both Turpin and Bevan became rather successful character performers well into the talkies. Turpin fared less well due to his reliance on physical deformity, which was geared more toward silent pictures.

Turpin died shortly after a brief role in Laurel and Hardy's last good feature film, *Saps at Sea* (1940). Bevan remained active in a variety of character roles until his death in 1958.

By the time talkies rolled in, Sennett had been totally eclipsed by Roach, and so he retired in 1935. He made brief appearances in movies and on television as late as the fifties and appeared with Steve Allen in a cinematic salute to Mack's work entitled *Down Memory Lane* in 1949. Probably the only really important productions for Sennett during the era of talking pictures were four W.C. Fields shorts made in 1932 and 1933. Mack Sennett died in 1960 at the age of 82.

While the Keystones were no more than wild live-action cartoons, with rarely any personality among the players, they are still highly essential in the development of screen comedy. These films initiated much of the physical humor that has since become basic and served as a starting ground for some of comedy's greatest talents.

Mack Sennett is the father of silent screen comedy because his productions are among the most inventive and original silent films — as essential to the evolution of the movie comedian as D.W. Griffith's silent epics are to filmmaking in general.

Hal Roach Productions

In the twenties Hal Roach was Sennett's rival. By the thirties Roach was the reigning king of comedy producers.

Laurel and Hardy, Charley Chase, and Harold Lloyd are all important staples of the Roach legacy and the development of screen comedy. Unlike Sennett's knockabout endeavors of the teens, the Roach-produced comedies had more polish and finesse—something that audiences desired after years of slapstick. Although Sennett mellowed in the twenties to compete, he had no chance, for by then his major comedy stars had left for greener pastures, while Roach had some of the most amazing minds in the business working for him.

The major stars who worked for Roach will be discussed more thoroughly in other chapters of the text, but one performer who should be mentioned right off is Harry "Snub" Pollard. Pollard got his start co-starring in Harold Lloyd's early short films and soon graduated to his own series of starring comedies.

Pollard, like Billy Bevan at Sennett's, had no distinct personality and relied on gags and his execution of same to make his films work. His prominence in the field of silent screen comedy does go just a bit further, however, due to the fact that he did make at least one film which is now considered a minor classic.

It's a Gift (1923) features Snub as an inventor who gets about in life with the help of some amusing gadgets, such as a bed which folds up into the wall and becomes a fireplace, and a motorless car which is controlled by the driver pointing a large magnet at the auto in front of him. An original and inventive film, *It's a Gift* shines because of its gags and not because of the personality of its star. It could have been made as well by any other similarly skilled comic.

Pollard enjoyed success as a star comic throughout the twenties, but when talkies came in he was relegated to minor roles in films featuring The Three Stooges and other leading clowns of the period. Snub died in 1962.

Will Rogers was another popular star on the Roach lot at this time. While he is a legendary figure in the history of entertainment, his immortality is due to the wit he used in his stage work during Ziegfeld Follies revues and such. Silent films couldn't use this facet of Will's talents, but were able to display his charm. Will gave very pleasant performances in films like *Don't Park There* (1924), *Hustling Hank* (1923), and *The Cake Eater* (1924), all of which allowed his charm to seep through the situations. His best films were movie satires like *Big Moments from Little Pictures* (1924), in which he spoofed Valentino, Fairbanks, even Sennett and the Keystone Cops.

Will's wit and charm were even more successful in the talkies he did for Fox from 1929 until his tragic death in 1935, when his private plane crashed, killing him and pilot Wiley Post.

Opposite: Cross-eyed Ben Turpin (left) and Billy Bevan were two of Sennett's popular clowns.

Snub Pollard had his own series at Hal Roach Productions.

Max Davidson was another name at Roach in comedy films during the twenties. A bearded, German-born actor, Max is yet another example of funny gags surrounding a puppet rather than a substantial character.

A good example of his work is *Call of the Cuckoo* (1927), which features cameos by Laurel and Hardy and Charley Chase as asylum inmates. The plot deals with Max and his family trying to live in a house that was built so hastily that nothing works properly (complete with a collapsing bathtub that reveals a nude Max in a quick shot ... surprising for 1927). Of course it is the gadgetry that is funny more than the comic.

Max Davidson did little work in talkies other than some minor roles in short films at Educational and Columbia studios. He died in 1950. A sampling of his work appears in the Robert Youngson compilation *Laurel & Hardy's Laughing Twenties* as does the work of Stan & Ollie and Charley Chase.

Aside from leading players, Roach had a wonderful stock of supporting comics, including the talents of Jimmy Finlayson, Tiny Sanford, Walter Long, Anita Garvin, Mae Busch, Charley Hall, Edgar Kennedy, Spec O'Donnell, and Billy Gilbert.

Dialogue was provided by H.M. Walker, while direction was performed by Fred Guiol, James Horne, Lloyd French, and three directors whose names meant even more as film developed in the future: George Stevens, George Marshall, and Leo McCarey. McCarey is one of the folks responsible for teaming Laurel with

Will Rogers' charm shone through even in silent films.

Hardy, as well as the credited director of the Marx Brothers' classic *Duck Soup* (1933). Stevens went from cameraman to director of comedies, and finally director of such screen classics as *Shane* (1953) and *Giant* (1956). Marshall is responsible for many of Bob Hope and Jerry Lewis's best films from the forties through the sixties and for directing Lucille Ball on television in the seventies.

Charley Chase directed under the name Charles Parrott. His brother, Jimmy Chase, directed as James Parrott and appeared in some films as Paul Parrott (yes, their real name was Chase, not Parrott).

Edgar Kennedy directed as E. Livingston Kennedy, and Stan Laurel was said to be the major creative force behind the direction of his films with and without Oliver Hardy, despite the fact that he never took a director's credit.

In the talkies, a musical store by Marvin Hately enhanced the action of the films perfectly.

Roach remained a highly successful producer for many years, eschewing shorts for forty-minute featurettes (known then as a streamlined features) and full-length feature films like Steinbeck's *Of Mice and Men* with Burgess Meredith and Lon Chaney, Jr. In the fifties, he and his son, the late Hal Roach, Jr., became active in producing such popular television shows as "My Little Margie," "The Trouble with Father," and "The Life of Riley."

The Hal Roach studios closed in the early 1960s, and Roach, even in his nineties, remained active with the distribution of his product to television and home collectors. It is a product which contains some of screen comedy's most priceless moments.

Al Christie Productions

The films made at the Christie studios are the least significant, but still deserve acknowledgement even if only for period popularity. While Roach had many secondary clowns (Clyde Cook, Max Davidson, et al.), Christie had all the rest.

One popular comedian at this studio was Larry Semon. Semon's comedies were slapstick endeavors with a faster pace, bigger gags, and, thus, wilder proceedings. These outrageous antics provide a lot of laughs, even if Semon is only a puppet in the Billy Bevan–Snub Pollard tradition, with no characterization of his own.

Larry loved hurling buckets of tar, doing pratfalls out of top-floor windows or airplanes, and pushing fat men into mud holes the size of the Pacific Ocean.

Bigger doesn't necessarily mean better, and the gags, while undeniably funny, can still be a bit overbearing. Semon films like *The Show* and *School Days* are typical two-reel examples of his work, with *The Perfect Clown* and the original *Wizard of Oz* being among his most notable features.

It should also be noted that Larry's stunts were all done by Wisconsin-born Bill Hauber, whose career ended when Semon died in 1928. Hauber died the following year.

The films of Larry Semon pop up at showings of silent comedies from time to time and always generate a substantial amount of laughter. But Semon's talents stopped short of placing him in the ranks of Chaplin, Keaton, Lloyd, or even Harry Langdon, and his use of stuntmen and overpowering sight gags hampers his credibility. Perhaps Semon is best considered one of the better minor clowns of the period.

Lupino Lane was another of the silent clowns who looked cute and did some funny bits, but without characterization. His work with objects in films like *Sword's Point* (1925) and *Wrong Way Willie* (1923) is impressive, but pales next to Keaton's similar antics.

Lane was trained in the British music halls that begat Stan Laurel and

Charlie Chaplin, but he didn't have the filmmaking genius of his two countrymen. Lane was not active in talkies but did work on stage frequently until his death in 1959 at age 67.

Lloyd "Ham" Hamilton started out as one half of the silent comedy team of Ham and Bud with Bud Duncan. Ham was a big, overgrown guy with bushy eyebrows, a big mustache, and no brains. Bud was a little wimpy upstart. Together they made one-reelers during the teens, and from the half-dozen or so that this writer has seen, it is quite evident that they never amounted to anything worth examination at all, ranking instead with such insignificant names in silent comedy as Fred Mace.

On his own in the Christie comedies, Hamilton is said to have been a very funny and very talented man. Charley Chase and Buster Keaton have both been quoted as admirers of Hamilton's work.

A fire at Christie's Educational studios destroyed a lot of the producer's filmed output including most of the Hamilton comedies, but in the few examples we have, one can see Ham's potential.

The first thing that strikes this writer is the walk. Hamilton had a walk that is virtually indescribable—more outrageous than even Chaplin's waddle. He resembled a fat kid in gym class with an excruciatingly tight jockstrap on as he ambled along from situation to situation.

Hamilton died in 1935, but had he lived, he may have been able to develop his potential further. If more of his sole work turns up (people are always finding isolated prints in remote locations, so there's always hope) we may someday have a chance to rediscover and re-evaluate his work.

As stated earlier, the Christie studios had a lot of secondary clowns. Eddie Lyons and Lee Moran, Neal Burns, Dorothy Devore, and Louise Fazenda all worked the Christie studios during the twenties, but none of their work is worth more than passing acknowledgement.

The studios hung around until 1938, with talking two-reelers featuring the likes of Shemp Howard, Billy Gilbert, Marie Dressler, Andy Clyde, and Buster Keaton at one time or another.

While containing nothing of the innovation that was found in the Roach or Sennett product, the Christie-produced comedies still do deserve at least marginal space when discussing the development of screen comedy during the teens, twenties, and thirties.

3

Charlie Chaplin

Charlie Chaplin is, without a doubt, the most important and most essential figure in the history of screen comedy, and one of the most essential figures in the whole of motion pictures. The first to rise above the term comedian and be hailed as an artist, even by those who looked upon movies as a foolish new medium, Chaplin made films that were immeasurably essential to the development of screen comedy and its comedians.

Born Charles Spencer Chaplin in England in 1889, Charlie became interested in show business early, due to his father's talents as a music hall entertainer. Joining Fred Karno's music hall troupe while still in his teens, Chaplin began working on the various comic techniques which he could later develop into milestones of screen humor. His understudy, Stan Laurel (later of Laurel and Hardy fame), replaced Chaplin as star comic of the troupe when Charlie left Karno to make films for Mack Sennett's Keystone studios in 1914.

While his screen debut, *Making a Living*, was a typical Keystone one-reeler, his second, *Kid Auto Races*, showed a glimmer of the characterization that Chaplin would soon develop into a legendary figure. Borrowing various ill-fitting garments from the wardrobes of other Sennett comics, Chaplin came up with a tramp costume, and *Kid Auto Races* marks the first appearance of Chaplin's immortal tramp.

Charlie worked on this character throughout his year at Keystone, and although he wrote and directed nearly all of his comedies, he needed more time to develop a lot of his creative ideas, which needed further exploration than the budget-minded Sennett would allow.

After some fine knockabout stuff in films like *His Trysting Place* with Mabel Normand, *The Rounders* with Fatty Arbuckle, *Dough & Dynamite* with Chester Conklin, *Gentlemen of Nerve* with Charley Chase, and *Tillie's Punctured Romance* (the first feature film comedy, which starred Chaplin, Marie Dressler, Mabel Normand, and The Keystone Cops), Charlie left Keystone for Essanay, on a promise of more money and even more creative control.

Chaplin's Essanay shorts, made throughout 1915, were even more important than those he made at Sennett's. While the tramp character was thought up and first put to use at Keystone, it was at Essanay that Charlie gave it a more substantial personality. His films had more substance, his character more real human qualities—two essential factors in the development of screen comedy.

The Tramp (1915) was Charlie's breakthrough film. Featuring a perfect blend of slapstick and sentiment, Chaplin had us not only laughing at the tramp but loving him as well. Not merely a faceless figure in a series of knockabout situations, Chaplin's tramp had the same feelings and emotions as any member of the audience.

Chaplin continued to polish his characterization in subsequent Essanay films like *Police, Shanghaied,* and *Work,* and by the time he left Essanay for Mutual studios in 1916, he had the tramp character, as well as his comedy, honed to absolute perfection.

The dozen films that Chaplin made for Mutual studios stand out as twelve of the most brilant screen treasures in the history of motion pictures. Screen historians unanimously agree that films like *The Count, The Floorwalker, Behind the Screen, The Pawnshop, The Cure, The Adventurer,* and *One A.M.* are among the medium's most influential works, essential examples of screen comedy, and the most important short subject contributions to the Chaplin screen legacy.

One A.M. is perhaps the most fascinating of the twelve Mutual productions. In it Chaplin works alone against a series of inanimate objects, something akin to the talents of Buster Keaton. Coming home in a drunken stupor, Charlie staggers into the house and tries to put himself to bed while being confronted with a series of mishaps with the various objects in his home. His battle with a bearskin rug and near-unsuccessful wrestling with a bed which pulls down out of the wall show a physical grace and talent for pantomime that remains unequalized by any other screen comic. By the time of this film, it was clear that Charlie Chaplin was indeed nothing less than a genius.

Chaplin had been writing and directing his own comedies ever since the Keystones, but in 1918, he decided to produce his own films as well. The control that Chaplin maintained over his works kept him from the troubles that beset Keaton in later years when he was forced to follow orders that were fatal to his creative talents.

By 1918, Chaplin's tramp had become a world-famous screen hero, the likes of which remained unmatched in the media until the Beatles appeared nearly a half-century later.

Theaters around the world would advertise the latest Chaplin releases merely by stating, "Charlie's Here Today" on their marquees, or by showing a huge display photo of the tramp outside of the building. The result was usually lines that went on for blocks. Many took time off work in order to see the films, products of a creative individual's reflections on human emotions, expressed through humor and good times. The films had already begun taking on classic proportions at the time of their initial release.

Chaplin continued his string of classics when producing his own films, which were first distributed by First National Studios. The short films *A Dog's Life,*

Charlie Chaplin in "Behind the Screen" (1916), one of his brilliant early comedies from Mutual.

Shoulder Arms, and Charlie's last short subject, *The Pilgrim*, are among the better examples of this period.

A Dog's Life shows the tramp getting about through the cruel world with a loyal, dedicated canine as presumably his only friend. Chaplin's relationship with the dog in this film served as something of a basis for the upcoming First National Chaplin feature *The Kid* (1921), which represents the definitive example of Chaplin's career at this point.

The dog becomes an abandoned child who captures Charlie's (and the viewer's) affections. The outline of *A Dog's Life* served as the basis for the format which Chaplin was to use in all subsequent features: a straight story with touches of comedy and sentiment, all of which blended exquisitely to form a work of communication through pantomime that is still outstanding in the field of motion pictures.

The Kid has Charlie finding an abandoned child, raising it on his own, and then balking when the infant's mother returns to reclaim him five years later. We see the tramp growing fond of the child throughout this upbringing and the infant's mutual feelings through a very skilled display of pantomime.

Charlie also explores all of the comic possibilities of his tramp trying to care for a baby and the relationship he has with the small boy who has developed, as it were, in the tramp's own image. Chaplin's comedy is up to its usual standards, and his acting is enhanced far beyond light pathos and well into skilled physical expression. *The Kid* remains one of Chaplin's finest works.

In 1923, Chaplin teamed with fellow silent stars Mary Pickford and Douglas Fairbanks to form what is now known as United Artists Studios, where he made his last films. Now not only writing, directing, producing, and starring in these efforts, Charlie also owned and controlled their distribution. It seemed that with each turn, a new facet of his genius was displayed.

The first feature at his own studio, *A Woman in Paris*, did not star Chaplin, although he did write, direct, and produce the film, but instead featured his oft-times leading lady Edna Purviance and actor Adolphe Menjou. It was the first of his films to perform poorly at the box office, although period critics labeled the enchanting romantic melodrama sheer genius. Chaplin then returned to his tramp character for four more films—four of the greatest films ever made.

The Gold Rush (1925) is the film which Chaplin stated he wanted to be remembered by. Set in the Klondike, *The Gold Rush* took Charlie two years to film. Striving for nothing less than absolute perfection, Chaplin achieved what he considered a printable scene after as many as one hundred takes. This practice has since been labeled artistic insanity, but apparently Chaplin knew what he wanted, for *The Gold Rush* is nothing short of outstanding.

The Circus (1928) is a very poignant, almost poetic look at big-top life, while continuing to display Chaplin's expertise at the creation and execution of gags, comic situations, and pure comic direction. *The Circus* won Charlie an Oscar at the first Academy Awards ceremonies, where best picture honors went to the movie classic *Wings*.

Charlie Chaplin's immortal tramp in "The Gold Rush" (1925).

City Lights began filming in late 1928 as a silent feature about the tramp's falling in love with a pretty blind girl and finding a doctor who restores her sight. Chaplin took three years on the film, and by the time he was ready to release it, silent movies had become obsolete with the coming of talking pictures. Refusing to transform his film into a talkie by hastily dubbing in voices and sound effects (a practice used on many late silents released after talkies had taken over), Chaplin issued *City Lights* as a silent film during an all-talking, all-singing, all-dancing year, 1931.

The results were just as Chaplin had predicted, for *City Lights* remains his masterpiece—one of the most beautiful motion pictures ever conceived. The very look on the tramp's face when the girl's eyesight is restored and she is seeing her benefactor for the first time is one of screen history's most powerful moments. *City Lights* is definitely one of the most perfect examples of filmmaking from all stages of acting and production.

Chaplin's next release, *Modern Times* (1936), showed the tramp caught up in various labor conditions at the hands of modern technology. A classic which is preferred by some even to *City Lights*, *Modern Times* was also a silent but did make use of music and sound effects, displaying yet another facet of Chaplin's genius. In this and all subsequent films, Chaplin wrote, arranged and scored the music as well as synchronizing all sound effects.

Charlie was not ready to let us hear the tramp speak in *Modern Times*, but he did let us hear his voice as he sang a gibberish novelty song. One of Chaplin's musical compositions for this film, "Smile" became a pop hit some two decades later for singer Nat King Cole. The only sad thing about *Modern Times* is that it marked the last appearance of the immortal tramp.

By 1940 Chaplin had conceeded his battle with talkies and made his first all-talking picture, *The Great Dictator*, which features him in a dual role as a meek soldier-barber and as the Hitleresque dictator of a mythical country. Ranking with such classic political satires as the Marx Brothers' *Duck Soup* (1933) and Stanley Kubrick's *Dr. Strangelove* (1963), *The Great Dictator* is said to have been seen by Hitler himself . . . twice! His reactions have not been recorded by history texts or memoirs.

Although it's a talkie, Chaplin did not eschew sight gags in *The Great Dictator*. One of the best occurs when Charlie, as a soldier, pulls the ring out of a grenade and rears back to throw it, only to have the live explosive slip down his sleeve. His comic timing and gag execution was still perfect.

Monsieur Verdoux (1947) was Chaplin's next film and even more offbeat. Considered appalling at the time of its initial release, this black comedy about a lecherous, womanizing murderer who ends up being executed was a bit ahead of its time. A bizarre, highly fascinating comedy, *Monsieur Verdoux* is a classic which seems quite tame today.

Limelight (1952) is definitely Chaplin's best talkie. As an aging music hall clown who attempts a comeback while introducing his protégée, a young ballerina (effectively played by Claire Bloom), Chaplin turned in a stunning performance in which he displayed as much skill for writing and delivering dialogue as he had exhibited so many times before with pantomime. Aside from the poignancy, Chaplin showed that his flair for comedy was still unbeatable as he performed a sketch with another giant of the silent screen, Buster Keaton. The result is a priceless piece of film.

Every possible aspect of Chaplin's genius shines through *Limelight* in acting, comedy, dialogue, pantomime, directing, production in general, use of music, and lighting. *Limelight* may very well be the greatest motion picture ever made.

Chaplin was ousted from America because of alleged Communist sympathies during the McCarthy era, so his last starring film, *A King in New York* (1957), was not released in the states. Considered at the time to be an offensive put-down of America, *A King in New York* is actually a harmless (especially by today's standards) satire of American ways of the fifties, including wide-screen movies and rock and roll among its targets.

Chaplin was off screen from then on except for a brief walk-on in the regrettable *A Countess from Hong Kong* (1967), which he wrote and directed.

He was given royal treatment upon his return to the states and honored once again by the Academy of Motion Picture Arts and Sciences with a special Oscar for his priceless contributions to the cinema. Chaplin was the hit of the 1971 ceremonies, receiving a thunderous standing ovation.

Chaplin retained ownership and control of his films but never made another. Conflicting reports state that he was working on another screen project in his later years, but failing health impaired his chances for completion. He married three times without success, finally finding the right mate in Oona, daughter of playwright Eugene O'Neill. Chaplin fathered his last child, James, in 1962 when he was seventy-two years old. His daughter Geraldine Chaplin became a rather successful actress, but his sons Sydney, Charlie Jr., and Michael were not as successful, though all were quite talented. Charlie Jr. died in 1968.

Charles Spencer Chaplin died on Christmas day, 1977, at the age of 88, leaving behind a screen legacy which says more about the development of humor and the expression of human emotions than any other contribution to fine arts. A truly gifted artist capable of consistent high quality, Charlie Chaplin remains immortal as the leading creator of our most popular form of culture, screen humor.

Chaplin Filmography

Keystone Films
All produced by Mack Sennett and released in 1914

Making a Living. *** With Henry Lehrman, Virginia Kirtley, Alice Davenport, Minita Durfee, Chester Conklin. Directed by Henry Lehrman. One Reel.

Kid Auto Races at Venice. **** Chaplin's first appearance as the tramp. A "split reel" comedy accompanied by the documentary *Olives and Their Oil* to make up a full reel. Directed by Henry Lehrman. 7 minutes.

Mabel's Strange Predicament. *** With Mabel Normand, Harry McCoy, Alice Davenport, Hank Mann, Chester Conklin, Al St. John. Directed by Henry Lehrman and Mack Sennett. One Reel.

Between Showers. *** With Ford Sterling, Chester Conklin, Emma Clifton. (Alternate titles: *The Flirts, Charlie and His Umbrella.*) Directed by Henry Lehrman. One Reel.

A Film Johnnie. *** With Fatty Arbuckle, Virginia Kirtley, Minita Durfee, Ford Sterling, Chester Conklin. (Alternate titles include *Movie Nut* and *Million Dollar Job*.) Directed by Mack Sennett. One reel.

Tango Tangles. **** With Ford Sterling, Fatty Arbuckle, Chester Conklin. (Alternate titles: *Charlie's Recreation* and *Music Hall*.) Directed by Mack Sennett. One reel.

His Favorite Pastime. **** With Peggy Pearce, Fatty Arbuckle. (Alternate title: *The Bone Head*.) Directed by George Nichols. One reel.

Cruel, Cruel Love. *** (Alternate title: *Lord Help Us*.) Directed by Mack Sennett. One reel.

The Star Boarder. **** With Edgar Kennedy, Alice Davenport, Gordon Griffith. (Alternate title: *A Hash House Hero*.) Directed by Mack Sennett. One reel.

Mabel at the Wheel. *** With Mabel Normand, Chester Conklin, Harry McCoy, Mack Sennett. Directed by Sennett and Normand. Two reels.

Twenty Minutes of Love. *** With Edgar Kennedy, Minita Durfee, Chester Conklin. (Alternate titles: *He Loved Her So, Love Friend, Cops & Watches*.) Directed by Mack Sennett. One reel (not two as often stated).

Caught in a Cabaret. *** With Mabel Normand, Harry McCoy, Alice Davenport, Chester Conklin, Mack Swain, Minita Durfee, Phyllis Allen, Gordon Griffith, Edgar Kennedy, Hank Mann, Alice Howell. (Alternate titles: *The Jazz Waiter, Faking in Society*.) Directed by Chaplin and Mabel Normand. Two reels.

Caught in the Rain. ***** With Alice Davenport, Mack Swain. (Alternate titles: *At It Again, Who Got Stung,* and *In the Park*, which is the title of a Chaplin Essanay comedy not related at all to this film.) Written and directed by Chaplin. One reel.

A Busy Day. ***** With Mack Swain. Chaplin's first dame masquerade, this is also a split reel released along with documentary *The Morning Papers*. Written and directed by Chaplin.

The Fatal Mallet. **** With Mabel Normand, Mack Sennett, Mack Swain. Written and directed by Chaplin. One reel.

Her Friend the Bandit. *** With Mabel Normand, Charles Murray. Directed by Chaplin and Normand. One reel.

The Knockout. **** With Fatty Arbuckle, Minita Durfee, Al St. John, Chester Conklin, Hank Mann, Alice Howell, Slim Summerville, Charley Chase, Mack Sennett, and the Keystone Cops. This is actually an Arbuckle starrer. Directed by Mack Sennett. Two reels.

Mabel's Busy Day. **** With Mabel Normand, Chester Conklin, Harry McCoy, Slim Summerville. Directed by Chaplin and Normand. One reel.

Mabel's Married Life. **** With Mabel Normand, Mack Swain, Charley Murray, Hank Mann, Harry McCoy, Alice Davenport, Alice Howell, Wallace McDonald. (Alternate title: *When You're Married.*) Directed by Chaplin and Normand. One reel.

Laughing Gas. **** With Fritz Schade, Alice Howell, Slim Summerville, Mack Swain, Joseph Swickard. Written and directed by Chaplin. One reel.

The Property Man. **** With Fritz Schade, Phyllis Allen, Mack Sennett. (Alternate title: *The Roustabout.*) Written and directed by Chaplin. Two reels (although a one-reel version entitled *Hits of the Past* exists).

The Face on the Barroom Floor. *** With Fritz Schade, Cecile Arnold, Chester Conklin. (Alternate title: *The Artist.*) Directed by Chaplin. One reel.

The Masquerader. **** With Fatty Arbuckle, Charley Murray. This is the infamous film which shows Chaplin sans makeup. Written and directed by Chaplin. One reel.

His New Profession. **** With Charley Chase. (Alternate titles: *The Good-for-Nothing, Helping Himself.*) Written and directed by Chaplin. One reel.

The Rounders. ***** With Fatty Arbuckle, Minita Durfee, Phyllis Allen, Al St. John, Charley Chase, Fritz Schade, Wallace McDonald. (Alternate title: *Oh What a Night!.*) Written and directed by Chaplin. One reel.

The New Janitor. **** With Al St. John. (Alternate titles: *The New Porter, The Blundering Boob, The Custodian.*) Written and directed by Chaplin. One reel.

Those Love Pangs. **** With Chester Conklin, Cecile Arnold. (Alternate title: *Love Pangs.*) Written and directed by Chaplin. One reel.

Dough & Dynamite. ***** With Chester Conklin, Fritz Schade, Phyllis Allen, Charley Chase, Slim Summerville, Wallace McDonald, Vivian Edwards, Norma Nichols, Cecile Arnold. Written and directed by Chaplin. 24 minutes.

Gentlemen of Nerve. **** With Mabel Normand, Chester Conklin, Mack Swain, Phyllis Allen, Charley Chase, Slim Summerville, Hank Mann. (Alternate title: *Some Nerve.*) Written and directed by Chaplin. One reel.

His Musical Career. **** With Mack Swain, Alice Howell. (Alternate title: *The Piano Movers.* Prototype for Oscar-winning Laurel and Hardy comedy *The Music Box* of 1932 and Three Stooges comedy *An Ache in Every Stake* of 1941. A Laurel and Hardy silent, *Hats Off*, is also said to be similar, but prints of that film no longer exist.) Written and directed by Chaplin. One reel.

His Trysting Place. ***** With Mack Swain, Mabel Normand, Phyllis Allen. Arguably Chaplin's best Keystone film. Written and directed by Chaplin. Two reels.

Tillie's Punctured Romance. ***** With Marie Dressler, Mabel Normand, Mack Swain, Charles Bennett, Chester Conklin, Edgar Kennedy, Charley Chase, Charley Murray, Minita Durfee, Gordon Griffith, Phyllis Allen, Alice Davenport, Harry McCoy, Alice Howell, Wallace McDonald, and the Keystone Cops (Slim Summerville, Hank Mann, Al St. John, Harry Gribbon). In this film, Chaplin does not play the tramp but instead is cast as a wily city slicker. Screenplay by Hampton Del Ruth, based on Edgar Smith's musical comedy *Tillie's Nightmare*, which starred Miss Dressler on stage. The sequel, *Tillie Wakes Up*, was not produced for Sennett and featured only Dressler among original cast. Directed by Mack Sennett. 57 minutes.

Getting Acquainted. **** With Phyllis Allen, Mabel Normand, Mack Swain, Edgar Kennedy, Harry McCoy, Cecile Arnold. Written and directed by Chaplin. One reel.

His Prehistoric Past. **** With Mack Swain, Gene Marsh, Fritz Schade. Written and directed by Chaplin. Two reels.

Essanay Films
All 1915.

His New Job. **** With Ben Turpin, Charlotte Mineau, Leo White, Gloria Swanson, Agnes Ayers. Written and directed by Chaplin. Two reels.

A Night Out. **** With Ben Turpin, Leo White, Bud Jamison, Edna Purviance. Written and directed by Chaplin. Two reels.

The Champion. **** With Bud Jamison, Edna Purviance, Leo White, Ben Turpin, Lloyd Bacon, Broncho Billy Anderson. (Distributed as two one-reelers entitled

Sparring Partner and *The Champion* by Official Films in 16mm during the 1960s and 70s.) Written and directed by Chaplin. Two reels.

In the Park. **** With Edna Purviance, Leo White, Bud Jamison, Lloyd Bacon. Written and directed by Chaplin. Two reels.

A Jitney Elopement. **** With Edna Purviance, Leo White, Lloyd Bacon. Written and directed by Chaplin. Two reels.

The Tramp. ***** With Edna Purviance, Bud Jamison, Leo White, Paddy McGuire, Lloyd Bacon. The most essential of Chaplin's Essanays. Written and directed by Chaplin. Two reels.

By The Sea. **** With Edna Purviance, Billy Armstrong, Bud Jamison. Written and directed by Chaplin. One reel.

Work. ***** With Charles Insley, Edna Purviance, Billy Armstrong, Marta Golden, Leo White, Paddy McGuire. (Alternate title: *The Paperhanger.*) Written and directed by Chaplin. Two reels.

A Woman. **** With Edna Purviance, Charles Insley, Marta Golden, Margie Reiger, Billy Armstrong, Leo White, Grant "Pancho" Rex. Written and directed by Chaplin. Two reels.

The Bank. ***** With Edna Purviance, Carl Stockdale, Billy Armstrong, John Rand, Charles Insley, Leo White, Fred Goodwins. Written and directed by Chaplin. Two reels.

Shanghaied. ***** With Edna Purviance, Wesley Ruggles, John Rand, Billy Armstrong, Paddy McGuire, Leo White, Fred Goodwins. Written and directed by Chaplin. Two reels.

A Night at the Show. ***** With Edna Purviance, Dee Hampton, Leo White, Bud Jamison. Chaplin plays two parts. Written and directed by Chaplin. Two reels.

Carmen (Charlie Chaplin's Burlesque on Carmen). *** With Edna Purviance, Ben Turpin, Jack Henderson, Leo White, John Rand, May White. Written and directed by Chaplin. 37 minutes.

Police. (1916) ***** With Edna Purviance, Wesley Ruggles, James Kelley, John Rand, Leo White, Billy Armstrong, Fred Goodwins, Bud Jamison. Written and directed by Chaplin. Two reels.

Triple Trouble. (1916) *** An unfinished Chaplin film that Essanay released including some outtakes from *Police*, when Charlie left the studios in 1916. Essanay went bankrupt two years later.

Mutual Films
All two-reel films.

The Floorwalker. (1916) ***** With Edna Purviance, Eric Campbell, Lloyd Bacon, Charlotte Mineau, Leo White, Albert Austin. Includes infamous escalator chase scene envied by Sennett. Written and directed by Chaplin.

The Fireman. (1916) *** With Edna Purviance, Eric Campbell, Lloyd Bacon, Leo White, John Rand, Frank Coleman. Weakest of the Chaplin Mutuals, though still good. Written and directed by Chaplin.

The Vagabond. (1916) **** Written and directed by Chaplin.

One A.M. (1916) ***** Chaplin alone in his best and most ingenious short film. Written and directed by Chaplin.

The Count. (1916) ***** With Edna Purviance, Eric Campbell, James T. Kelley, Leo White, Albert Austin. Written and directed by Chaplin.

The Pawnshop. (1916) ***** With Edna Purviance, John Rand, Henry Bergeman, Albert Austin, Eric Campbell. Written and directed by Chaplin.

Behind the Screen. (1916) ***** With Eric Campbell, Edna Purviance, Frank Coleman, Albert Austin, Henry Bergeman. Written and directed by Chaplin.

The Rink. (1916) ***** With Edna Purviance, Eric Campbell, James T. Kelley, Henry Bergeman, Charlotte Mineau. Written and directed by Chaplin, who also shows remarkable skating skills.

Easy Street. (1917) ***** With Edna Purviance, Eric Campbell, Albert Austin. Considered by many the definitive short. Written and directed by Chaplin.

The Cure. (1917) ***** With Edna Purviance, Eric Campbell, John Rand. Written and directed by Chaplin.

The Immigrant. (1917) ***** With Edna Purviance, Albert Austin, Henry Bergeman, Tiny Sanford, Eric Campbell. Includes infamous dining on the ship sequence. Written and directed by Chaplin.

Chaplin tries to reason with comic "heavy" Eric Campbell in "The Fireman" (1916).

The Adventurer. (1918) ***** With Edna Purviance, Eric Campbell, Henry
  Bergeman, Albert Austin, Frank Coleman. Written and directed by Chaplin.

First National Films
*These and all subsequent releases written and directed by Chaplin
unless otherwise noted.*

A Dog's Life. (1918) ***** With Edna Purviance, Tom Wilson, Sydney Chaplin,

(Charlie's half-brother), Albert Austin, Henry Bergeman, Chuck Risener, Billy White, James T. Kelley. 33 minutes.

The Bond. (1918) *** Split-reel film made for Liberty Loan Committee, with Chaplin and Edna Purviance.

Shoulder Arms. (1918) ***** With Edna Purviance, Sydney Chaplin, Henry Bergeman, Albert Austin. Lou Costello once cited this as his candidate for the greatest comedy film ever. 35 minutes.

Sunnyside. (1919) **** With Edna Purviance, Tom Wilson, Henry Bergeman. 29 minutes.

A Day's Pleasure. (1919) ***** With Jackie Coogan, Babe London, Edna Purviance, Henry Bergeman. Two reels.

The Kid. (1921) ***** Feature, with Jackie Coogan, Edna Purviance, Carl Miller, Tom Wilson, Chuck Reisner, Albert Austin, Nellie Blye Baker, Henry Bergeman, Lita Grey. Assistant director Chuck Reisner. Photographed by Rollie Totheroe.

The Idle Class. (1921) **** With Edna Purviance, Mack Swain, Allan Garcia, Loyal Underwood, Henry Bergeman, John Rand, Lita Grey, and Lita Grey's mother, Lillian McMurray. Two reels.

Pay Day. (1922) ***** With Phyllis Allen, Mack Swain, Edna Purviance, Sydney Chaplin. Two reels.

The Pilgrim. (1923) ***** With Edna Purviance, Kitty Bradbury, Mack Swain, Dinky Dean Reisner. The last Chaplin film which was not a full-length feature. 43 minutes.

United Artists Films

A Woman of Paris. (1923) ***** With Adolphe Menjou, Edna Purviance, Carl Miller, Lydia Knott, Charles French, Henry Bergeman. Charlie does not star, but he does write and direct. He makes a brief appearance in the film as a porter. 77 minutes.

The Gold Rush. (1925) ***** With Mack Swain, Georgia Hale, Tom Murray, Malcom White, Henry Bergeman. 88 minutes.

The Circus. (1928) ***** With Allen Garcia, Merna Kennedy, Harry Crocker, Henry Bergeman. 66 minutes.

City Lights. (1931) ***** With Virginia Cherrill, Florence Lee, Harry Myers, Allan Garcia, Hank Mann, Henry Bergeman. Assistant directors: Henry Bergeman, Harry Crocker, Albert Austin. Music composed by Chaplin, conducted by Alfred Newman. 87 minutes.

Modern Times. (1936) ***** With Paulette Goddard, Tiny Sanford, Chester Conklin, Hank Mann, Henry Bergeman. Assistant directors: Henry Bergeman and Carter DeHaven (Gloria's father). Music composed by Chaplin. 85 minutes.

The Great Dictator. (1940) ***** With Jack Oakie, Paulette Goddard, Reginald Garner, Henry Daniell, Bernard Gorcey, Billy Gilbert, Carter DeHaven, Emma Dunn, Eddie Gribbon, Hank Mann, Chester Conklin. 126 minutes.

Monsieur Verdoux. (1947) ***** With Martha Raye, Mady Correll, Allison Rodan, Marjorie Bennett. 122 minutes.

Limelight. (1952) ***** With Claire Bloom, Buster Keaton. 143 minutes.

A King in New York. (1957) ***** With Dawn Addams, Michael Chaplin, Phil Brown. Banned from American cinemas for over fifteen years. 122 minutes.

A Countess from Hong Kong. (1967) ** With Marlon Brando, Sophia Loren, Sydney Chaplin (Charlie's son). Charlie plays a small role in his one and only regret. 126 minutes.

Anthologies Containing Chaplin's Work

The Essanay Revue of 1916. (1916) No director credited.

Chase Me Charlie (1932). Narrated by Terry Bergeman.

Charlie Chaplin Carnival. (1938; uncut Mutual shorts *Behind the Screen, The Count, The Vagabond, The Fireman*)

Charlie Chaplin Cavalcade. (1938; uncut Mutual shorts *One A.M., The Pawnshop, The Rink, The Floorwalker*)

Charlie Chaplin Festival. (1938; uncut Mutual shorts *The Adventurer, The Cure, The Immigrant, Easy Street*)

Gaslight Follies. (1955) Directed by Joseph E. Levine.

When Comedy Was King. (1960) Robert Youngson Productions.

The Chaplin Revue. (1958) (uncut *A Dog's Life, Shoulder Arms,* and *The Pilgrim*)

Days of Thrills and Laughter. (1961) Robert Youngson Productions.

30 Years of Fun. (1963) Robert Youngson Productions.

The Funniest Man in the World. (1970) Narrated by Douglas Fairbanks, Jr.

The Gold Rush (1925) was rereleased in 1942 with music, sound effects (both scored by Chaplin), and Charlie's own narration.

4

Buster Keaton

For the most part, Charlie Chaplin is the undisputed king of motion picture comedy, but there are those who argue that Joseph Francis "Buster" Keaton is every bit as talented. Often these arguments seem quite justified, for Keaton is definitely a major artist.

Born in 1893 to vaudeville parents, Buster learned the knockabout skills which were essential to early screen comedy at a young age. He performed with his parents in their wild slapstick stage act, The Three Keatons.

Discovered by silent star Roscoe "Fatty" Arbuckle, Buster made his screen debut in Fatty's *The Butcher Boy* in 1917. Keaton's activities would often outshine those of the agile fat man in this and other Arbuckle starrers in which he appeared. Finally, he got a starring series of his own in 1920.

Buster's lack of facial expression garnered him the nickname "The Great Stone Face," but also enhanced the gags that he performed and created for his films. Rather than characterizing himself to specification, Buster would instead use himself as an object, a prop, putting himself in situations which would make even his very appearance funny. He utilized the medium for all that he could, his gags and situations taking the silent screen to its furthest boundaries.

His creativity shone in his own starring short films, including *One Week* (1920), *The Playhouse* (1921), and *The Balloonatic* (1923).

One Week has Buster building a honeymoon cottage using plans which have been sabotaged by the man his bride left behind. Since Keaton's prowess always seemed to thrive best when working with objects, the building of the house and Keaton's attempt to live in it once it's been built are poetic in their comic execution.

The film opens with Buster and his bride being pelted with rice and old shoes as they leave the church. Buster stops, finds a pair of shoes that look like they'll fit, and decides to keep them.

After a run-in on the road with the man she left behind, Buster and the new Mrs. Keaton arrive at the site where their house is to be, only to find that they must build it themselves. The wily ex-boyfriend then paints different numbers on the boxes so that they will not go according to the building directions. After a series of fascinating circumstances, Buster completes a house that looks so bizarre it

34

makes the viewer think of some distorted human face as found in early silent horror films.

In building the house, Buster's acrobatic skills are demonstrated in a variety of little incidents, including a scene where he climbs down a ladder, leans backwards so that the ladder pulls away from the house it's propped up against, and resumes his climb down from the other side of the ladder.

Once the house is built, Buster invites friends over for a housewarming party, which turns into a disaster as a terrible storm occurs. The house is no match for the weather and begins turning around like a top, spitting all of its occupants out one by one. Buster attempts to get back into the spinning house but keeps missing the door as it comes around. Once he does manage to get back in, he is propelled about and ultimately spit out again.

Keaton's gags in *One Week* are far better seen than described, and this, his first starring short film, was an excellent example of the prime quality work that was to come from this talented little man with the stone face.

The Playhouse is almost too amazing for words. While not quite Buster's best short film, it is certainly one of the most unusual, fascinating films ever conceived, especially the opening, which deals with a stage show presentation.

Buster plays absolutely every part of this film, including the orchestra leader, every member of the orchestra, every performer in the stage show being presented, and every man, woman, and child in the audience watching the show.

After a few gags, there is a shot of Keaton sleeping backstage in a theater where he is working as a stage hand; it was all a dream, a fabrication of what this lowly stagehand would like to occur in reality.

A later scene has Keaton replacing an ailing monkey in a man-animal act, with the make-up and mannerisms done to perfection. Another bizarre incident is a shot of two one-armed men in the audience applauding by hitting each other's hands together. Keaton later stated that *The Playhouse* was conceived in an attempt to satirize then-contemporary film producer Thomas Ince, who used to give himself so many screen credits in his pictures.

The Balloonatic is another one of Buster's best short films, especially in the opening sequences, these show Buster cavorting in a carnival fun house, trying both to understand and to outsmart the various little gags that he is confronted with.

Throughout all of his short films Buster's work is flawless. Like the Chaplin Mutual series, Buster's work needed no improvement.

The best example of the short films is *Cops* (1922), which features the greatest chase sequence in all of film comedy, choreographed perfectly by Buster Keaton. A series of unrelated circumstances soon has the entire police force, hundreds of cops, all chasing Keaton. Sight gags include Buster balancing on a board atop a high fence, with a cop on either side teeter-tottering the board in their attempts to get their hands on him.

Buster performed more amazing acrobatic skills in this comedy than in any

Buster Keaton vs. the universe in "One Week" (top, 1920) and vs. Phyllis Haver in "The Balloonatic" (bottom, 1923).

other short film. The gags were beautifully executed, the chase choreographed with all the style and grace of a ballet, and the film remains one of the silent screen's most important short comedies.

In 1923, shorts were abandoned for features, where Buster showed even more of his comic brilliance while proving that these more ambitious projects were no threat.

Seven Chances (1925) features a classic climax that has shades of *Cops*, but instead of policemen, Buster is running from falling boulders. Hundreds of large rocks, small rocks, and medium-sized rocks come rolling down a hill after Buster, who must dodge them while hurrying to get to his wedding, for he is already late.

By this time, Keaton had proven again and again that he was one of the screen's most creative comic minds when it came to the creation and execution of gags. In 1927, he also proved his capabilities as a filmmaker in the same league as Chaplin.

The General is one of the undisputed classics of motion picture history, ranking with Chaplin's *City Lights*, as well as with such American screen milestones as *Citizen Kane, Birth of a Nation, Intolerance*, and *All Quiet on the Western Front*. With its brilliant use of editing, camerawork, and basic cinematic structure, *The General* was better than even Keaton had seemed capable of doing. It displayed a filmmaking brilliance that very, very few in the history of screen comedy have achieved. Unfortunatley, time didn't allow Buster any more films that came near to the caliber of *The General*. In 1927, the year *The General* was released, Warner Brothers released *The Jazz Singer*, which made history as the first talking picture.

Keaton went over to MGM in 1928 to make the silent features *The Cameraman* and *Spite Marriage*, which were both magnificent works. Then, in 1929, something hit Keaton that compared with that year's stock market crash. He was stripped of his screen authority and forced to eschew pantomime for dialogue in his forthcoming films, which would all be talkies.

Unlike Chaplin, who by this time had complete ownership and control over his product, Buster had to cater to studio rulers who were too budget-minded to allow Keaton the creative control he sorely needed. His first talkie shows it.

Easy Go (1929) is perhaps the worst comedy made by a major comic artist. Almost none of Keaton's talents survive this dull musical comedy, which is now more dated than films Buster made a decade before. Unfortunately, the ensuing MGM features weren't much better.

Doughboys (1930), an army comedy with predictable gags done better by others before, was Keaton's next film for Metro. It was better than his first, but not by much.

Sidewalks of New York (1931) was written in collaboration with Jules White, whose taste for violence didn't fit Buster's work at all. White's later work with The Three Stooges showed his lack of artistic discipline even more clearly.

Parlor, Bedroom, and Bath (1931) was better due to some clever gags and a good supporting cast, but the fact remained that these films could have been made by any less capable comic.

Buster's next three films for MGM—*Speak Easily, The Passionate Plumber* (both 1932), and *What! No Beer?* (1933) had him teamed with Jimmy Durante, a combination that went together about as well as pickles and chocolate. Buster then left MGM.

Keaton starred in a series of talking shorts for Al Christie's Educational studios from 1934 to 1937 and another for Columbia from 1939 to 1941. He also acted as consultant on some comedy features (including some of the best Red Skelton vehicles) and did bits in feature films. He had sunk to the level that Harry Langdon had sunk to, but not due to ego. Buster was a victim of the studio system—a genius not allowed full reign to create what he knew best. It was a terribly frustrating time.

Despite the unfairness, Buster did remain active and even did some television work in the fifties and sixties. In one of his last films, *Sergeant Deadhead* (1965), which starred Frankie Avalon, Buster fumbled his way around a bunch of contemporary teen idols who may or may not have known that they were working with one of the screen's greatest legends.

Buster Keaton died in 1966, but toward the end saw a rekindling of interest in his old silent comedies. He began making public appearances at various institutions, and a thunderous standing ovation he received at one of these appearances reduced the comedian to tears.

Finally given the recognition denied him for so long, Buster Keaton was again being hailed as the brilliant movie clown he'll always be. If any motion picture artist could even begin to equal Chaplin, Buster Keaton would perhaps be the only one, for, like Chaplin, his contribution to the cinema is priceless and his artistry is timeless.

Keaton Filmography

Short Subjects Starring Keaton
All run two reels (15 to 20 minutes) and are directed by Keaton and Eddie Cline.

One Week. (1920) ***** With Sybil Seely, Joe Roberts.

Convict 13. (1920) ***** With Sybil Seely, Eddie Roberts, Joe Keaton, Eddie Cline.

The Scarecrow. (1920) **** With Sybil Seely, Joe Roberts, Al St. John.

Neighbors. (1920) **** With Joe Roberts, Virginia Fox, Eddie Cline, Jack Duffy. (Alternate title: *The Back Yard.*)

The Haunted House. (1921) ***** With Virginia Fox, Joe Roberts, Eddie Cline.

The High Sign. (1921) **** With Al St. John.

The Goat. (1921) ***** With Virginia Fox, Joe Roberts, Mal St. Clair.

The Playhouse. (1921) ***** With Virginia Fox, Joe Roberts.

The Boat. (1921) ***** With Sybil Seely, Eddie Cline.

The Paleface. (1921) ***** With Joe Roberts.

Cops. (1922) ***** With Virginia Fox, Joe Roberts, Eddie Cline, 300 extras.

My Wife's Relations. (1922) ***** With Kate Price, Monty Collins, Tommy Willson.

The Blacksmith. (1922) ***** With Virginia Fox, Joe Roberts.

The Frozen North. (1922) **** With Virginia Fox, Joe Roberts.

Electric House. (1922) **** With Joe, Myra, and Lousie Keaton.

Daydreams. (1922) A complete print of this three-reel film is no longer in existence.

The Balloonatic. (1923) ***** With Phyllis Haver.

The Love Nest. (1923) **** With Virginia Fox, Joe Roberts.

Silent Feature Films

The Saphead. (1920) *** With William Crane, Irving Cummings, Carol Holloway, Beaulah Booker, Jeff Williams, Ed Jobson, Eddie Alexander, Jack Livingstone, Henry Clauss. Directed by Herbert Blanche. 66 minutes.

The Three Ages. (1923) ***** With Margaret Leahy, Wallace Beery, Joe Roberts, Horace Morgan, Lionel Bellmore. Directed by Keaton with Eddie Cline. 54 minutes.

Our Hospitality. (1923) ***** With Natalie Talmadge (Mrs. Keaton), Buster Keaton, Jr., Joseph Keaton (Buster's father). Directed by Keaton with John Blystone. 68 minutes.

Sherlock Jr. (1924) ***** With Kathy McGuire, Ward Crane, Joe Keaton, Horace Morgan, Ford West. Directed by Keaton with William B. Goodrich (Fatty Arbuckle). 49 minutes.

The Navigator (1924) ***** With Kathy McGuire, Fred Vroom, Noble Johnson, Clarence Burton. Directed by Keaton with Donald Crisp. 55 minutes.

Seven Chances. (1925) ***** With Roy Barnes, Snitz Edwards, Ruth Dwyer, Franke Raymond, Erwin Connelly. Directed by Keaton. 57 minutes.

Go West. (1925) ***** With Howard Truesdale, Kathy Myers, Ray Thompson. Directed by Keaton. 73 minutes.

Battling Butler. (1926) ***** With Sally O'Neil, Snitz Edwards, Francis McDonald, Mary O'Brien, Walter James. Directed by Keaton. 75 minutes.

The General. (1927) ***** With Glen Cavender, Jim Farley, Fred Vroom, Marian Mack, Charles Smith. Unquestionably Keaton's masterpiece. Directed by Keaton and Clyde Bruckman. 81 minutes.

College. (1927) *** With Ann Cornwall, Flora Bramley, Harold Goodwin, Buddy Mason, Grant Withers. Directed by James Horne. 63 minutes.

Steamboat Bill Jr. (1928) *** With Ernest Torrence, Tom Lewis, Tom McGuire, Marion Byron. Directed by Charles Reisner. 73 minutes.

The Cameraman. (1928) ***** With Marceline Day, Harold Goodwin, Harry Gribbon, Sid Bracy. Directed by Edward Sedgwick. 84 minutes.

Spite Marriage. (1929) ***** With Dorothy Sebastian, Edward Earle, Leila Hyams, William Betchel, John Byron. Keaton's last silent released with musical score and sound effects. Directed by Edward Sedgwick. 92 minutes.

The Talkies

Easy Go. (1929) * With Robert Montgomery, Anita Page, Trixie Friganza, Edward Brophy. (Alternate titles: *Le metteur en scene* in France and *Estrellados* in Spanish.) Directed by Edward Sedgwick. 93 minutes.

Doughboys. (1930) ** With Edward Brophy, Sally Eilers, Cliff "Ukelele Ike" Edwards, Frank Mayo. Directed by Edward Sedgwick.

Parlor, Bedroom, and Bath. (1931) *** With Charlotte Greenwood, Reginald

Denny, Cliff Edwards, Dorothy Christy. Directed by Edward Sedgwick. (Alternate titles: *Buster se marie* in France, *Casanova wilder willen* in Germany.)

Sidewalks of New York. (1931) ** With Anita Page, Cliff Edwards, Frank Rowan, Norman Phillips, Frank LaRue. The film Keaton hated most. Directed by Jules White. 70 minutes.

The Passionate Plumber. (1932) ** With Jimmy Durante, Irene Purcell, Polly Moran, Gilbert Roland, Maude Eburne. Directed by Edward Sedgwick. 73 minutes. (Alternate title: *Le plombier amoureux* in France.)

Speak Easily. (1932) *** With Jimmy Durante, Thelma Todd, Hedda Hopper, William Pawley, Sidney Toler, Henry Armetta, Edward Brophy, Ruth Selwyn. Directed by Edward Sedgwick. 80 minutes.

What! No Beer? (1933) ** With Jimmy Durante, Roscoe Ates, Phyllis Barry, John Mijian, Henry Armetta. Directed by Edward Sedgwick. 70 minutes.

Le roi des champs elysées. (1934) French film not released in the United States.

An Old Spanish Custom. (1936) With Lupita Tovar, Esme Percy, Lyn Harding. British feature film, also known as *The Invader*. Directed by Adrian Brunel. 60 minutes.

El moderno barba azul. (1946) Mexican production not released in the United States.

Educational Films
All two reels and directed by Charles Lamont.

The Gold Ghost. (1934) *** With Dorothy Dix, William Worthington.

Allez Oop. (1934) *** With Dorothy Sebastian, Harry Myers.

Palooka from Paducha. (1935) ** With Joe, Myra, and Louise Keaton.

One Run Elmer. (1935) *** With Lola Andre, Dewey Robertson.

Hayseed Romance. (1935) ** With Jane Jones, Dorthea Kent.

Tars and Stripes. (1935) ** With Vernon Dent, Dorthea Kent.

The E-Flat Man. (1935) ** With Dorthea Kent, Broderick O'Farrell.

The Timid Young Man. (1935) *** With Lola Andre, Tiny Sanford.

Three on a Limb. (1936) ** With Lola Andre, Grant Withers.

Grand Slam Opera. (1936) *** With Diana Lewis, Harold Goodwin.

Blue Blazes. (1936) ** With Arthur Jarrett, Rose Kessner.

The Chemist. (1936) ** Directed by Al Christie.

Mixed Magic. (1936) ** With Eddie Lambert, Marilyn Stewart.

Jail Bait. (1937) *** With Harold Goodwin, Bud Jamison.

Ditto. (1937) *** With Barbara and Gloria Brewster.

Love Nest on Wheels. (1937) *** With Al St. John, Bud Jamison.

Columbia Short Subjects
All two reels and directed by Jules White.

Pest From the West. (1939) *** With Lorna Gray, Gino Corrado. Directed by Del
  Lord.

Mooching Through Georgia. (1939) *** With Monty Collins, Bud Jamison.

Nothing but Pleasure. (1940) *** With Dorothy Appelby, Bud Jamison.

Pardon My Berth Marks. (1940) *** With Dorothy Appelby, Elsie Ames.

Taming of the Snood. (1940) ** With Dorothy Appelby, Elsie Ames.

The Spook Speaks. (1940) ** With Dorothy Appelby, Elsie Ames.

His Ex Marks The Spot. (1940) ** With Dorothy Appelby, Matt McHugh.

So You Won't Squawk. (1941) *** With Matt McHugh, Bud Jamison.

General Nuisance. (1941) *** With Elsie Ames, Monty Collins.

She's Oil Mine. (1941) ** With Monty Collins, Eddie Laughton.

Supporting Roles (Features)

Hollywood Cavalcade. (1939) Directed by Irving Cummings. 96 minutes.

The Villain Still Pursued Her. (1940) Directed by Eddie Cline. 65 minutes.

Li'l Abner. (1940) Directed by Albert Rogell. 78 minutes.

Forever & a Day. (1943) Directed by Cedric Hardwicke. 104 minutes.

San Diego I Love You. (1944) Directed by Reginald LeBorg. 83 minutes.

That's the Spirit. (1945) Directed by Charles Lamont. 93 minutes.

That Night With You. (1945) Directed by William Sieter. 84 minutes.

God's Country. (1946) Directed by Robert Tansey. 65 minutes. Color.

The Loveable Cheat. (1949) Directed by Richard Oswald. 74 minutes.

In The Good Old Summertime. (1949) Directed by Robert Z. Leonard. 102 minutes. Color.

You're My Everything. (1949) Directed by Walter Lang. 94 minutes. Color.

Sunset Boulevard. (1950) Directed by Billy Wilder, 110 minutes.

Limelight. (1952) Directed by Charles Chaplin. 143 minutes.

Around the World in 80 Days. Directed by Michael Anderson. 148 minutes. Color.

Adventures of Huckleberry Finn. (1960) Directed by Michael Curtiz. 107 minutes. Color.

Ten Girls Ago. (1962) Directed by Harold Daniels. (Never released.)

It's a Mad Mad Mad World. (1962) Directed by Stanley Kramer. 192 minutes. Color.

Pajama Party. (1964) Directed by Don Weis. 85 minutes. Color.

Beach Blanket Bingo. (1965) Directed by William Asher. 98 minutes. Color.

Beach Blanket Bingo. (1965) Directed by William Asher. 98 minutes. Color.

How to Stuff a Wild Bikini. (1965) Directed by William Asher. Color.

Sergeant Deadhead. (1965) Directed by Norman Taurog.

A Funny Thing Happened on the Way to the Forum. (1966) Directed by Richard Lester. 99 minutes. Color.

War Italian Style. (1967) Directed by Luigi Scattini. 84 minutes. Color.

(The last two films were released posthumously.)

Miscellaneous Short Subject Appearances

Buster had supporting roles in the following Fatty Arbuckle starrers (all two reels):

The Butcher Boy (1917), Coney Island (1917), Out West (1918), The Bellboys (1918), Moonshine (1918), Good Night Nurse (1918), The Hayseed (1919), The Garage (1919).

Buster also made the following 16mm shorts for industrial purposes:

Paradise for Buster. (1952) Directed by Del Lord. 39 minutes.

The Devil to Pay. (1960) Directed by Herb Skoble. 28 minutes.

Triumph of Lester Snapwell. (1963) Color, with no director credit. 22 minutes.

Film. (1965) Directed by Alan Schneider. 22 minutes.

Railrodder. (1965) Directed by Gerald Petterton. 21 minutes. Color.

The Scribe. (1966) Directed by John Sebert. 30 minutes. Color. (Posthumously released.)

Anthologies Containing Keaton's Work

When Comedy Was King. (1960) Produced by Robert Youngson. 80 minutes.

The Great Chase. (1962) Presented by Paul Killiam. 79 minutes. Tinted color.

Thirty Years of Fun. (1963) Produced by Robert Youngson. 85 minutes.

The Sound of Laughter. (1963) Narrated by Ed Wynn. 75 minutes.

MGM's Big Parade of Comedy. (1965) Produced by Robert Youngson. 82 minutes.

Four Clowns. (1970) Produced by Robert Youngson. (The other three clowns are Laurel, Hardy, and Charley Chase.) 97 minutes.

The Three Stooges Follies. (1974) Columbia release featuring short films starring Stooges and others. Keaton's *Nothing but Pleasure* (1940) shown intact. 116 minutes.

Documentaries Containing Keaton's Work

The Sad Clowns. (1961) 16mm production by Sterling Educational Films also features work by Chaplin and Harry Langdon. 27 minutes.

Buster Keaton Rides Again. (1965) 56-minute feature showing Keaton working on *The Railrodder.* (1965). Produced by the National Board of Canada.

5

Harold Lloyd

When one discusses the greats of silent screen comedy, the names Chaplin, Keaton, and Lloyd are always mentioned in the same breath, as if the speaker were referring to something singular rather than a group of three different artists.

Chaplin was the king of comedy, Keaton a serious rival, and Harold Lloyd another strong contender for the crown. There is no reason to begrudge Harold his stance among film buffs as one of the greats, because he is, quite frankly, a genius.

There are nevertheless a few things to consider. Lloyd was very popular in his heyday (the twenties), every bit as much as Chaplin or Keaton, and is fondly remembered today. He did not, however, achieve this greatness as rapidly as Buster or Charlie.

Chaplin's expertise was still in development when his did his first films at Keystone, but the genius still showed, and many of his earliest films are among his best.

In literally stealing films right out from under talented Fatty Arbuckle, Keaton's genius shone, and his first solo efforts are among his finest.

Lloyd had growing pains. At first he played a character named Lonesome Luke in a series of slapstick one-reelers with Bebe Daniels and Bud Jamison. These films were similar to the Chaplin Keystones, but relied too heavily on the kicks and rock-throwing antics that get a little too silly and annoying after a while.

A lot of Lonesome Lukes came and went with almost no development (other than slapstick experience) before Harold discovered the glasses. A pair of horn-rimmed glasses turned Lloyd into the youthful go-getter with the never-say-die attitude, a character as important to silent comedy as Chaplin's tramp.

But Harold made little progress in the ensuing shorts, most of which had him teamed with Snub Pollard. There are funny moments in *Spring Fever, Just Neighbors*, and *The Big Idea*, among others, but Harold still hadn't hit his stride.

After four years and hundreds of one-reelers, Harold began making little gems every so often. Most notable was *Don't Shove*, which reminds one of Chaplin's *The Rink*.

Graduating to two-reelers in 1920, Lloyd discovered the thrill element in silent comedy and began experimenting with it. While a film like *Haunted Spooks* was only semi-successful, films like *High & Dizzy* and *Never Weaken* showed the potential of a real master comic.

Never Weaken, Lloyd's last short film, was a priceless thriller of a comedy in which Lloyd is teetering helplessly on a skyscraper, trying desperately to get down without falling. Repeated a few years later by Laurel and Hardy in *Liberty*, this thrill element enhanced the silent comedy of Lloyd perfectly, and nobody played it better. Films like this were test runs for his classic feature *Safety Last* which was forthcoming.

When Harold began making features in 1921, he really hit his stride. Lloyd turned out eighteen feature films, the majority being among the screen's greatest triumphs, while the others were at the very least thoroughly enjoyable.

His first feature, *A Sailor Made Man*, was an excellent work running just under five reels. His next, *Grandma's Boy*, was a wonderful example of the type of comedy audiences could expect from Lloyd in the future.

Lloyd was a go-getter who never gave up. Whether teetering on a ledge or beating up a bully three times his size, Harold always won out with good-natured determination. Without using pathos, Harold was also capable of a poignancy that caused viewers to sympathize with him, laughing all the way.

Safety Last (1923) is considered by some his masterpiece; others believe it to be the greatest silent comedy ever made. The thrill element is used to its fullest potential in this exciting film, which features Harold climbing a tall downtown building as a publicity stunt to impress his girl. After over sixty years, *Safety Last* is still as thrilling and exciting a picture as one could ever hope for. Photos from *Saftey Last* of Harold climbing the building or hanging from the hand of a large clock are perhaps more famous than stills from any other silent film.

Another brilliant Lloyd feature was *Hot Water* (1924), which utilized the type of frustration found in Charley Chase's best vehicles. Harold has a wife in this one (unusual, since he is more often in pursuit of a girl whom he wins in the end through sheer determination), and is beset by problems with meddling in-laws, traffic jams, and a crowded bus on which he tries to calm the live wild turkey he is bringing home for supper.

In terms of laughs, *Hot Water* is just an outstanding film, and Harold plays it beautifully. It is also the first in a string of four silent comedies which display his genius to absolute perfection.

Poignancy without pathos or sappy sentiment is one of the highlights of *The Freshman*. Oddly underrated by Lloydists, it is in fact a beautiful film. Harold gives one of his most moving performances as a naive young man who dreams of going to college, only to finally attend and become a laughingstock due to silly carrying on which he believes to be sincere. Corny in that it allows Harold to emerge as a football hero, the film still exemplifies the "go-getter" factor in Harold's work, and the football game in the end is very exciting.

Next to last in this string of four classics is *For Heaven's Sake* (1926), and if there's a better chase in a silent film (or a talkie, *The French Connection* notwithstanding), this writer would sure like to hear about it. A runaway bus, a dog pound wagon, a revolving door, and Lloyd all add up to more thrills than found in virtually any other comedy from this period. Only Chaplin, Keaton, or Laurel and Hardy could ever make a silent picture as funny as this.

Finally, *The Kid Brother* (1927) is perhaps Harold Lloyd's greatest film. It has simply everything: story, gags, poignancy, thrills, and fine characterization. As a skinny weakling in a family of macho men, Lloyd proves himself by emerging victorious in the exciting finale involving a fist fight that will cause even the most critical viewer to cheer.

Speedy (1928) is Harold's last silent film, and it shows a mellower demeanor in his character and a slower pace with fewer gags. The film is a big comedown from the four gems that preceeded it, although it is still quite enjoyable.

The talkies were next, and Lloyd's silent feature *Welcome Danger* was hastily re-dubbed for release as a sound picture. Longer than the usual Lloyd offering (nearly two hours), *Welcome Danger* did not garner very good reviews, although it did big box office, presumably due to the fact that Harold's massive throngs of fans were dying to hear him talk. *Welcome Danger* is no longer available for screening, owners of Harold's estate stating that they will probably never release it.

Feet First (1930) is a rehash of old schtick, not up to Lloyd's standards. While still thrilling in the building-ledge sequences, it can't measure up to the classic *Safety Last* or even the short film *Never Weaken*.

Movie Crazy (1932) is usually hailed as Lloyd's best talkie, and it is magnificent. One of its priceless sequences has Harold attending a party wearing a magician's coat, with all of his various tricks and gags springing one by one. This sequence is brilliant, and was lifted almost verbatim by the Three Stooges for their short subject *Loco Boy Makes Good* (1942). Lloyd, of course, sued.

The Cat's Paw (1934) has been blatantly overlooked, although it is another example of Lloyd's genius. Very offbeat, this bizarre little item features Harold as a missionary's son who has been reared in China. When the naive lad returns to his homeland of America, mobsters pull strings to get the far-from-streetwise Lloyd elected as town mayor so that they can go about their underworld doings uninterrupted.

When Harold does get wise to what's going on, he devises a bizarre and elaborate plan to get the mobsters to confess to all past crimes. With the help of several Chinese-American friends, Lloyd rounds up every crook in town, chains them up in a store basement, and threatens to chop off their heads in a mass execution.

While sticking to the basic little-guy-who-rises-from-object-of-ridicule premise, *The Cat's Paw* is still the most offbeat and one of the most fascinating Harold Lloyd talking comedies.

Then it was back to the old formula with *The Milky Way* (1936), another of Lloyd's greatest films, remade by Danny Kaye in 1946 as *The Kid from Brooklyn*. Lloyd is a meek milkman who is duped into becoming a prizefighter. The usual

Harold Lloyd in a famous moment from "Safety Last" (1923).

gags about training, fighting, and inevitable gangster interruptions are all played to their fullest potential.

Harold planned to retire after *Professor Beware* (1938), another overlooked gem that more closely resembles his silent classics of the go-getter who wins by determination (complete with chase sequence) than any of his talkies. He did lay off film for years until he was coaxed back by ace writer-director Preston Sturges, whose work included such classics as *Sullivan's Travels* and *Hail the Conquering Hero*.

The Sins of Harold Diddlebock (1947) is a good comedy with a great supporting cast, but not up to Lloyd's or Sturges's talents. Both were great individual forces in screen comedy, and together they should have made one of the best films in American screen history. The film was released in an abridged version in 1951 under the title *Mad Wednesday*. Both versions still exist today. Lloyd then retired, never to make another film other than two compilations of his work. He received a special Academy Award in 1952. Lloyd died of cancer in 1971.

In looking over the filmography of Harold Lloyd, one is reminded of Stan Laurel, as Lloyd too would assume full supervision over his product without getting script or directorial credit. He does receive producer credit, and most films were made for his own company, for Lloyd had as much say in his screen work as Chaplin, Keaton, or Laurel and Hardy.

Harold Lloyd's work represents a group of some very impressive screen comedies, strong enough to immortalize their creator. As stated in the beginning of this chapter, Harold Lloyd was a genius, and the films he has left behind more than prove such a claim.

Lloyd Filmography

NOTE: As Lloyd made hundreds of one- and two-reel films, few of which are substantial representations of his talents (and those few which do merit such attention are discussed in the text), only his features are given star ratings. A title listing of his short films in chronological order follows the feature listing.

The Harold Lloyd Features (silents)

A Sailor Made Man. (1921) **** With Mildred Davis, Noah Young, Dick Sutherland, Gus Leonard, Leo Willis. Directed by Fred Newmeyer. 49 minutes.

Grandma's Boy. (1922) **** With Mildred Davis, Anna Townsend, Charles Stevenson, Noah Young, Dick Sutherland. Directed by Fred Newmeyer. 61 minutes.

Doctor Jack. (1922) **** With Mildred Davis, John T. Prince, Eric Mayne, C. Norman Hammond. Directed by Fred Newmeyer. 57 minutes.

Safety Last. (1923) ***** With Mildred Davis, Bill Strothers, Noah Young, Westcott B. Clarke. Directed by Fred Newmeyer and Sam Taylor. 74 minutes.

Why Worry. (1923) **** With Jobyana Ralston, John Aasen, Leo White, Wallace Howe. Directed by Fred Newmeyer and Sam Taylor. 66 minutes.

Girl Shy. (1924) *** With Jobyana Ralston, Richard Daniels, Carlton Griffin. Directed by Fred Newmeyer and Sam Taylor. 82 minutes.

Hot Water. (1924) ***** With Jobyana Ralston, Josephine Crowell, Charles

Harold Lloyd has all the problems he can handle in "Hot Water" (1924).

Stevenson, Mickey McBann. Directed by Fred Newmeyer and Sam Taylor. 57 minutes.

The Freshman. (1925) ***** With Jobyana Ralston, Brooks Benedict, James Anderson, Joseph Harrington. Directed by Fred Newmeyer and Sam Taylor. 80 minutes.

For Heaven's Sake. (1926) ***** With Jobyana Ralston, Noah Young, James Mason, Paul Weigel. Directed by Sam Taylor. 66 minutes.

The Kid Brother. (1927) ***** With Jobyana Ralston, Walter James, Leo Willis, Olin Francis, Eddie Boland. Directed by Lewis Milestone and Ted Wilde. 83 minutes.

Speedy. (1928) *** With Ann Christy, Ben Woodruff, Brooks Benedict, Babe Ruth, Dan Wolheim. Directed by Ted Wilde. 87 minutes.

Sound Feature Films

Welcome Danger. (1929) With Barbara Kent, Noah Young, Charles Middleton, William Walling. Originally a silent which was then dubbed and released as a talkie, *Welcome Danger* is no longer available for screening. Directed by Mal St. Clair and Clyde Bruckman. 115 minutes.

Feet First. (1930) *** With Barbara Kent, Robert McWade, Lillianne Leighton, Henry Hall, Noah Young. Directed by Clyde Bruckman. 93 minutes.

Movie Crazy. (1932) ***** With Constance Cummings, Kenneth Thompson, Sydney Jarvis, Eddie Featherstone. Directed by Clyde Bruckman. 84 minutes.

The Cat's Paw. (1934) ***** With Una Merkel, George Barbier, Alan Dinehart, Grace Bradley, Nat Pendelton. Directed by Sam Taylor. 102 minutes.

The Milky Way. (1936) ***** With Adolphe Menjou, Veree Teasedale, Helen Mack, William Gargan, George Barbier. Directed by Leo McCarey. 89 minutes.

Professor Beware. (1938) **** With Phyllis Welch, Raymond Walburn, Lionel Stander, William Frawley, Thurston Hall. Directed by Elliot Nugent. 87 minutes.

The Sins of Harold Diddlebock. (1947) *** With Frances Ramsde, Jimmy Conlin, Raymond Walburn, Rudy Vallee, Edgar Kennedy. Directed by Preston Sturges. 89 minutes. (Released in 1951 as *Mad Wednesday* at 76 minutes.)

Lonesome Luke one-reelers

1915

Lonesome Luke
A Mixup for Maisie
Some Baby
Giving Them Fits
Bughouse Bellhops
Great While It Lasted
Ragtime Snapshots
Foozle at the Tea Party
Rhymes and Roughnecks
Patient's Pranks
Social Gangster
Leans to the Literary
Lugs Luggage
Lolls in Luxury

1916

The Candy Cutup
• Foils the Villain
• Rural Roughnecks
• Pipes the Pippens
Circus King
• Double
Happy Days
• Bomb Throwers
• Late Lunchers
• Laughs Last
• Fatal Flivver
• Society Mixup
• Washful Waiting
• Ride Roughshod

• Crystal Gazer
• Lost Lamb
• Does the Midway
• Joins the Navy
• And the Mermaids
• Speedy Club Life
• Bangtails
• The Chauffeur
• The Gladiator
• Patient Provider
• Newsie Knockout
• Movie Muddle
Rank Impersonater
• Firework Fizzle
• Locates the Loot
• Shattered Sleep
• Lost Liberty
• Busy Day

1917

• Stop Luke and Listen
• Messenger
• Mechanic
• Trolley Troubles
• Wild Women
• Loses Patients
• London to Laramie
• Clubs Are Trump
• Lively Life
• Tin Can Alley
• Honeymoon
• We Never Sleep

The one-reel silents featuring the "glasses" character:

1918

• All Aboard
• Move On
• Bashful

• The Tip
• The Big Idea
• The Lamb
• At Him Again
• Beat It

Gasoline Wedding
Look Pleasant *Please*
Here Come the Girls
Let's Go
On The Jump
Follow the Crowd
Pipe the Whiskers
It's a Wild Life
Hey There
Kicked Out
Non Stop Kid
Two Gun Gussie
City Slicker
Sic 'Em *Towser*
Are Crooks Dishonest
Ozark Romance
That's Him
Bride and Gloom
Two Scrambled
Bees in His ~~Parlor~~ *Bonnett*
Why ~~Me~~ *Pick on Me*
Har 'Em Rave
Take a Chance
She Loves Me Not

1919

Going Going Gone
Ask Father
On the Fire
I'm on My Way
Look Out Below

The Dutiful Fub
Next Aisle Over
Sammy in Siberia
Just Dropped In
Crack Your Heels
Ring Up the Curtain
Young Mr. Jazz
Si Señor
Before Breakfast
The Marathon
Back to the Woods
Pistols for Breakfast
Swat the Crook
Off the Trolley
Spring Fever
Just Neighbors
At the Old Stage Door
Never Touched Me
A Jazzed Honeymoon
Count Your Change
Chop Suey & Co.
Heap Big Chief
Don't Shove
Be My Wife
The Rajah
He Leads, Others Follow
Soft Money
Count the Votes
Pay Your Dues
His Only Father

Two-reel comedies:

1919

Bumping Into Broadway
Captain Kidd's Kids
From Hand to Mouth

1920

His Royal Slyness
Haunted Spooks
Eastern Westerner

High and Dizzy
Get Out and Get Under
Number Please
Now or Never
Among Those Present

1921

I Do
Never Weaken

Lloyd's work also appeared in the following self-produced compilations:

Harold Lloyd's World of Comedy (1962)

Harold Lloyd's Funny Side of Life (1963)

Lloyd said possibly to have appeared in the following early Roach comedies as Lonesome Luke, but reports are unconfirmed:

Every Ten Minutes, Spitball Sadic, Soaking His Clothes, Pressing His Suit, Terrible Stuck Up, Fresh from the Farm, Tinkering with Trouble (all 1915)

6

Charley Chase

Charley Chase was not a slapstick comedian, but instead used a comedy of situation similar to what was later on television. Using a timid, fidgety character in most of his films and a youthful, go-getter, Harold Lloyd–type character in others, Charley managed to make some very entertaining short comedies.

Now, to compare Chase's short films with television isn't to belittle them (not even TV's greatest moments match Chase's work); instead the comparison is meant as an example.

In all of his films, Charley is trying to accomplish something which he finds quite important, but he is constantly beset with little obstacles which he has difficulty in overcoming. Even those which are easy to defeat are so much in the way that the frustration builds nonetheless.

Chase made some brilliant, some good, and some average comedies, but never an out-and-out bad one, and the brilliant ones sprang up quite often, not only in the twenties but also in the thirties when Chase began an equally delightful series of talking shorts.

Today Charley Chase is revered by those who know his work, which includes a mere handful of film students and comedy buffs. He really should be more noted, but his oblivion is apparently the result of several factors.

First: Chase made short comedies, his feature film appearances being limited to small roles in films like Laurel and Hardy's *Sons of the Desert* (1934). It is often stated that Chase was tried in a feature by Hal Roach and failed, but how can one judge by one feature (which is available only in an abridged, two-reel form today)? Laurel and Hardy's first feature, *Pardon Us* (1931), was also quite weak, but the duo proved themselves with subsequent attempts before Roach decided to eschew short films in 1935. Perhaps if Laurel and Hardy had made *Pardon Us* in 1935 as their first feature, Roach would have found them unsuitable and they would have been forced to take refuge at Columbia studios as Chase did. It's almost scary to imagine Stan and Oliver in violent short films directed by Jules White.

Another reason for Chase's being so little known today is that although his films are available, they are seldom run. Even on college campuses, where presenting older films (especially comedies) is a standard practice, Chase's work has been neglected for revivals of anyone from Fields, the Marx Brothers and Laurel and Hardy to the Three Stooges, the Ritz Brothers, and the Bowery Boys.

Charley got his early training as a bit player at Sennett's Keystone studio in films like *Love Loot & Crash* (1913) and Chaplin's *Gentlemen of Nerve* (1914). After many of these standard Keystone knockabout shorts and no forseeable increase in roles or development, Chase went off to the Hal Roach studios, where he worked as a writer, director, and comedian.

Chase didn't take long at all to establish his screen persons. Unlike Harold Lloyd, who toiled for years in countless one-reelers, he seemed to know right off just how he wanted to present himself on screen.

While his earlier one-reelers were more slapstick-oriented, they maintained the same order of situations replete with mounting frustrations that Chase was to use in his later two- and three-reel comedies on into the talky revolution.

All Wet (1924) is one of Charley's earliest vehicles as well as one of his greatest. Hurrying to meet a train, Charley gets his auto stuck in a huge mud hole. He tries getting it out, but only succeeds in getting it stuck worse and getting himself full of mud. He tries to get help from a nearby gas station, but even their tow truck is powerless, for soon the auto is completely underwater. Chase dives under to fasten the towing hook to the car's axle, but when the tow truck pulls, it succeeds only in pulling off the axle.

Chase finally gives up and heads for the train station on foot, getting there just as a load of caged circus animals are being carried off of the train. Chase realizes he has run his errand on the wrong day. As if this weren't enough, Charley then stands too close to a lion's cage, and the beast reaches out and rips off Chase's trousers, leaving the hapless clown to run home in his underwear.

After more enjoyable one-reelers like *Young Oldfield* and *Ten Minute Egg*, Chase graduated to two-reel films. Effectively using situations involving embarass-ment and frustration, Charley continued to make such fine vehicles as *The Way of All Pants* (1926), which has him caught without pants under a dinner table where people are eating, making it impossible to leave without being discovered; and *Limousine Love* (1927), a hilarious short which has Charley driving to his wedding not knowing that there is a naked woman in the back seat of his car.

Charley was a box office favorite by the time he made his masterpiece, *Movie Night*, in 1929. His last silent film, *Movie Night* is a perfect example of humor in mounting frustration.

It opens with family man Charley discovering that his child has the hic-coughs. Knowing that a good scare is a cure, Chase dons a sheet and poses as a ghost. His efforts are a bit too convincing, for the child faints and Chase is bawled out by his wife.

The family then heads for the movies, where Charley finds that the cashier is also suffering from the hiccoughs. Undaunted by his earlier results, Chase decides to pose as a burglar in order to scare away her hiccoughs. He succeeds only in nearly getting himself thrown in jail by a cop.

Charley Chase is the most notoriously underrated screen comic of them all.

Inside the theater, Charley himself develops a severe case of the hiccoughs, which prove to be so annoying to the other patrons that he is forced to leave the building.

When talking pictures came into prominence, Chase was far from threatened. He not only adapted beautifully, he enhanced his films with a pleasant singing voice. He continued at Roach, with *Now We'll Tell One* (1932), *You Said a Hatful* (1933), *The Nickel Nurser* (1933), *Public Ghost Number One* (1934), and *It Happened One Day* (1935) among his better efforts.

Charley's best talking short, by far, is *Girl Grief* (1932), which ranks as high as Laurel and Hardy's Oscar-winning *The Music Box* (1932) and Buster Keaton's brilliant *Cops* (1923). Experiments conducted by this writer show that this Chase film will receive more laughs than any other comedy from an audience of any age group. It's a big claim to make, but these experiments seem to prove that *Girl Grief* is about the best short comedy ever made.

The premise has timid Charley substituting for his ailing mother as a singing teacher at an all-girl school. The only problem is that Charley is afraid of girls.

One of the first scenes at the school has Chase teaching his mother's class to sing "I Was Seeing Nellie Home." The two spinster school principals listen closely outside the classroom door as the class gives a nice, easy rendition of the song.

Slowly the girls start speeding up the beat, adding be-bop gibberish along with the actual lyrics. This appalls the eavesdropping principals, but seems to delight innocent Charley, who gets so caught up in the beat he begins dancing about the room. When the principals storm in, Charley stops dead in his tracks, hastily returns the girls to the proper pace for the last line of the song, and then, stammering about and dying of embarassment, Charley stumbles out of a large open window, lands on a diving board, and bounces fully clothed into the school pool.

Another priceless scene in *Girl Grief* has two mischievous students sneaking into Charley's room and pouring large amounts of catnip on his bed. Dozens of stray cats enter Charley's room during the night through an open window and dive into his bed. Chase later awakens with a start to find all these cats hopping about playfully on his bed.

Girl Grief is an extremely funny comedy, better constructed than even some prestigious comedy classics. This film alone is sufficient reason to rank Chase alongside Chaplin, Keaton, and Laurel and Hardy in the front ranks of movie comedians.

The feature Roach tried Chase in was *Bank Night* (1936). Conflicting stories result in confusion over why it was not released and why Chase was given no more work in features.

Some accounts state that the folks who actually held bank night at the theatres would not allow many of the scenes, and therefore the film had to be edited to two reels and issued as a short subject. Other accounts claim that the bank night people objected only to the title, and that Roach's editing the film to two reels was due to Chase's inability to sustain a feature film. *Bank Night* was released as *Neighborhood House*, and there seems to be no indication of Chase faltering. If Charley had been given the same freedom in a feature series as he had been given in short films . . . in fact, if Chase had been given a feature series at all, he just may have proven himself eventually. That he was not given the chance is perhaps the greatest injustice in film history.

Chase sought refuge at Columbia and was fortunately given the freedom to control his own short films, but despite an above-average output quality-wise, Charley seemed to be in a bit of a rut, unable to progress any further. Years of heavy drinking (due, some say, to marital difficulties) hampered his health, but his films remained on par right up until his untimely death in 1940.

Charley Chase is easily the best of the unfairly neglected screen comics of the past, and deserves a lot more recognition. Hopefully his work will eventually be rediscovered by the masses and given its due, for Chase is one of history's most engaging show business personalities.

Chase Filmography

The Silent Shorts

At First Sight. (1924) *** Directed by James Parrott (Jimmy Chase, Charley's brother.) One reel.

One of the Family. (1924) *** Directed by James Parrott. One reel.

Just a Minute. (1924) *** Directed by James Parrott. One reel.

Powder and Smoke. (1924) *** Directed by James Parrott. One reel.

A Perfect Lady. (1924) *** Directed by James Parrott. One reel.

Hard Knocks. (1924) **** Directed by James Parrott. One reel.

Love's Detour. (1924) ** Directed by James Parrott. One reel.

Don't Forget. (1924) *** Directed by James Parrott. One reel.

The Fraidy Cat. (1924) *** Directed by James Parrott. One reel.

Publicity Pays. (1924) *** Directed by Leo McCarey. One reel.

April Fool. (1924) *** Directed by Leo McCarey. One reel.

Position Wanted. (1924) *** Directed by Leo McCarey. One reel.

Young Oldfield. (1924) **** Directed by Leo McCarey. One reel.

Stolen Goods. (1924) *** Directed by Leo McCarey. One reel.

Jeffries, Jr. (1924) **** Directed by Leo McCarey. One reel.

Why Husbands Go Mad. (1924) *** Directed by Leo McCarey. One reel.

Ten Minute Egg. (1924) **** Directed by Leo McCarey. One reel.

Seeing Nellie Home. (1924) *** Directed by Leo McCarey. One reel.

Sweet Daddy. (1924) *** Directed by Leo McCarey. One reel.

Why Men Work. (1924) *** Directed by Leo McCarey. One reel.

Outdoor Pajamas. (1924) *** Directed by Leo McCarey. One reel.

Sittin' Pretty. (1924) *** Directed by Leo McCarey. One reel.

Too Many Mamas. (1924) **** Directed by Leo McCarey. One reel.

Bungalow Boobs. (1924) *** Directed by Leo McCarey. One reel.

Accidental Accidents. (1924) *** Directed by Leo McCarey. One reel.

All Wet. (1924) ***** Directed by Leo McCarey. One reel.

The Poor Fish. (1924) *** Directed by Leo McCarey. One reel.

The Royal Razz. (1924) **** Directed by Leo McCarey. One reel.

Hello Baby. (1925) **** Directed by Leo McCarey. One reel.

Fighting Fluid. (1925) *** Directed by Leo McCarey. One reel.

The Family Entrance. (1925) *** Directed by Leo McCarey. One reel.

Plain and Fancy Girls. (1925) *** Directed by Leo McCarey. One reel.

Should Husbands Be Watched. (1925) *** Directed by Leo McCarey. One reel.

Hard Boiled. (1925) *** Directed by Leo McCarey. One reel.

Is Marriage the Bunk? (1925) **** Directed by Leo McCarey. One reel.

Bad Boy. (1925) **** Directed by Leo McCarey. One reel.

Big Red Riding Hood. (1925) *** Directed by Leo McCarey. One reel.

Looking for Sally. (1925) **** Directed by Leo McCarey. Two reels.

What Price Goofy? (1925) **** Directed by Leo McCarey. Two reels.

Isn't Life Terrible? (1925) *** Directed by Leo McCarey. Two reels.

Innocent Husbands. (1925) *** Directed by Leo McCarey. Two reels.

No Father to Guide Him. (1925) *** Directed by Leo McCarey. Two reels.

The Caretaker's Daughter. (1925) *** Directed by Leo McCarey. Two reels.

The Uneasy Three. (1925) *** Directed by Leo McCarey. Two reels.

His Wooden Wedding. (1925) ***** Directed by Leo McCarey. Two reels.

Charley My Boy. (1926) *** Directed by Leo McCarey. Two reels.

Mama Behave. (1926) *** Directed by Leo McCarey. Two reels.

Dog Shy. (1926) **** Directed by Leo McCarey. Two reels.

Mum's The Word. (1926) **** Directed by Leo McCarey. Two reels.

Long Fliv the King. (1926) **** Directed by Leo McCarey. Two reels.

Mighty Like a Moose. (1926) ***** Directed by Leo McCarey. Two reels.

Crazy Like a Fox. (1926) *** Directed by Leo McCarey. Two reels.

Bromo and Juliet. (1926) **** Directed by Charles Parrott (Charley Chase). Two reels.

Tell'em Nothing. (1926) *** Directed by James Parrott. Two reels.

Be Your Age. (1926) **** Directed by Leo McCarey. Two reels.

There Ain't No Santa Claus. (1926) *** Directed by Fred Guiol. Two reels.

Many Scrappy Returns. (1927) *** Directed by Fred Guiol. Two reels.

Are Brunette Safe? (1927) *** Directed by Fred Guiol. Two reels.

One Mama Man. (1927) *** Directed by Fred Guiol. Two reels.

Forgotten Sweeties. (1927) *** Directed by Fred Guiol. Two reels.

Bigger and Better Blondes. (1927) *** Directed by Fred Guiol. Two reels.

Fluttering Hearts. (1927) *** Directed by Fred Guiol. Two reels.

What Women Did for Me. (1927) **** Directed by Fred Guiol. Two reels.

Now I'll Tell One. (1927) *** Directed by Fred Guiol. Two reels.

Assistant Wives. (1927) *** Directed by Fred Guiol. Two reels.

The String of Strings. (1927) *** Directed by Fred Guiol. Two reels.

The Lighter That Failed. (1927) *** Directed by Fred Guiol. Two reels.

The Way of All Pants. (1927) ***** Directed by Fred Guiol. Two reels.

Never the Dames Shall Meet. (1927) **** Directed by Fred Guiol. Two reels.

All for Nothing. (1928) **** Directed by Fred Guiol. Two reels.

Aching Youths. (1928) **** Directed by Fred Guiol. Two reels.

Limousine Love. (1928) ***** Directed by Fred Guiol. Two reels.

The Fight Pest. (1928) **** Directed by Fred Guiol. Two reels.

Imagine My Embarrassment. (1928) **** Directed by Fred Guiol. Two reels.

Is Everybody Happy? (1928) **** Directed by Fred Guiol. Two reels.

The Booster. (1928) **** Directed by Fred Guiol. Two reels.

All Parts. (1928) *** Directed by Fred Guiol. Two reels.

Chasing Husbands. (1928) **** Directed by Fred Guiol. Two reels.

Ruby Love. (1929) *** Directed by Fred Guiol. Two reels.

Off to Buffalo. (1929) **** Directed by Fred Guiol. Two reels.

Movie Night. (1929) ***** Directed by Fred Guiol. Two reels.

The Sound Shorts

All produced by Hal Roach studios, and running two reels in length except as otherwise noted.

The Big Squawk. (1929) *** With Nena Quartero, Gale Henry. Directed by Warren Doane.

Leaping Love. (1929) *** With Isabelle Keith, Dixie Gay, Barbara Leonard, Maurice Black. Directed by Warren Doane.

Snappy Sneezer. (1929) **** With Anders Randolf, Thelma Todd. (Also released in silent form under the title *Hay Fever.*) Directed by Warren Doane.

Crazy Feet. (1929) *** With Thelma Todd, Anita Garvin. Directed by Warren Doane.

Stepping Out. (1929) *** With Thelma Todd, Anita Garvin. Directed by Warren Doane.

Great Gobs. (1929) ** With Edgar Kennedy, Linda Laredo, Mildred Costello, William Guiler. Directed by Warren Doane.

The Real McCoy. (1930) ** With Edgar Kennedy, Thelma Todd, Charley Hall. Directed by Warren Doane.

Whispering Whoopee. (1930) **** With Thelma Todd, Anita Garvin, Eddie Dunn, Kay Delsys. Directed by James Horne.

All Teed Up. (1930) **** With Edgar Kennedy, Thelma Todd, Dell Henderson. Directed by James Horne.

Fifty Million Husbands. (1930) *** With Ruth Hiatt, Tiny Sanford, Christine Maple, Edgar Kennedy. Directed by Edgar Kennedy.

Fast Work. (1930) ** With June Marlowe, Dell Henderson, Charles French, Pat Harmon. Directed by James Horne.

Girl Shock. (1930) **** With Elinor Vandivere, Edgar Kennedy, Jerry Mandy, Catherine Courtney. Directed by James Horne.

Dollar Dizzy. (1930) *** With Thelma Todd, Edgar Kennedy, James Finlayson. Directed by James Horne. Three reels.

Looser Than Loose. (1930) **** With Thelma Todd, Dorothy Granger, Dell Henderson, Wilfred Lucas, Edgar Kennedy, Eddie Dunn, Gordon Douglas. Directed by James Horne.

High C's. (1931) *** With Thelma Todd, Carlton Griffin, Jimmy Adams and the Ranch Boys. Directed by James Horne. Three reels.

Thundering Tenors. (1931) ***** With Lillian Elliot, Elizabeth Forrester, Dorothy Granger, Lena Malena, Eddie Dillon. Directed by James Horne.

The Pip From Pittsburgh. (1931) ***** With Thelma Todd, Dorothy Granger, Kay Deslys, Carlton Griffin, Charley Hall. Directed by James Parrott.

Rough Seas. (1931) *** With Thelma Todd, Carlton Griffin, Frank Brownlee. A sequel to *High C's.* Directed by James Parrott. Three reels.

One of the Smiths. (1931) *** With James Finlayson, Louise Carver. Leo Willis. Directed by James Parrott. Three reels.

The Panic Is On. (1931) ***** With Billy Gilbert, Leo Willis, Margaret Mann. Directed by James Parrott.

Skip the Maloo! (1931) **** With Julie Bishop, Gale Henry, Dell Henderson. Remake of the 1927 *One Mama Man.* Directed by James Parrott.

What a Bozo! (1931) ***** With Gay Seabrook, Liz Forrester, Charley Hall. Directed by James Parrott.

Hasty Marriage. (1931) ***** With Jimmy Finlayson, Billy Gilbert, Harry Bernard, Lillian Elliott. Directed by Gil Pratt.

The Tabasco Kid. (1932) **** With Frances Lee, Billy Gilbert, Wilfred Lucas. Directed by James Horne.

The Nickel Nurser. (1932) ***** With Thelma Todd, Billy Gilbert, Harry Bowen, Eddie Dillon. Directed by Warren Doane.

In Walked Charley. (1932) ***** With Julie Bishop, Gertrude Astor, Dell Henderson. Directed by Warren Doane.

First in War. (1932) *** With Carlton Griffin, Nancy Torres, Billy Gilbert. Directed by Warren Doane.

Young Ironsides. (1932) ***** With Muriel Evans, Clarence Wilson, Billy Gilbert, Charley Hall. Directed by James Parrott.

Girl Grief. (1932) ***** With Muriel Evans, Nora Cecil, Ida Schumacher. Directed by James Parrott.

Now We'll Tell One. (1932) ***** With Muriel Evans, Lillian Elliot, Frank Darien, Gale Henry. Directed by James Parrott.

Mr. Bride. (1932) ***** With Dell Henderson, Charley Hall, Gale Henry, Harry Bernard. Directed by James Parrott.

Fallen Arches. (1933) ***** With Muriel Evans, Billy Gilbert, Eddie Dunn, Charley Hall, James C. Morton. Directed by Gus Meins.

Nature in the Wrong. (1933) ** With Muriel Evans, Carlton Griffin, Nora Cecil. Directed by Charles Parrott (Charley Chase).

His Silent Racket. (1933) ***** With Muriel Evans, Jimmy Finlayson, Anita Garvin, Harry Bernard. Directed by Chase.

Arabian Tights. (1933) **** With Muriel Evans, Rolfe Sedan, Carlton Griffin, Eddie Baker. Directed by Chase.

Sherman Said It. (1933) ***** With Nita Pike, Jimmy Adams and the Ranch Boys, Marvin Hatley, Harry Bernard. Directed by Chase.

Midsummer Mush. (1933) ***** With Betty Mack, Eddie Baker, the Ranch Boys. Directed by Chase.

Luncheon at Twelve. (1933) ***** With Betty Mack, Gale Henry, Billy Gilbert, Charley Hall. Sections of this film were used by the Stooges in the Chase-directed short *Tassles in the Air*. Directed by Chase.

The Cracked Iceman. (1934) ***** With Betty Mack, Billy Gilbert, Harry Bowen, Spanky MacFarland, Stymie Beard. Directed by Chase.

Four Parts. (1934) **** With Betty Mack, Florence Roberts. Directed by Chase and Eddie Dunn.

I'll Take Vanilla. (1934) **** With Tommy Bond, Betty Mack, Harry Bowen. Directed by Chase.

Another Wild Idea. (1934) ***** With Betty Mack, Frank Austin, Tiny Sanford, Harry Bernard. Directed by Chase.

It Happened One Day. (1934) **** With Betty Mack, Oscar Apfel, Charley Hall, James C. Morton, Eddie Baker. Directed by Chase.

Something Simple. (1934) **** With Betty Mack, Dell Henderson, Arthur Houseman, Lew Kelly, Charley Hall. Directed by Chase.

You Said a Hatful! (1934) **** With Dorothy Appelby, Oscar Apfel, Clarence Wilson, Harry Bernard, Tiny Sanford. Directed by Chase.

Fate's Fathead. (1934) **** With Dorothy Appelby, Dorothy Granger, Dick Alexander, Hattie McDaniel. Directed by Chase.

The Chases of Pimple Street. (1934) ***** With Betty Mack, Ruthelma Stevens, Gertrude Astor, Wilfred Lucas. Directed by Chase.

Okay Toots! (1935) **** With Jeanie Roberts, Constance Bergen, Harry Bernard. Directed by Chase and Bill Terhune.

Poker at Eight. (1935) **** With Constance Bergen, Bernadene Hayes, Tom Dugan, Harry Bernard. Directed by Chase.

Southern Exposure. (1935) *** With Constance Bergen, Alfalfa Switzer, Max Davidson. Directed by Chase.

The Four-Star Border. (1935) *** With Constance Bergen, T. Roy Barnes, Grace Goodall. Directed by Chase.

Nurse to You. (1935) ***** With Muriel Evans, Clarence Wilson, Billy Gilbert, Fred Kelsey. Directed by Chase.

Manhattan Monkey Business. (1935) **** With Joyce Compton, James Finlayson, Gertrude Astor. Directed by Chase and Harold Law.

Public Ghost Number One. (1935) ***** With Joyce Compton, Clarence Wilson, Ed Maxwell, Harry Bowen. Directed by Chase and Harold Law.

Life Hesitates at 40. (1936) **** With Joyce Compton, James Finlayson, Alfalfa Switzer. Directed by Chase and Harold Law.

The Count Takes the Count. (1936) **** With Antoinette Lees, Kewpie Morgan, Harry Bowen, Dorothy Granger. Directed by Chase and Harold Law.

Vamp 'Til Ready. (1936) *** With Wilma Cox, Brooks Benedict, Harry Bowen. Remade by Leon Errol as *Let's Go Stepping*. Directed by Chase and Harold Law.

On the Wrong Trek. (1936) *** With Rosiana Lawrence, Bonita Weber, Clarence Wilson, Bud Jamison, cameo by Laurel and Hardy. Directed by Chase and Harold Law.

Neighborhood House. (1936) **** With Darla Hood, George Meeker, Ben Taggart. Originally a 59-minute feature entitled *Bank Night*. Directed by Chase and Harold Law.

Chase left the Roach studios and began writing, directing, and starring in short comedies at Columbia studios following the release of Neighborhood House. *The following films are all two-reelers which were released by Columbia Pictures. All were directed by Del Lord except where otherwise noted.*

The Grand Hooter. (1937) **** With Peggy Stafford, Harry Semels, Bud Jamison.

From Bad to Worse. (1937) **** With Peggy Stafford.

The Wrong Miss Wright. (1937) ***** With Peggy Stafford, John Murray, Bud Jamison. Remake of Chase's 1926 silent *Crazy Like a Fox*. Directed by Charles Lamont.

Calling All Doctors. (1937) ***** With Lucille Lund, Bobby Watson, John Murray. Directed by Charles Lamont.

The Big Squirt. (1937) ***** With Leora Thatcher, Eddie Featherstone, Bud Jamison, Ted Lorch.

Man Bites Lovebug. (1937) **** With Mary Russell, John Murray, Frank Lackteen. Remade by Billy Gilbert as *Wedded Bliss*.

Time Out for Trouble. (1938) **** With Louise Stanley, Bess Flowers, Dick Curtis, Vernon Dent, Bud Jamison.

The Mind Needer. (1938) **** With Ann Doran, Bess Flowers, Vernon Dent.

The Nightshirt Bandit. (1938) *** With Phyllis Barry, Eva McKenzie, James C. Morton, Fred "Snowflake" Toomes. Directed by Jules White.

Pie ala Maid. (1938) **** With Ann Doran, John Tyrell, Lionel Belmore.

The Sap Takes a Rap. (1939) *** With Gloria Blondell, Ethel Clayton, George Cleveland.

Chump Takes the Bump. (1939) *** With Ann Doran, John Murray, Vernon Dent. Remade by Hugh Herbert as *Who's Hugh.*

Rattling Romeo. (1939) ***** With Ann Doran, John Tyrell, Harry Bernard, Bud Jamison.

Skinny the Moocher. (1939) *** With Ann Doran, John Murray, Richard Fiske, John Tyrell.

Teacher's Pest. (1939) **** With Richard Fiske, Chester Conklin.

The Awful Goof. (1939) **** With Linda Winters (Dorothy Comingore), Dick Curtis, Bud Jamison.

The Heckler. (1940) ***** With Monty Collins, Vernon Dent, Richard Fiske. Remade by Shemp Howard as *Mr. Noisy.*

South of the Boudoir. (1940) *** With Ann Doran, Helen Lynde, Arthur Q. Bryan.

His Bridal Fright. (1940) *** Iris Meredith, Bruce Bennett, Richard Fiske.

Chase also did bit roles in dozens of Sennett-Keystone films like Chaplin's *Gentlemen of Nerve,* and *Love Loot & Crash* with the Keystone Cops, as well as directing several Fox films during the late teens. He made guest appearances in the following films:

Thundering Fleas (1926) with Our Gang
Call of the Cuckoo (1927) with Max Davidson
Sons of the Desert (1934) with Laurel and Hardy
Kelly the Second (1935) with Patsy Kelly

Chase also directed dozens of films with the likes of Andy Clyde, Smith & Dale, The Three Stooges, and Harry Langdon at Columbia.

7

Laurel and Hardy

Stan Laurel and Oliver Hardy epitomized the word *team*. Any two actors in anything even semi-funny always have shades of Laurel and Hardy, with Jackie Gleason's "The Honeymooners," Neil Simon's *The Odd Couple*, and even Johnny Carson and Ed McMahon's clowning on "The Tonight Show" as examples.

Laurel and Hardy developed these influential characterizations rather quickly and perfected them with each performance. Their film series contains among the most impressive samplings of consistent high quality in screen history, and their contribution to fine arts is as great as Chaplin's.

Stan Laurel (born Arthur Jefferson, 1890) came from a show business background, making his stage debut in 1906 in his homeland of England. He came to the states as Chaplin's understudy in Fred Karno's music hall troupe, eventually finding work at the Hal Roach studios as a writer, gagman, director, and actor in comedies.

Laurel's character in early films is very similar to Chaplin's. One of these early solo efforts, *Lucky Dog* (1918), featured an actor named Oliver Hardy as the heavy, marking their first appearance together. They weren't a team yet; they just happened to be in the same film.

Hardy (born Oliver Norvelle Hardy, 1892) did not come from a show business background and originally planned to become a lawyer like his father. But a fine singing voice got him interested in show business, and he eventually found work in movies as a heavy to Chaplin imitator Billy West and popular Al Christie comic Larry Semon. Hardy had been active in motion pictures for five years by the time he appeared in *Lucky Dog*.

Stan and Ollie happend to be in the same film quite a few times, especially during the mid-twenties, and seemed to work rather well together. Hal Roach and director Leo McCarey noticed an interesting rapport, a chemistry that just seemed to stand out whenever Stan and Ollie shared a scene.

After a few experiments, the boys worked as a team in *Do Detectives Think?* (1927), a comedy which features them as bumbling detectives trying to protect a judge from an escaped killer whom he just sent up. By now the boys had developed the screen characterizations they would continue to utilize and improve upon.

Laurel was the quiet, meek, slow-witted skinny kid and Hardy the big, pompous, overbearing fat kid. Like children, they would stick together through thick and thin, but were not above sacrificing each other to extricate themselves from danger.

Laurel's character would often unwittingly get the boys into trouble, and it would be up to the slightly more clever Hardy to get them out, with whatever painful backfiring he had to take. In the process we saw that Stan liked Ollie and looked up to him as a skinny weakling would look up to his stronger, more experienced big brother.

In reality, both were immensely talented professionals who enjoyed the complete freedom of supervising their own films. They would add ideas, make revisions on the script, and ad-lib entire scenes on the spot, creating some of their most important work extemporaneously as the cameras rolled.

Laurel would be the director of all comedy scenes, with the credited director acting only as a veritable traffic cop to keep things moving along. Although he wished no screen credits for his behind-the-scenes endeavors, Stan, like Chaplin, had complete control over the creation of his films.

Throughout their entire career, Stan and Ollie worked beautifully together on screen and never battled or argued off screen. Such a relationship was a rarity among comedy teams.

The first short to be issued as an official Laurel and Hardy release was *The Second Hundred Years* (1927), which features the boys as prisoners who don painters' clothes and try to paint their way out of prison. When noticed by a suspicious street cop, Laurel and Hardy try to convince him of their innocence by painting everything in sight including bricks, windows, trees, and a girl's bottom.

The Battle of the Century (1927) ranks with their best early silents due to a mammoth pie-throwing climax. The first reel of this two-reeler has yet to be discovered and is thought to be lost forever, but the second reel has survived.

A pie man carrying a tray of pies slips on a banana peel with which Ollie has littered his path. He gets up and pushes a pie into Oliver's face. Ollie then grabs a pie to hurl at the pie man, who ducks, causing it to hit an innocent passerby. One thing leads to another until dozens of people are crowded around the pie truck, hurling pies wildly at each other, with stray pastries flying into dentists' offices, barbershops, etc. This scene builds perfectly and is an excellent example of the construction and pacing Laurel and Hardy were to use in similar comic situations throughout their film career.

Laurel and Hardy continued to make top quality short comedies like *That's My Wife* (1928), *Leave 'Em Laughing* (1928), *The Finishing Touch* (1928), *Bacon Grabbers* (1929), and *Angora Love* (1929), all including techniques which were to become mainstays of screen comedy. But *Two Tars* (1928), *You're Darn Tootin'* (1928), and *Big Business* (1929) remain their three finest silent shorts as well as three of the greatest comedies in screen history.

You're Dam Tootin' features the boys as musicians, and, like *The Battle of the Century*, builds gradually to a climax, from small battle to a large war that involves the entire block. Stan and Oliver get into an argument which soon has Stan destroying Ollie's instrument and Ollie destroying Stan's. This leads to mock violence with punching and kicking. When bystanders and passersby try to break up the fight, they succeed only in getting involved, the battle culminating with everybody ripping each other's pants off.

Two Tars is an even better example of how Laurel and Hardy could develop a small incident into something big. The film has the boys caught in a traffic jam. Everyone gets impatient and arguments ensue, one of which involves the duo and the motorist behind them (Edgar Kennedy). Arguing soon leads to violence in any Laurel and Hardy comedy, and this film is no exception. The boys do some damage to Kennedy's auto; he comes back and does some to theirs; and this goes back and forth, getting gradually more serious until finally everybody is destroying each other's car in another well-paced, perfectly executed example of reciprocal destruction.

Of all Laurel and Hardy's silent films, *Big Business* is probably best considered their masterpiece (some would argue *Two Tars*, which is justified). As Christmas tree salesmen, Stan and Ollie have no luck at all, especially when they come to the home of James Finlayson (or Fin). Fin doesn't want a tree either, but when he closes his door, he manages to close it on the team's tree, so they must ring his doorbell and bother him again.

Fin mistakes this for peristence and reacts by throwing their tree out into the street. This gets the boys mad, so Laurel takes out a pocket knife and peels the address numbers off of Fin's house. Fin reacts by cutting off Oliver's tie. One thing leads to another until Laurel and Hardy are tearing apart Fin's house and yard while Fin destroys their car and stock of Christmas trees.

One of the really fascinating things about these battles is that in their early stages, each combatant takes turns performing some act of destruction on the other's person or property. The receiver stands by patiently until it is his turn to strike back. With each bit of business more damage is done, and it seemingly becomes harder and harder for the receiver to wait his turn. This enhances the gradual buildup from petty destruction of minor things to the ultimate full-fledged war with the receiver no longer standing and waiting his turn. Like children, Stan and Ollie and their combatants believe there is all the logic in the world in their violent actions.

This basic structure, the escalation of violence, is often used on today's TV programs which dabble in slapstick; but Laurel and Hardy's perfecting of it with the actions deliberate and the pacing always gradual, shows its most important and influential use. Theirs was definitely the work of supreme comic artists. Like Charley Chase, Laurel and Hardy made a splendid transition to talking

Opposite: Stanley Laurel (left) and Oliver Hardy, one of the screen's greatest comedy teams.

pictures when silent films were being eschewed for the new medium. Their voices matched their screen characterizations perfectly, and although they still relied heavily on physical humor, they enhanced their comedy with dialogue.

The basic structure of their best sound shorts showed them trying to accomplish some ordinarily easy task, but having no luck at all in achieving their goal.

A Perfect Day (1929) has them trying to start their car and head out on a picnic. First they can't get the car started. When they take care of that, they get a flat tire. When the tire is changed, they notice the neighborhood preacher coming down the street, so they must hide in the house (it's Sunday, of course). At last, when they finally get the car going, they drive into a huge mud hole and slowly sink right in, defeated.

Hog Wild (1930) has the team trying to install a radio serial on the roof to improve the reception on Mrs. Hardy's radio. Falling off into the lily pond or down the chimney are among the problems they have. After all their toil and trouble, a man comes to take the radio away because the payments have not been made.

Helpmates (1931) has them trying to straighten up Ollie's house after a wild party so that the vacationing Mrs. Hardy doesn't find it in a shambles when she returns later that day. After dozens of slapstick misadventures, the house is finally burned to the ground.

The above three shorts are brilliant contributions to screen comedy and among the duo's best work, all using the same basic idea of trying to accomplish something that's simple, yet failing due to various circumstances.

In 1932, Laurel and Hardy took this same premise and made what many consider the all-time greatest comedy featurette: a three-reeler entitled *The Music Box* which ultimately won the boys an Academy Award.

The first half of this comedy has Laurel and Hardy assigned to deliver a piano to a home which is located atop a huge flight of stairs. They painfully try to get the instrument to its destination but are forever interrupted by people on their way down the stairs who can't get through with the piano in the way. They make it to the top a couple of times, but always lose control of the piano, which goes rolling all the way back down the stairs.

The second half has them arriving with the piano, finally, and finding that the parties are not home. Undaunted, the boys decide to break in and put the piano in the living room. Now, this doesn't sound like a difficult task, but for Laurel and Hardy it's impossible, and eventually the entire home is demolished.

As if this weren't enough, the owner of the home is one of the people Stan and Ollie got into a battle with on their way up the stairs. When he sees what they have done to his home, he takes out an ax and demolishes the piano.

The Music Box is Laurel and Hardy's masterpiece as well as one of the finest comedies ever conceived. Even non-devotees of the team are amused by this landmark comedy. Its pacing and general construction is still unequaled.

Laurel and Hardy also fared quite well in feature films. A possible exception is *Pardon Us* (1931), which is slowly paced and a bit dated. Often called a two-reel story stretched over five reels, *Pardon Us* is not a good example of Laurel and Hardy features despite many very funny sequences.

Pack Up Your Troubles (1932) is far better, ranking with their best features and bearing similarities to two Chaplin classics, *Shoulder Arms* and *The Kid*.

The first half of this film has the boys in basic training, fouling up the way one would expect. Eventually they are used as sacrifices at the front during a raid, only to accidentally capture an entire enemy troupe and become heroes. A friend, however, is less fortunate and becomes a battle casualty.

The second half finds the boys back in the states and appointing themselves as guardians of their deceased friend's orphaned little girl. With evil orphanage officials after them all the time, the boys must conceal the fact that they're taking care of her while looking for her grandparents.

Aside from the excellent comedy sequences, *Pack Up Your Troubles* shows a poignancy, especially in Ollie, that no other Laurel and Hardy films have to such a striking degree. This emotion remains one of the feature's strongest points.

Stan and Ollie continued to make excellent shorts like *Busy Bodies* (1933), *Midnight Patrol*, (1933), *Towed in a Hole* (1933), *Them Thar Hills* (1934), and *Tit for Tat* (1935 – nominated for an Oscar), until Roach made the decision to eschew all short films and switch exclusively to features.

Laurel and Hardy had no worries, having proven themselves in the past with such features as *Sons of the Desert* (1934), which along with *Way Out West* (1937) ranks as their finest work in a feature film.

It's interesting to compare *Sons of the Desert* and *Way Out West*. The choice as to which film is the better Laurel and Hardy vehicle is split down the middle among film students and comedy aficionados as well as average Laurel and Hardy fans.

Sons of the Desert, which was made first, features the boys as members of a fraternal lodge who take an oath to attend a convention in Chicago. Mrs. Laurel complies, but Mrs. Hardy won't hear of it. Oliver feigns illness, and Stan arranges for a phony doctor to diagnose the illness and state that a trip to Honolulu is the only cure. Realizing that his wife detests ocean voyages, Ollie tells her that he will have Stan accompany him, and the two sneak off to the convention.

Not long after they leave, the papers come out with headlines reading that the ship which sailed for Honolulu has sunk, and the duo's wives fear the worst. That is, until they go to the movies to calm their anxiety and see their spouses in a newsreel that covers the convention.

When Stan and Ollie return home and notice the paper which details the shipwreck, they come up with an elaborate story about how they "ship-hiked" home after the terrible ordeal, not knowing that the wives are on to them.

Sons of the Desert is a subtle domestic comedy, paced perfectly and performed even better by the team and their supporting cast, which includes Mae

Busch and Charley Chase. Rather than using gags, Laurel and Hardy depend more on situation and their reaction to events which take place. While there are some priceless gags containing some of the duo's funniest moments, the basis of this film is much more subtle than any of their other vehicles.

Way Out West has the boys traveling out west to Brushwood Gulch to deliver a valuable gold mining deed. Swindled into giving it to the wrong people, Stan and Ollie decide to right things once they get wise, and barge in to retrieve the deed. Their efforts are unsuccessful.

Returning later that night, the boys sneak in (none too subtly) to the crooks' apartment. They ultimately retrieve the deed and restore it to its rightful owner.

The plot is simpler in this film, relying more on gags, and is therefore a more typical Laurel and Hardy vehicle. Not paced or constructed cinematically as well as *Sons of the Desert*, *Way Out West* does contain more belly laughs, the strongest of which occur during the scene in which Stan and Ollie try recovering the deed for the first time.

After much running around and wrestling to get hold of the deed, Laurel finally grabs it and runs into the bedroom with it stuck down his shirt, followed closely by one of the crooks, a saloon girl. In a most unladylike manner she reaches right down Laurel's shirt and grabs for it, but this tickles Stan, who falls onto the bed kicking and screaming helplessly. Meanwhile, Oliver is being held outside the door at gunpoint, so he can be of no help.

Another plus for *Way Out West* is that it has two very pleasant musical interludes which show other facets of the duo's talents.

All in all, it just isn't possible to choose whether *Sons of the Desert* or *Way Out West* should be considered the team's masterpiece among their feature films. Let us just sit back and praise the boys for having not one, but two features which rank among the screen's greatest comedies.

In their other feature films, Laurel and Hardy seemed to fare best when sticking to their tried-and-true formula as they did in *Our Relations* (1936), *Blockheads* (1938), *A Chump at Oxford* (1940), and *Saps at Sea* (1940), which are some of their better features.

Tiresome musical numbers got in the way of priceless comedy sequences in *The Devil's Brother* (1933), *March of the Wooden Soldiers* (1934), and *The Bohemian Girl* (1936), three films based on operettas. All three should have been gems, thanks to their great comedy scenes, but the music seems to serve largely as an intermission.

Romantic subplots not directly involving the duo plagued *Swiss Miss* (1938) and *Bonnie Scotland* (1935), but even these films had enough good comedy to make them worthwhile.

One other feature, *The Flying Deuces* (1939), made for Boris Morros produc-

Opposite: Laurel and Hardy with Billy Gilbert and demolished piano in the Oscar-winning classic, "The Music Box" (1932).

tions, is also less exciting due to a heavy reliance on old gags that the boys had done better in earlier films.

All of these features were still good works, and each contained essential comedy material. It wasn't until 1941, when Laurel and Hardy left the Hal Roach studio due to money matters and signed with the more prestigious 20th Century Fox and MGM, that they finally fell victim to anti-creative authority and began to appear in works which were far below their talents.

No longer given the freedom to work out new ideas and make full use of their creativity to explore possibilities for the situations, Laurel and Hardy suffered the same fate as Buster Keaton. They were forced to do the script as written, without wasting precious studio time on comic innovation or creativity. These films were thrown together as cheaply and as quickly as possible so as to turn a profit on the Laurel and Hardy name. After nearly fifteen years, in which they made over eighty of the most priceless contributions to screen history, Laurel and Hardy became victims of the Hollywood system.

Great Guns (1941), for Fox, was a tired army comedy full of old predictable gags which could have been performed by any lesser comedians. *A-Haunting We Will Go* (1942), also for Fox, was even worse, casting the team as bumbling assistants to a hammy magician.

Air Raid Wardens (1943), for MGM, falters even more than the Fox films, despite a cast which includes Edgar Kennedy. *Jitterbugs* (1943) remains the weakest of their Fox films, with nothing even remotely appropriate to the duo's talents contained in the script. The only thing preventing any of these later works from being outright dogs is the incredible talent of Laurel and Hardy, which still managed to shine through even with the weakest material.

The Dancing Masters (1943), for Fox, has the boys playing dance instructors with Laurel teaching ballet. It is a situation with great comic potential, which was, unfortunately, unexplored. *The Big Noise* (1944) was an improvement and easily the best of the later films. Casting the boys as janitors who pose as detectives and are hired by a wacky scientist to guard a highly powerful explosive, *The Big Noise* contains more chances for the duo to utilize the humor within their characterizations than any of the films in which they were stuck during this time.

Nothing But Trouble (1944), for MGM, has the boys coming to the aid of a boy king whose uncle is plotting to kill him for an inheritance. Although still below par, this one does seem to please the kiddies.

The Bullfighters (1945), for Fox, was to be their last American film. Like *The Big Noise*, it contains a good amount of Laurel-and-Hardy-oriented comedy material. While not a great film (thanks to the studio's refusal to give the boys time to develop fresh comic ideas), it is still amusing due to its inclusion of slapstick sequences, which the team had the ability to perform perfectly under any circumstances. Although these films were made directly after Roach's *Saps at Sea*, Laurel and Hardy look about ten years older. Perhaps this was a fault of the makeup department, or perhaps the team aged ten years when looking at their scripts (it would be no surprise).

Tired of the treatment they were getting, Laurel and Hardy left pictures to concentrate on a series of tours throughout the United States and Europe during which they would perform their own material live. They made one more film, *Atoll K* (1952), in France, but this foreign production, which concerns a group of lowlifes who set up housekeeping on a deserted island that they intend to keep government-free, isn't up to standard. One of the major faults is that Stan was very ill during the filming, and his screen appearance shows it. Thinner and weaker-looking than in photos taken ten years later, Laurel's appearance takes away from his performance.

Hardy had made two appearances without Stan, in *The Fighting Kentuckian* (1949) with John Wayne and *Riding High* (1950) with Bing Crosby, when Hal Roach, Jr., proposed a Laurel and Hardy television series. The series would be in color, shot the same way as their old shorts had been done years before, with the duo in charge of their own material.

Arrangements were being made for this series when Stan was felled by a stroke. The stroke was a serious one, and Stan recovered almost completely, but his illness was enough to put a temporary halt on plans for the series.

Sadly, once Stan had recovered, Oliver fell ill. Having had heart trouble in the past, Hardy now suffered a stroke so devastating that it left him incapable of movement or speech. Stan, who has stated that Oliver was more like a brother than a friend, visited his former partner regularly until the jovial and wonderfully talented fat man died on August 7, 1957.

Stan's later years were busy ones, with the Laurel and Hardy comedies being revived in theaters and on television. Laurel would receive hundreds of pieces of fan mail from all over the world, and he insisted upon answering each one. Other entertainers, including Dick Van Dyke, Jerry Lewis, Red Skelton, Marcel Marceau, and Buster Keaton would visit Stan for lengthy discussions on their mutual art. Stan Laurel died on February 23, 1965.

The best adjectives in the English language are used so often for such small things that it's impossible to describe Laurel and Hardy's profound importance to screen comedy with mere words. There has never been a team that worked so beautifully together, with such perfect cohesion, nor will there ever be another pair of comedians with such brilliant insights or exceptional talents in the realm of screen comedy. Laurel and Hardy made up the greatest comedy team ever.

Laurel and Hardy Filmography

The Silent Shorts
All running two reels in length

The duo's films together prior to their teaming up:

Duck Soup. (1927) Not available for screening.

Slipping Wives. (1927) *** With Priscilla Dean, Albert Conti. Directed by Fred Guiol.

Love 'Em and Weep. (1927) ** With Mae Busch, James Finlayson. Laurel in a large role; Hardy does small bit part. Remade as *Chickens Come Home* in 1931. Directed by Fred Guiol.

Why Girls Love Sailors. (1927) Not available for screening.

With Love and Hisses. (1927) *** With James Finlayson, Frank Brownlee. Directed by Fred Guiol.

Sugar Daddies. (1927) *** With James Finlayson, Noah Young, Charlotte Mineau. Directed by Fred Guiol.

Sailor Beware. (1927) *** With Anita Garvin, Tiny Sanford, Lupe Velez. Directed by Hal Yates.

Flying Elephants. (1927) ** With Dorothy Coburn, Leo Willis, Tiny Sanford, James Finlayson. Directed by Fred Butler.

Putting Pants on Phillip. (1927) *** With Sam Lufkin, Harvey Clark. Directed by Clyde Bruckman.

Silent shorts made as a team:

Do Detectives Think? (1927) **** With James Finlayson, Viola Richard, Noah Young. The duo's first film as a team. Directed by Fred Guiol.

The Second Hundred Years. (1927) ***** With James Finlayson, Eugene Pallette, Tiny Sanford. First "official" Laurel & Hardy comedy. Directed by Fred Guiol.

Hats Off. (1927) With James Finlayson, Anita Garvin, Dorothy Coburn. No known print of this film exists. Directed by Hal Yates and Leo McCarey.

The Battle of the Century. (1927) ***** With Eugene Pallette, Charley Hall, Anita Garvin. Only the second reel of this film is known to exist. Directed by Clyde Bruckman.

Leave 'Em Laughing. (1928) ***** With Edgar Kennedy, Otto Fries, Charley Hall. Directed by Clyde Bruckman and Leo McCarey.

The Finishing Touch. (1928) ***** With Edgar Kennedy, Dorothy Coburn, Sam Lufkin. Directed by Clyde Bruckman and Leo McCarey.

From Soup to Nuts. (1928) **** With Anita Garvin, Tiny Sanford, Edna Marian, Otto Fries. Directed by E. Livingston Kennedy (Edgar Kennedy).

You're Darn Tootin'. (1928) ***** With Otto Lederer, Christian Frank. Directed by E. Livingston Kennedy (Edgar Kennedy).

Their Purple Moment. (1928) **** With Anita Garvin, Kay Delsys. Directed by James Parrott.

Should Married Men Go Home. (1928) **** With Anita Garvin, Edgar Kennedy, Dorothy Coburn. Directed by James Parrott.

Early to Bed. (1928) ** No supporting cast. Directed by Emmett Flynn and Leo McCarey.

Two Tars. (1928) ***** With Thelma Hill, Ruby Blaine, Edgar Kennedy, Charley Hall. Directed by James Parrott and Leo McCarey.

Habeas Corpus. (1928) ***** With Richard Carle. Directed by James Parrott and Leo McCarey.

We Faw Down. (1928) **** With Kay Delsys, Vivien Oakland. (Also released as *We Slip Up.*) Directed by Leo McCarey.

Liberty. (1929) **** With Tom Kennedy, James Finlayson. Clearly inspired by Harold Lloyd's *Never Weaken*. Directed by Leo McCarey.

Wrong Again. (1929) *** With Dell Henderson. Directed by Leo McCarey.

That's My Wife. (1929) ***** With Vivien Oakland. Directed by Leo McCarey and Lloyd French.

Big Business. (1929) ***** With James Finlayson, Tiny Sanford. Directed by Leo McCarey and James Horne.

Double Whoopee. (1929) **** With Jean Harlow, Tiny Sanford. It is said that a "dubbed" version is available with voices by actor and avid Laurel and Hardy buff Chuck McCann. This is unconfirmed. Directed by Lewis Foster.

Bacon Grabbers. (1929) ***** With Edgar Kennedy, Jean Harlow. Directed by Lewis Foster.

Angora Love. (1929) ***** With Charley Hall, Edgar Kennedy, Harry Bernard. Directed by Lewis Foster.

The Sound Films

Unaccustomed As We Are. (1929) *** With Mae Busch, Edgar Kennedy, Charley Hall, Thelma Todd. Directed by Lewis Foster. Two reels.

Berth Marks. (1929) *** With Pat Harmon, Charley Hall, Harry Bernard. Directed by Lewis Foster. Two reels.

Men O' War. (1929) *** With Anne Cornwall, Gloria Greer, James Finlayson, Charley Hall, Harry Bernard. Directed by Lewis Foster. Two reels.

A Perfect Day. (1929) ***** With Edgar Kennedy, Kay Delsys, Harry Bernard, Baldwin Cooke. Directed by James Parrott. Two reels.

They Go Boom. (1929) *** With Charley Hall, Sam Lufkin. Directed by James Parrott. Two reels.

The Hoosegow. (1929) *** With James Finlayson, Tiny Sanford, Leo Willis, Charley Hall. Directed by James Parrott. Two reels.

Night Owls. (1930) ***** With Edgar Kennedy, James Finlayson, Anders Randolph. Directed by James Parrott. Two reels.

Blotto. (1930) ***** With Anita Garvin, Tiny Sanford, Charley Hall, Frank Holliday. Directed by James Parrott. Three reels.

Brats. (1930) ***** No supporting cast. Directed by James Parrott. Two reels.

Below Zero. (1930) *** With Charley Hall, Frank Holliday, Tiny Sanford, Leo Willis, Blanch Payson. Directed by James Parrott. Two reels.

Hog Wild. (1930) ***** With Fay Holdreness, Dorothy Granger. Directed by James Parrott. Two reels.

The Laurel & Hardy Murder Case. (1930) ** With Fred Kelsey, Stanley Blystone, Tiny Sanford, Dell Henderson. Directed by James Parrott. Three reels.

Another Fine Mess. (1930) *** With Thelma Todd, Charles Gerard, James Finlayson. Directed by James Parrott. Three reels.

Be Big. (1930) *** With Anita Garvin, Isabelle Keith. Directed by James Parrott. Three reels.

Chickens Come Home. (1931) **** With Mae Busch, Thelma Todd, James Finlayson. Directed by James Horne. Three reels.

Laughing Gravy. (1931) ***** With Charley Hall, Harry Bernard. Directed by James Horne. Two reels.

Our Wife. (1931) ***** With Babe London, James Finlayson. Directed by James Horne. Two reels.

Pardon Us. (1931) *** With Wilfred Lucas, Walter Long, June Marlowe, James Finlayson, Charley Hall, Otto Fries, Tiny Sanford. (Alternate titles: *Hinter Schloss und Riegel* in Germany, *Sous les verrous* in France, *Gaol Birds*, and *Jail Birds*. On television often cut up into two-reelers entitled *Whatta Stir* and *Tooth Trouble*.) Directed by James Parrott. 56 minutes.

Come Clean. (1931) ***** With Gertrude Astor, Linda Loredo, Mae Busch, Charlie Hall. Directed by James Horne. Two reels.

One Good Turn. (1931) *** With Mary Carr, James Finlayson, Billy Gilbert. Directed by James Horne. Two reels.

Beau Hunks. (1931) **** With Charles Middleton, Broderick O'Farrell, Charley Hall, Tiny Sanford. Directed by James Horne. Four reels.

Helpmates. (1931) ***** With Blanche Payson, Bobby Burns, Robert Callahan. Directed by James Parrott. Two reels.

Any Old Port. (1932) ***** With Walter Long, Jaqueline Wells, Harry Bernard, Charley Hall, Sam Lufkin. Directed by James Horne. Two reels.

The Music Box. (1932) ***** With Billy Gilbert, Charley Hall, Sam Lufkin, Lilyan Irene, Gladys Gale. Academy Award winner for best live action short subject. Same basic idea used by Chaplin in *His Musical Career* (1914) and later by the Three Stooges in *An Ache in Every Stake* (1941). Considered by many to be the duo's masterpiece. Directed by James Parrott. Three reels.

The Chimp. (1932) **** With Billy Gilbert, James Finlayson, Charles Gamora. Directed by James Parrott. Three reels.

County Hospital. (1932) *** With Billy Gilbert, William Austin. Directed by James Parrott. Two reels.

Scram. (1932) *** With Arthur Housman, Dick Cramer, Vivien Oakland. Directed by Ray McCarey. Two reels.

Pack Up Your Troubles. (1932) ***** With Jaquie Lyn, Donald Dillaway, Tom Kennedy, James Finlayson, George Marshall, Mary Carr, Muriel Evans, Billy

Gilbert, Grady Sutton, Frank Brownlee, Charles Middleton. (On television often cut up into short subjects titled *Doughboy Daze* and *Smitherines*.) Directed by George Marshall and Ray McCarey. 70 minutes.

Their First Mistake. (1933) *** With Mae Busch, Billy Gilbert, George Marshall. Directed by George Marshall. Two reels.

Towed in a Hole. (1933) ***** With Billy Gilbert. Directed by George Marshall. Two reels.

Twice Two. (1933) **** With Baldwin Cooke, Charley Hall. Directed by James Parrott. Two reels.

Me & My Pal. (1933) **** With James Finlayson, James C. Morton, Charley Hall, Bobby Dunn. Directed by Charles Rogers. Two reels.

The Devil's Brother. (1933) **** With Dennis King, Thelma Todd, James Finlayson, Henry Armetta, Tiny Sanford, Lane Chandler, Arthur Pierson, Lucille Browne. (Alternate titles: *Bogus Bandits, The Virtuous Tramps*. Originally titled *Fra Diavolo* and based on that opera by Daniel F. Auber. On television often cut up into short subjects titled *Easy Come Easy Go, In Trouble*, and *Cry Babies*.) Directed by Charles Rogers and Hal Roach. 90 minutes.

The Midnight Patrol. (1933) **** With Charley Hall, Frank Brownlee, Eddie Dunn, Marion Bardell. Directed by Lloyd French. Two reels.

Busy Bodies. (1933) ***** With Charley Hall, Tiny Sanford. Directed by Lloyd French. Two reels.

Dirty Work. (1933) ***** With Lucien Littlefield, Sam Addams. Directed by Lloyd French. Two reels.

Sons of the Desert. (1934) ***** With Mae Busch, Dorothy Christie, Charley Chase, Lucien Littlefield, John Elliot. On television often edited to two reels and titled *Fun on the Run*. Considered along with *Way Out West* (1937) to be the duo's feature masterpiece. (Alternate titles: *Fraternally Yours, Sons of the Legion*.) Directed by William Seiter. 70 minutes.

Oliver the Eighth. (1934) **** With Mae Busch, Jack Barty. Directed by Lloyd French. Three reels.

Going Bye Bye. (1934) **** With Mae Busch, Walter Long. Directed by Charles Rogers. Two reels.

Them Thar Hills. (1934) ***** With Charley Hall, Mae Busch, Billy Gilbert. Directed by Charles Rogers. Two reels.

March of the Wooden Soldiers. (1934) **** With Charlotte Henry, Felix Knight, Henry Brandon, Florence Roberts, Johnny Downs, Marie Wilson, Jean Darling, Kewpie Morgan, Billy Bletcher. Originally titled *Babes in Toyland* and based on that operetta by Victor Herbert, remade by Walt Disney in 1962. (Alternate title: *Revenge is Sweet.* Available as a one-reeler, *Banished to Bogeyland*). Directed by Charles Rogers and Gus Meins. 79 minutes.

The Live Ghost. (1934) **** With Walter Long, Mae Busch, Charley Hall, Arthur Housman. Directed by Charles Rogers. Two reels.

Tit for Tat. (1935) ***** With Mae Busch, Charley Hall, Bobby Burns, James C. Morton. Sequel to *Them Thar Hills.* Directed by Charles Rogers. Two reels. Nominated for an Academy Award.

The Fixer Uppers. (1935) *** With Charles Middleton, Mae Busch, Arthur Housman, Noah Young. Directed by Charles Rogers. Two reels.

Thicker Than Water. (1935) **** With Daphne Pollard, James Finlayson, Harry Bowen. The duo's last short film. All subsequent films are features. Directed by Charles Rogers. Two reels.

Bonnie Scotland. (1935) *** With June Lang, William Janney, Mary Howard, James Finlayson, Lionel Bellmore, Daphne Pollard, Marvin Hatley. (Alternate title: *Heroes of the Regiment.* For television sometimes broken into shorts: *In a Mess, The Rookies, Bang Bang, All Wet.*) Directed by James Horne. 80 minutes.

The Bohemian Girl. (1936) **** With Mae Busch, Antonio Moreno, Darla Hood, Jacqueline Wells, James Finlayson, Eddie Borden, Bobby Dunn. Based on Balfe's operetta. For television sometimes cut up into shorts: *Gyp the Gypsy* and *Kidnapped.* Directed by James Horne. 70 minutes.

Our Relations. (1936) ***** With Daphne Pollard, Betty Healy, Sidney Toler, Alan Hale, Arthur Housman, James Finlayson, Dell Henderson. A two-reel abridgement *Twin Trouble* is available to TV. Directed by Henry Lachman. 75 minutes.

Way Out West. (1937) ***** With James Finlayson, Rosina Lawrence, Sharon Lynne, Chill Wills, Stanley Fields, the Avalon Boys, James C. Morton, Tex Driscoll, Flora Finch, Vivien Oakland. Considered, along with *Sons of the Desert*, to be the duo's feature masterpiece. A three-reel abridgement entitled *Wacky*

Gag publicity shot for Laurel and Hardy's 1935 "Bonnie Scotland."

Westerners or *The Wacky West* is available to television. Directed by James Horne. 65 minutes. Released in computerized color in 1985.

Swiss Miss. (1938) *** With Walter Woolf King, Della Lind, Eric Blore, Doodles Weaver, Stanley Blystone. A two-reel abridgement entitled *Alpine Antics* is available to TV. Directed by John Blystone. 73 minutes.

Blockheads. (1938) ***** With Billy Gilbert, Minna Gombell, Patricia Ellis, James Finlayson, Tommy Bond. On television often cut up into two short subjects, *Do It Yourself* and *What Next*. Directed by John Blystone. 58 minutes.

The Flying Deuces. (1939) *** With Jean Parker, Reginald Gardner, Charles Middleton, James Finlayson. A two-reel abridgement entitled *In The Guardhouse* is available to TV. Released by Boris Morros Productions for RKO Radio Pictures. Directed by A. Edward Sutherland. 70 minutes.

A Chump at Oxford. (1940) **** With Wilfred Lucas, Charley Hall, Peter Cushing, Anita Garvin, James Finlayson. Originally released in America at 42 minutes. A two-reel abridgement entitled *Alter Ego* is available to television. Directed by Alf Goulding. 63 minutes.

Saps at Sea. (1940) **** With Dick Cramer, James Finlayson, Ben Turpin (his last role), Charley Hall. The duo's last film for Hal Roach studios, and their last real quality work. On TV often broken into two-reelers, *Horn Hero* and *Where to Now.* Directed by Gordon Douglas. 57 minutes.

Great Guns. (1941) ** With Sheila Ryan, Dick Nelson, Edmund McDonald, Ludwig Stossel, Kane Richmond. Directed by Monty Banks. 75 minutes.

A-Haunting We Will Go. (1942) ** With Sheila Ryan, Dante the Magician, John Shelton, Elisha Cook, Jr. Directed by Alf Werker. 67 minutes.

Air Raid Wardens. (1943) ** With Edgar Kennedy, Jaqueline White, Stephen McNally, Donald Meek. Directed by Edward Sedgwick. 67 minutes.

Jitterbugs. (1943) ** With Vivien Blaine, Bob Bailey, Lee Patrick, Noel Madison. Directed by Mal St. Clair. 75 minutes.

The Dancing Masters. (1943) ** With Trudy Marshall, Bob Bailey, Margaret Dumont, Daphne Pollard. Directed by Mal St. Clair. 60 minutes.

The Big Noise. (1944) *** With Arthur Space, Doris Merrick, Veda Ann Borg, Bobby Blake, Esther Howard. Directed by Mal St. Clair. 75 minutes.

Nothing But Trouble. (1944) ** With Mary Boland, David Leland, Phillip Merivale, Henry O'Neill. Directed by Sam Taylor. 70 minutes.

The Bullfighters. (1945) *** With Richard Lane, Ralph Sanford, Margo Woode, Carol Andrews, Rory Calhoun. Directed by Mal St. Clair. 70 minutes.

Atoll K. (1951) ** With Suzy Delair, Max Elloy, Felix Oudart, Luigi Tosi. Released at 82 minutes in America under the title *Utopia*, while known as *Robinson Crusoe Land* in England. Directed by Leo Joannon and John Berry. 98 minutes.

Laurel and Hardy made guest appearances in the following films:

Forty Five Minutes From Hollywood. (1926) In separate roles. Directed by Fred Guiol.

Call of the Cuckoo. (1927) starring Max Davidson. Directed by Clyde Bruckman. Two reels.

Hollywood Revue of 1929. All-star film directed by Charles Reisner. 82 minutes.

Rogue Song. (1930) Color Lawrence Tibbett vehicle directed by Lionel Barrymore. 115 minutes.

Stolen Jools. (1931) All-star film directed by William McGann. Two reels.

On the Loose. (1931) Starring Thelma Todd & ZaSu Pitts. Directed by Hal Roach. Two reels.

Wild Poses. (1933) Our Gang comedy directed by Robert McGowan. Two reels.

Hollywood Party. (1934) Jimmy Durante feature directed by Richard Boleslavsky. 70 minutes.

On the Wrong Trek. (1936) Written by, directed by and starring Charley Chase. Two reels.

Pick a Star. (1937 aka *Movie Struck*) starring Rosina Lawrence & Patsy Kelly. Directed by Edward Sedgwick. 70 minutes.

Tree in a Test Tube. (1943) Color government short by Pete Smith. Two reels.

A super 8mm color home movie, circa 1955, entitled Stan Visits Ollie *as well as* Laurel & Hardy On Tour *from about 1952 are both floating around among collectors.*

Anthologies Containing Laurel & Hardy's Work

The Golden Age of Comedy. (1958) Produced by Robert Youngson.

When Comedy Was King. (1960) Produced by Robert Youngson.

Days of Thrills & Laughter. (1961) Produced by Robert Youngson.

Thirty Years of Fun. (1963) Produced by Robert Youngson.

MGM's Big Parade of Comedy. (1965) Produced by Robert Youngson.

Laurel & Hardy's Laughing Twenties. (1965) Produced by Robert Youngson.

Crazy World of Laurel & Hardy. (1965) Produced by Jay Ward.

Further Perils of Laurel & Hardy. (1966) Produced by Robert Youngson.

Four Clowns. (1970) Produced by Robert Youngson (the other two clowns are
   Keaton and Chase).

The Best of Laurel & Hardy. (1982) Produced by Hal Roach Studios, Inc.

   *Laurel and Hardy also appeared in cartoon form in many Disney, Warner
Brothers, and Ub Iwerks productions as well as a ton of Larry Harmon–produced
cartoons during the late sixties.*
   *Laurel and Hardy have also been played on commercials and in movies over
the years. The most memorable is probably Dick Van Dyke and Henry Calvin's rendition on a 1964 episode of "The Dick Van Dyke Show," which was seen and enjoyed
by Stan Laurel.*

Stan Laurel appeared in the following films without Oliver Hardy.

One- and two-reelers:

1917

Nuts In May
Lucky Dog
Hickory Hiram
Phoney Photos
Whose Zoo

1918

Huns and Hyphens
Just Rambling Along
Bears and Badmen

Frauds and Frenzies
Hoot Man

1921

The Rent Collector

1922

The Egg
The Weak-End Party
Mud and Sand
The Pest

1923

When Knights Were Gold
The Handy Man
Noon Whistle
White Wings
Under Two Jags
Pick and Shovel
Collars and Cuffs
Kill or Cure
Gas and Air
Oranges and Lemons
Short Orders
Man About Town
Roughest Africa
Frozen Hearts
The Whole Truth
Save the Ship
Scorching Sands
Mother's Joy

1924

Smithy
Postage Due
Brothers Under the Chin
Zeb Vs. Paprika
Near Dublin
Rupert of Hee-Haw
Wide Open Spaces
Short Kilts
Mixed Nuts
Madam Mixup
Detained
Monsieur Don't Care
West of Hot Dog

1925

Somewhere In Wrong
Twins
Pie Eyes
Snow Hawk
Navy Blue Days
The Sleuth
Yes Yes Nanette
Dr. Pyckle and Mr. Pride
Half a Man
Friendly Enemies
Moonlight and Noses
Wandering Papas
Enough To Do
Madame Mystery

1926

Never Too Old
Merry Widower
Wise Guys Prefer Brunettes
Get 'Em Young
Raggedy Rose
On the Front Page
Seeing the World
Eve's Love Letters
Now I'll Tell One
Should Tall Men Marry

Features:

Atta Boy (1926). Directed by Edward Griffith.

Oliver Hardy appeared in the following films without Stan Laurel.

One and two reelers:

1914

Outwitting Dad
Back to the Farm
Pins are Lucky
The Smugglers Daughter
The Female Cop
What He Forgot
Cupid's Target
Shaddy the Tailor
The Paperhanger's Helper
Charley's Aunt
Artists and Models

1915

The Tramps
Prize Baby
An Expensive Visit
Cleaning Time
Mixed Flats
Safety Worst
Twins Sisters
Baby
Who Stole the Doggies
A Lucky Strike
The New Butler
Matilda's Legacy
Her Choice
The Cannibal King
What a Cinch!
Clothes Make the Man
The Dead Letter
Avenging Bill
The Haunted Hat
Simp and the Sophomores
Babe's School Daze
Ehtel's Romeos
Bungalow Bungle
Three Rings and a Goat
The Rheumatic Joint
Something in Her Eye
Nanitor's Joyful Job

Fatty's Fatal Fun
Ups and Down
This Way Out

1916

Chickens
Bungles Rainy Day
The Tryout
One Two Amany
Serenade
Bungles Elopement
Bungles Lands a Job
Mama's Boys
Water Cure
Sea Dogs
Hungry Hearts
Never Again
A Day At School
Spaghetti
Side Tracked
Stranded
The Reformer
Royal Blood
Twin Flats
The Guilty One
He Winked and Won
Fat and Fickle

1917

Wanted a Bad Man
The Other Girl
Love Bugs
Lucky Dog
Back Stage
The Hero
Dough Nuts
The Goat
Genius
The Star Boarder
Chief Cook
Candy Kid

1918

Handy Man
Bright and Early
Playmates

1919

Freckled Fish
Hop the Bellhop
Lions and Ladies
Mules and Mortgages
Tottsies and Tamales
Healthy and Happy
Dames and Dentists
He Laughs Last
Springtime
Decorator
His Jonah Day

1921

The Little Wildcat
Counter Jomper
Three Ages
King of the Wild Horses

1922

Her Boyfriend
Kid Speed
Stick Around

1925

Is Marriage the Bunk
Hop To It
Stick Around
Isn't Life Terrible
Stop Look and Listen
Say It With Babies

1926

Long Fliv the King
Crazy Like a Fox
Be Your Age
Fluttering Herts

1928

Galloping Ghosts
Barnum and Ringling Inc.

Features:

The Wizard of Oz. (1925) as the Tin Man. 55 minutes.

The Perfect Clown. (1926) with Larry Semon. 66 minutes.

Stop, Look, and Listen. (1927) with Larry Semon. 67 minutes.

Zenobia. (1939) with Harry Langdon. 70 minutes.

The Fighting Kentuckian. (1949) with John Wayne. 77 minutes.

Riding High. (1950) with Bing Crosby; a Frank Capra film. 80 minutes.

8

The Marx Brothers

Brash, witty, uncontrolled, and exciting; the Marx Brothers are all of these. Perhaps the most influential talking comedians, the brothers have influenced such latter-day television comedy as "M*A*S*H," "Welcome Back Kotter," and "Barney Miller."

Pushed into a stage career by their mother, Minnie, the five siblings developed their basic characterizations early in their careers and had perfected them quite well, through vaudeville and Broadway engagements, by the time they made their first motion picture, *Coconuts*, in 1929. (A silent film, *Humor Risk*, made some years before, was never released and has since been lost.)

Groucho (born Julius, 1890) was the wisecracking punster who would override all authoritative figures with verbal brutalities that caused viewers to admire and respect his gall. Unlike that of W.C. Fields, Groucho's rudeness was rather playful and less justified. Where Fields would lash out at the very unscrupulous, Groucho would instead tease.

Harpo (born Adolph, later Arthur, 1888) was an expert harpist and pantomimist. Never speaking in the act (except in their early days on stage, when he was said to have used a mock Irish accent), Harpo showed enormous skills in pantomime and physical comedy — often as impressive as the work such silent masters as Chaplin and Keaton had accomplished in previous decades.

Chico (born Leonard, 1886) was an enchanting con man with an Italian accent and a captivating twinkle in his eye which hid the larceny in his heart. His piano playing was second to none, and as the much-needed link between the Harpo and Groucho characters, he was an indispensible part of the group.

Zeppo (born Herbert, 1901) was said to be very funny off screen, but was given nothing to do in any of the films he appeared in. His acting is very bland, his appearance unnecessary.

Gummo (born Milton, 1897) left the act before they did movies; no comments can be made concerning his contribution to the screen.

The Marx Brothers' first films, *Coconuts* (1929) and *Animal Crackers* (1930), were both based on Broadway shows they starred in. Both suffer from staginess and primitive sound production, as well as some embarrassingly bad musical numbers (although *Coconuts* was scored by Irving Berlin and *Animal Crackers* by

Bert Kalmar and Harry Ruby). *Animal Crackers* did provide Groucho with what was to remain his theme song for the rest of his life: "Hooray for Captain Spaulding."

Monkey Business (1931) is their third film and first genuine classic in a string of five. Cast as four stowaways on a luxury liner, the brothers manage to get mixed up in a feud between two rival gangsters while dodging the captain and his crew who want to throw them off the boat. *Monkey Business* moves quickly and features some excellent routines. Groucho's depression-era one-liners about food shortages and unemployment may never become dated.

Horse Feathers (1932) is even better. Groucho is cast as the dean of a college who attends a speakeasy to arrange for two pro football players to serve as ringers for the school team. Instead, he ends up with Chico and Harpo. *Horse Feathers* remains one of the group's best and most popular features. Zeppo's small role as Groucho's son was incidental, but all three other siblings shone.

Duck Soup (1933) is considered by many to be their masterpiece. A political satire that was light years ahead of its time, *Duck Soup*'s originality was powerful enough to leave a strong impression on virtually every other politically inclined comedy that has been made since, from *To Be or Not to Be* (1942) with Jack Benny to Stanley Kubrick's incredible *Dr. Strangelove* (1963). Harpo's battle of wits with co-star Edgar Kennedy ranks among silent comedy's greatest moments in pantomime, while Groucho's scenes with Margaret Dumont are beyond compliment.

Despite its stance as an American screen classic today, *Duck Soup* performed poorly at the box office at the time of its initial release, causing Paramount to drop the brothers later that year (1933). Zeppo also left the act to go into the agency business.

Chico then searched for another studio and found one in MGM. Legendary film producer Irving Thalberg believed that what the brothers needed was a purpose in their films — a reason to care for them. Thalberg's idea was to incorporate the brothers into a substantial plot and show off genuine feelings and emotions so that they could express more human qualities rather than just run rampant with wild gags.

The sheer insanity and comic spontaneity of *Duck Soup* found an audience years later, but at the time audiences wanted a quieter craziness. The answer turned out to be *A Night At the Opera*, one of the most wonderful screen comedies of all time.

The Marx Brothers were given a purpose: aiding and befriending a young tenor and his girl, thwarting villians, and doing so in their usual fashion, only this time with enough reason to attract period moviegoers. The gags are first-rate all the way, and the overall production is much more elaborate than any of the Paramounts. Marx fans are always split in their decision as to whether *Duck Soup* or *A Night at the Opera* is the team's masterpiece.

It just may very well be *A Day at the Races* (1937) another elaborately constructed excursion into music, romance, and sheer insanity. Better supporting

The three best-known Marx Brothers: Groucho (seated), Chico, and Harpo.

players and sometimes better gags enhance *A Day at the Races*, and even the musical bits (including a marvelously entertaining song and dance number featuring Harpo and a group of talented young blacks, which some seem to think is racist) aren't so bad.

While *A Day at the Races* was being filmed, Irving Thalberg died. It was a blow to Hollywood when the 37-year-old producer succumbed to pneumonia (also reported as tuberculosis) leaving MGM, and especially the Marxes, in a terrible state of shock.

After *Races*, the boys went over to RKO studios to film *Room Service* (1938) with Lucille Ball and Ann Miller. An enjoyable comedy with its share of good schtick, *Room Service* just didn't quite live up to the group's previous films and was a throwback to the quality of *Coconuts* and *Animal Crackers*. Since *Room Service* had also originally been a stage production, it suffered from the same staginess as the earlier films.

Back at MGM in 1939, the Marx Brothers found that reigning head Louis B. Mayer was more intent on killing their career than enhancing it as Thalberg had. Their final three MGM efforts were their three weakest films. *At the Circus* (1939), *Go West* (1941), and *The Big Store* (1942) all had their moments of hilarity, but these were buried under awful music and even worse romantic leads. The Marx Brothers decided to retire after *The Big Store*.

Throughout the war years, Groucho busied himself with a quiz show, Chico led his own band, Harpo was doing stage appearances, and all three were taking their turn at entertaining the troops.

The 1946 they were approached by United Artists to do another film. *A Night in Casablanca* turned out to be their best film since *A Day at the Races*, but its poor box office reaction didn't warrant a full-fledged return to the screen.

Harpo was to star alone in *Love Happy* (1949), one of Marilyn Monroe's early appearances, but Chico managed to land a small part and thus Groucho was asked to appear in a few unrelated scenes. The results were only fair.

All three appeared briefly (and separately) in the ghastly all-star *The Story of Mankind* and did a stint on television's "General Electric Theater" in something called "The Incredible Jewel Robbery," their last appearance together.

Chico died in 1961 and Harpo in 1964. Groucho remained active on television with "You Bet Your Life," a quiz show. He also made frequent guest appearances on various game and talk shows and played character roles in many films throughout the fifties and sixties.

He lived to see the huge revival of interest in the Marx Brothers films, wrote a couple of books, and performed to a sellout crowd at Carnegie Hall after passing his eightieth birthday.

When told that a survey among college students revealed that their three favorite men of all time were God, their father, and Groucho Marx, Groucho replied that he didn't mind coming in third on that list.

Groucho died in 1977, two months after Gummo's death. Zeppo died in 1979.

The energy of the Marx Brothers is still unequaled in the entertainment world, along with their gift for spontaneity and their incredible influence on comedy. The brothers made only thirteen films, with five true classics among them. Yet they managed to achieve a level of talent and professionalism, as well as an incredible amount of comic charisma, the likes of which we will never see again.

Harpo and Susan Marx with Barbara and Zeppo Marx in a rare off-screen shot.

Marx Brothers Filmography

Paramount

Coconuts. (1929) *** With Margaret Dumont, Kay Francis, Oscar Shaw, Mary Eaton, Basil Rueysdale. Directed by Joe Santley and Robert Florey. 96 minutes.

Animal Crackers. (1930) *** With Margaret Dumont, Lillian Roth, Louis Sorin, Hal Thompson. Directed by Victor Heerman. 98 minutes.

Monkey Business. (1931) ***** With Thelma Todd, Tom Kennedy, Ruth Hall, Otto Fries. Directed by Norman McLeod. 77 minutes.

Horse Feathers. (1932) ***** With Thelma Todd, Nat Pendelton, James Pierce. Directed by Norman McLeod. 70 minutes.

Duck Soup. (1933) ***** With Margaret Dumont, Louis Calhearn, Edgar Kennedy, Charles Middleton. Directed by Leo McCarey. 70 minutes.

MGM films

A Night at the Opera. (1935) ***** With Allan Jones, Margaret Dumont, Kitty Carlisle, Walter Woolf King, Billy Gilbert, Jonathan Hale, Sigfried Ruman. Directed by Sam Wood. 92 minutes.

A Day at the Races. (1937) ***** With Margaret Dumont, Allan Jones, Maureen O'Sullivan, Sigfried Ruman, Douglas Dumbrille, Leonard Ceely, Esther Muir. Directed by Sam Wood. 109 minutes.

RKO Radio Pictures:

Room Service. (1938) *** With Lucille Ball, Ann Miller, Frank Albertson, Donald MacBride. Directed by William Seiter. 78 minutes.

Back at MGM:

At the Circus. (1939) ** With Eve Arden, Margaret Dumont, Kenny Baker, Florence Rice, Nat Pendelton. Directed by Edward Buzzell. 87 minutes.

Go West. (1941) ** With Walter Woolf King, John Carrol, Diana Lewis. Directed by Edward Buzzell. 80 minutes.

The Big Store. (1942) ** With Margaret Dumont, Tony Martin, Douglas Dumbrille, Virginia Grey. Directed by Charles Reisner. 83 minutes.

United Artists

A Night in Casablanca. (1946) **** With Sigfried Ruman, Lisette Verea, Charles Drake, Lois Collier. Directed by Archie Mayo. 85 minutes.

Love Happy. (1949) ** With Vera Ellen, Illona Massey, Raymond Burr, Melville Cooper, Eric Blore, Marilyn Monroe. Directed by David Miller. 85 minutes.

Anthologies containing the Marx Brothers' work

MGM's Big Parade of Comedy. (1965) Produced by Robert Youngson.

The Marx Brothers in a Nutshell. (1982) Presented on PBS television.

Groucho appeared alone in the following features:

Copacabana. (1947) Directed by Alfred Green. 93 minutes.

Mr. Music. (1950) Directed by Richard Hayden. 113 minutes.

Double Dynamite. (1951) Directed by Irving Cummings, Jr. 80 minutes.

A Girl in Every Port. (1952) Directed by Chester Erskine. 86 minutes.

Skiddo. (1969) Directed by Otto Preminger. 98 minutes. Color.

Harpo did make one appearance on Groucho's TV game show "You Bet Your Life." Chico never appeared.

The brothers also appeared fleetingly in *The Story of Mankind* (1957), directed by Irwin Allen. 100 minutes.

9

W.C. Fields

W.C. Fields is more than just a great movie comedian; he is, like Mark Twain, one of America's greatest humorists. Fields had a strong impact on the development of screen comedy and made profound discoveries in satire.

Fields usually cast himself as an innocent Everyman and then surrounded his character with every possible offensive stereotype. Crooked politicians and businessmen, ethnic stereotypes, nagging wives and mothers-in-law, sponging relatives, slow-witted employees, pesky children, nosy neighbors, and self-righteous senior citizens would plague this Everyman as they plague so many of us in everyday life; but unrestrained by good manners, Fields seldom held his tongue and eventually would lash out at these stereotypes, making examples of them even further than their screen appearance.

Viewers would always side with Fields, sharing his frustrations and often wishing they had the power to fight back like him. While most of his hatred for these individuals came out through grumblings under his breath, there was a limit to his patience and he would ultimately tell them what he thought, sometimes not as much as the viewer would have liked (as in *You Can't Cheat an Honest Man*) and other times more than he probably should have (as in the widely banned *The Dentist*).

Fields' childhood and upbringing sounds like a Dickens story, but it's quite true. A rough childhood led to an ultimate brawl with his father and caused him to run away from his Philadelphia home at the age of eleven. Born William Claude Dukenfeld in 1979, Fields didn't shorten his name until landing stage roles as a juggler, trick golfer, and pool player (after spending his childhood on the streets and in pool halls honing his craft). His talents in vaudeville led to a spot in the Ziegfeld Follies and a film short, *Pool Sharks* (1915), a standard one-reeler which had nothing to do with his later screen success.

Fields landed steady film employment at Paramount studios in 1925, and films like *Sally of the Sawdust, It's the Old Army Game*, and *So's Your Old Man* showed many facets of the characterization he was to use once he began making talkies.

Fields' reputation as a legendary drinker was in every way accurate, but his drinking reportedly was not the reason for his big red nose. Years later, in interviews, Fields revealed that a street fight he was engaged in as a child was the reason for his enlarged proboscis, and his embarrassment prompted him to wear a big bushy mustache on stage and in all of his films until 1932.

Basically a dialogue comedian, Fields could also hold his own with pantomime and performs rather well in all of his silent pictures, though none of them are the landmarks that his talkies became. Having less control than he would in later years, Fields perfected basic mannerisms and bits of business for the development of his character in the silent films, but it wasn't until the talkies that he was given the opportunity to utilize his comic genius to its furthest boundaries.

His first talkie was *The Golf Specialist* (1930), a filmed version of his golf act that is interesting only as an example of how the act looked on stage (Fields performed a shorter version of the act in his later feature *You're Telling Me*).

Her Majesty Love (1931), his first feature, was a love story with amusing comic touches by Fields and Leon Errol (who appeared to even better advantage in Fields' later *Never Give a Sucker an Even Break*), but their talents couldn't save the film from its limitations.

Million Dollar Legs (1932) is the first really great Fields picture and has become a nonsense classic. Playing the ruler of a mythical kingdom where all of the men have the same name, as do the women, and all of the townfolk are capable of tremendous athletic skill, Fields is talked into holding a track meet by an enterprising young man (Jack Oakie in one of his finest performances) and ultimately entering in the Olympics.

Fields was teamed with Allison Skipworth in one of the better sequences featured in the all-star classic *If I Had a Million* (1932), which showed, in a series of episodes, different peoples' reactions to receiving a million dollars. Fields then made four brilliant two-reelers for Mack Sennett.

The Dentist (1932) is the best and most controversial, showing Fields as a crabby, hard-hearted dentist who fights with his friends on the golf course, fights with his daughter at home, and treats his patients in the shoddiest manner imaginable. Professionals in the dental fields at that time were very offended, and subsequent releases of the film edit it down to ten minutes, cutting out most of the offensive material. Today it ranks as one of the screen's greatest examples of satire.

The Pharmacist and *The Barber Shop* (both 1933) are also top satires on those professions. *The Fatal Glass of Beer* (1933) is a knock at melodrama complete with bad dialogue and poor production quality—the work of a genius.

After appearing with Burns and Allen, Bela Lugosi, Stu Erwin, Rudy Vallee, and a host of others in the wonderfully funny all-star *International House* (1933), which dealt with the invention of television, Fields began a series of screen classics which showed his character to greater perfection each time.

You're Telling Me (1933) contains the priceless scene where Fields is standing in front of a pet store when a friend of his comes out with a caged

W.C. Fields, 1879–1946.

parakeet. The bird is intended as a peace offering, for the man has had a fight with his wife. Fields, also plagued with marital difficulties, states, "It'll take a bigger bird than that to cheer my wife up." The next scene shows him being pulled down the street by an ostrich with a leash around its neck.

Larry "Buster" Crabbe, famous as Flash Gordon, Buck Rogers, Captain Gallant, and a host of other screen heroes, made one of his first screen appearances as the juvenile in *You're Telling Me.*

In an interview shortly before his death, Crabbe said that Fields "Drank all day and never showed it, I don't know how he did it. He wasn't a particularly friendly man, he could've cared less about me or anybody else. And his drinking never caused him to forget his lines. Often he would ad-lib something funnier than what was originally in the script."

Fields' best two films at Paramount were the classics *It's a Gift* (1934) and *Man on the Flying Trapeze* (1935), both of which cast him as a henpecked husband beset by the various stereotypes, and both of which included some of the most essential representatives of the comedian's objectives.

Fields doesn't just all of a sudden hate kids and old ladies in these films. Instead, he shows them as unbearable pests who deserve nothing but utter contempt. This is done with such total perfection that the viewer never quite realizes that by laughing he's condoning hatred.

After *Poppy* (1936), based on his stage act, and *The Big Broadcast of 1938*, which was the film that introduced Bob Hope singing "Thanks For The Memory," Fields left Paramount for Universal studios.

His first two films for Universal, *You Can't Cheat an Honest Man* (1939) and *My Little Chickadee* (1940), have become classics but are not up to his usual standards.

You Can't Cheat an Honest Man featured Edgar Bergen and dummy Charlie McCarthy, whose feud with Fields on radio prompted a pretty good screen match (Fields wrote the dialogue); but Bergen was no ventriloquist. This failing takes away from the material, which, thusly, is better suited for radio.

My Little Chickadee had Fields collaborating on the screenplay and the lead role with Mae West. This pairing just didn't work, because the strong personalities of the stars clashed rather than blended, despite their reported great respect for each other. Both stated in later years that they considered the film to be one of the most pleasant experiences either had enjoyed in show business.

The Bank Dick (1940) is Fields' undisputed masterpiece. While he had made high caliber films for nearly a decade, *The Bank Dick* ranks as one of the most fascinating and important contributions to American humor.

An almost poetic look the average man's hatred for, and manipulation by, every conceivable stereotype, Fields managed to give every viewer a target for his or her inner frustrations. The bartender (played by Shemp Howard) is the only individual other than Fields without any despicable characteristics.

Constructed perfectly, with a slow, realistic pace, *The Bank Dick* again shows Fields as the meek family man with devastatingly honest perceptions of the human inadequacies which surround us all. It is an absolutely incredible film.

Never Give a Sucker an Even Break (1941) was Fields' next film and last starring vehicle. The film is in many ways as brilliant as *The Bank Dick*, but it falters—because, believe it or not, of its intelligence.

As a satire on filmmaking, Fields decided simply to make a bad film with *Never Give a Sucker an Even Break*. Playing himself, Fields takes a script to a producer to read, and as the producer reads it, we see the script as a film. In his script, Fields casts himself as a superhero to satirize Hollywood's star system at the time, and also manages to attack the sudden bursting into song in musicals and the instant falling in love of romantic drama. These satirizations are performed with such careful subtlety and played with such sincerity that not every viewer realizes what Fields is trying to do. An ingenious work for those capable of understanding the comedian's objectives, *Never Give a Sucker an Even Break* is usually remembered for the slapstick car chase that is the climax of the film.

In failing health brought on by years of heavy drinking, Fields made brief appearances in a handful of revue films during the next few years. He died on Christmas day in 1946, putting an end to one of the most perceptive, original and amazing comic minds ever.

W.C. Fields has become a cult figure, a respected comedian, and is con-

Fields clowns with the legendary John Barrymore.

sidered a fine humorist. His screen legacy features a host of characters whose personalities are the foundation for everyone's inner frustrations, and in the middle of it all, a large-nosed drunk who doesn't ask for sympathy but instead fights back. Fields' work will remain timeless, and the man will remain an immortal figure in the history of American fine arts.

Fields Filmography

The Silent Films

(The writer has seen only a handful of Fields' silents, many are no longer in existence. For this reason, some have not received ratings.)

Pool Sharks. (1915) *** Directed by Edwin Middleton. One reel.

His Lordship's Dilemma. (1916) Directed by William Haddock. One reel. (No longer in existence.)

Janice Meredith. (1923) With Marion Davies, Ken Maynard. Directed by D.W. Griffith. 80 minutes. (No longer in existence.)

Sally of the Sawdust. (1925) *** With Carol Dempster, Erville Alderson, Alfred Lunt, Glenn Anders, Effie Shannon. Directed by D.W. Griffith. 75 minutes.

That Royale Girl. (1926) With Carol Dempster, Harrison Ford (no relation to today's popular actor). Directed by D.W. Griffith. 75 minutes. (No longer in existence.)

It's the Old Army Game. (1926) With Louise Brooks. Directed by A. Edward Sutherland. 75 minutes. (No longer in existence.)

So's Your Old Man. (1926) ** With Alice Joyce. Directed by Gregory LaCava. 67 minutes. (Remade in 1932 as *You're Telling Me.*)

The Potters. (1927) Directed by Fred Newmeyer. 70 minutes. (No longer in existence. Remade in 1934 as *It's a Gift.*)

Running Wild. (1927) Mary Brian. Directed by Gregory LaCava. 77 minutes. (No longer in existence. Remade in 1935 as *The Man on the Flying Trapeze.*)

Two Flaming Youths. (1928) ** Directed by John Waters. 85 minutes. (Remade in 1939 as *You Can't Cheat an Honest Man.*)

Tillie's Punctured Romance. (1928) ** With Louise Fazenda, Mack Swain, Chester Conklin. Remake of the marvelous Chaplin film for Sennett. Directed by Al Christie. 57 minutes.

Fools for Luck. (1928) ** With Chester Conklin. Directed by Chuck Reisner. 60 minutes.

The Talkies
All for Paramount unless otherwise stated.

The Golf Specialist. (1930, RKO) *** Directed by Monte Brice. Two reels.

Her Majesty Love. (1931, RKO) ** With Marilyn Miller, Leon Errol, Ford Sterling, Chester Conklin, Ben Lyon, Virginia Sale. Directed by William Dietrle. 75 minutes.

Million Dollar Legs. (1932) ***** With Susan Fleming, Lyda Roberti, Jack Oakie, Hugh Herbert, Andy Clyde, Billy Gilbert. Directed by Eddie Cline. 65 minutes.

If I Had a Million. (1932) ***** With Alison Skipworth, Gary Cooper, Jack Oakie, Charlie Ruggles, Mary Boland, George Raft, Gene Raymond, Wynne Gibson, Charles Laughton. Directed by James Cruze, Bruce Humberstone, Norman Taurog, Stephen Roberts, Ernst Lubitsch, William Seiter. 88 minutes.

The Dentist. (1932) ***** With Elise Cavannah, Babe Kane, Bud Jamison. Directed by Leslie Pierce. Two reels.

The Fatal Glass of Beer. (1933) ***** With George Chandler, Rychard Cramer. Directed by Clyde Bruckman. Two reels.

The Pharmacist. (1933) ***** With Grady Sutton, Babe Kane. Directed by Arthur Ripley. Two reels.

The Barber Shop. (1933) ***** With Elise Cavannah, Harry Watson. Directed by Art Ripley. Two reels.

International House. (1933) ***** With George Burns & Gracie Allen, Stu Erwin, Peggy Hopkins Joyce, Bela Lugosi, Rudy Vallee, Franklin Pangborn, Rose Marie, Sterling Holloway, Cab Calloway and his Orchestra. Directed by Eddie Sutherland. 70 minutes.

Tillie and Gus. (1933) ***** With Alison Skipworth, Baby LeRoy, Clarence Wilson. Directed by Frances Martin. 58 minutes.

Alice in Wonderland. (1933) ** With Charlotte Henry, Richard Arlen, Cary Grant, Gary Cooper, Jack Oakie, Edna May Oliver. Directed by Norman McLeod. 77 minutes.

Six of a Kind. (1933) **** With Charlie Ruggles, Mary Boland, George Burns, Gracie Allen, Allison Skipworth. Directed by Leo McCarey. 62 minutes.

You're Telling Me. (1933) ***** With Joan Marsh, Buster Crabbe, Louise Carter, Kathleen Howard. Directed by Erle C. Kenton. 67 minutes.

Old Fashioned Way. (1934) **** With Baby LeRoy, Judith Allen, Joe Morrison, Jack MulHall. Directed by William Beaudine. 65 minutes.

Mrs. Wiggs of the Cabbage Patch. (1934) ** With ZaSu Pitts, Pauline Lord, Donald Meek. Directed by Norman Taurog. 80 minutes.

It's a Gift. (1934) ***** With Kathleen Howard, Baby LeRoy, Morgan Wallace, Tommy Bupp, Tammanay Young. Directed by Norman McLeod. 75 minutes.

Fields' decidedly unsportsmanlike conduct won him fame as a comedian.

David Copperfield. (1934, MGM) **** With Ethel Barrymore, Freddie Bartholemew, Lionel Barrymore, Edna May Oliver. Directed by George Cukor. 133 minutes.

Mississippi. (1934) **** With Bing Crosby, Joan Bennett, Gail Patrick, Queenie Smith, Claude Gillingwater. Directed by Eddie Sutherland. 75 minutes.

The Man on the Flying Trapeze. (1935) *****With Kathleen Howard, Mary Brian, Grady Sutton, Walter Brennan, Vera Lewis. Directed by Clyde Bruckman. 65 minutes.

Poppy. (1936) ****With Rochelle Hudson, Richard Cromwell, Lynne Overman, Catherine Doucet. Directed by Eddie Sutherland. 75 minutes.

The Big Broadcast of 1938. (1938) *** With Bob Hope, Martha Raye, Shirley Ross, Dorothy Lamour, Leif Erickson, Ben Blue. Directed by Mitchell Leisen. 90 minutes.

Universal

You Can't Cheat an Honest Man. (1939) **** With Edgar Bergen, Constance Moore, James Bush, Thurston Hall. Directed by George Marshall and Eddie Cline. 76 minutes.

The Bank Dick. (1940) ***** With Grady Sutton, Evelyn DelRio, Franklin Pangborn, Shemp Howard, Bill Wolfe, Jack Norton, Una Merkel. Directed by Eddie Cline. 74 minutes.

My Little Chickadee. (1940) *** With Mae West, Joseph Calleia, Dick Foran, Margaret Hamilton. Directed by Eddie Cline. 83 minutes.

Never Give a Sucker an Even Break. (1941) ***** With Gloria Jean, Franklin Pangborn, Leon Errol, Margaret Dumont, Butch and Buddy, Bill Wolfe. Directed by Eddie Cline. 70 minutes.

Fields made a guest appearance in the following revue films:

Tales of Manhattan. (1942) Directed by Julien Duviver. 118 minutes. (The Fields episode, which also featured Phil Silvers, was cut from the final release print but has been recently reissued as a one-reeler.)

Follow the Boys. (1944) Directed by Eddie Sutherland. 122 minutes.

Song of the Open Road. (1944) Directed by S. Sylvan Simon. 93 minutes.

Sensations. (1945) Directed by Andrew Stone. 86 minutes.

A sequence from David Copperfield *with Fields was included in Robert Youngson's anthology* MGM's Big Parade of Comedy *(1964).*

10

The Three Stooges

Of all the great comedians in this book, the Stooges are in one sense probably the most amazing. Not great clowns like Chaplin, Keaton, or Laurel and Hardy, the Stooges are nevertheless highly popular comedians. Their popularity has given rise to fan clubs, books, and film festivals, and they are even the objects of serious study.

The Three Stooges starred in 190 two-reelers for Columbia studios over a 24-year period, the longest running film series of all time. Does this alone mean that they deserve to be considered leading comedy stars? No! Volume is meaningless (look how many episodes of "The Brady Bunch" and "The Dukes of Hazzard" were filmed); it is quality, not quantity, that matters in screen comedy.

And what about the quality? The Three Stooges had the privilege of working with such top directors as Clyde Bruckman, Charley Chase, Edward Bernds and Del Lord, as well as supporting players like Snub Pollard, Emil Sitka, Bud Jamison, Symona Boniface, and Vernon Dent. They made many very enjoyable comedies as well as many flops (when you make 190 films, there's bound to be a good number of both), but even their best efforts— *Men in Black, Hoi Polloi, Pardon My Clutch*, and *Goof on the Roof* among them — are hampered by an overall silliness that is rather disconcerting.

Their forte was slapstick and their timing was good, but their use of violence was not planned as well as Chaplin's or Laurel and Hardy's. The violence was usually overdone, sometimes to the point of looking downright cruel.

As for material, the Stooges had their share of innovative gags, but these were repeated in many films. The group was often trapped by old, wheezy gags, bad one-liners, and some really embarrassing shortcomings in the technical department (most notably in *Hot Scots*, where the action in a fight scene is speeded up, and so are the actors' voices, causing the Stooges to sound more like the Chipmunks).

The Stooges came to Columbia in 1934 after having performed on stage and in a few films with Ted Healy, who played the lead in their act, with the Stooges being just what their name states. Since they had little chance to develop any genuine characterization in their early days, the Stooges' most essential development can be found in their Columbia two-reelers.

109

The act consisted of Moe Howard (Moses Harry Horowitz, born 1897), his brother Shemp Howard (Samuel Horowitz, born 1895) and Larry Fine (Lawrence Feinberg, born 1902). They had made stage appearances and one film, *Soup to Nuts* (1930) for Fox, when Shemp decided to leave the group and go off as a single.

The boys then hired Moe's younger brother Jerome Horowitz (born 1903), who shaved his head and became known as Curly Howard. They did more stage work and minor screen work with Healy at MGM before leaving for Columbia to star in their own series. (Healy remained a highly paid vaudeville star and motion picture character actor until his tragic death in 1937.)

The trio's first Columbia short, *Woman Haters* (1934), was a tired musical with the dialogue done in rhyme. *Punch Drunks* (1934), written by the trio, shows some important character development. *Men in Black* (1934) was nominated for an Oscar as best short subject, but lost to Disney's animated *Three Little Pigs*. In retaliation, the Stooges titled their next comedy *Three Little Pigskins* (1935). It was a football film, and it featured a young Lucille Ball.

By the mid-thirties, the Stooges had developed their characters and continued to polish them throughout their film career. While not as essential to the evolution of the movie comedian as Chaplin's tramp, the Stooges did create characters which have remained popular to this day.

Moe was the short, pug-faced bully and self-appointed leader of the group. Believing himself to have more brains than the others, Moe would keep Curly or Larry in line with a brand of childish violence that ranges from amusingly silly to just plain cruel. There was always a fine line between comic attacks that were funny and those that were pointlessly overdone (for example, a slap in the face as opposed to Moe's running a cheese grater over Curly's face). Unfortunately, these boundaries were ignored a bit too often.

Larry was the bewildered innocent, the middleman who was constantly caught in the middle of Moe and Curly's scraps, siding with whichever one he believed to be in the right. While Larry is the most limited stooge, he is also the most quietly endearing.

Curly was a bizarre, frustrated child-man whose reactions were those of a none-too-bright infant. Gurgling when pleased, growling and slapping his forehead when annoyed, and shrieking and hooting when excited or frightened were among his most predominant mannerisms. Curly is the most interesting character; he is the reason why many fans like the Stooges, as well as why others detest them.

Curly would eat sloppily, resort to disturbing noises that sounded like a sick jungle animal, and employ spastic gestures that were often bothersome in their painful resemblance to actual physical deformity. His reactions were usually stupidly overdone and never acquired a sense of artistic discipline.

On the other hand, Curly also showed signs of comic skill when guided by a top director, or even by brother Moe (who was responsible for some of the trio's gags), and his timing was often quite good. Curly was not a genius, but he does deserve some respect for the talent he did have.

Men in Black is the trio's first really great comedy, fast-paced with good construction and enjoyable comedy performances. Set in a hospital, *Men in Black* features the Stooges as doctors and relies more on gags and one-liners, which occur between the Stooges and the various weird patients, than on violence. The timing and pacing in *Men in Black* ranks it among the trio's very best efforts.

Hoi Polloi (1935) dealt with a professor trying to transform the Stooges into gentlemen, teaching them proper enunciation of the English language, table etiquette, and knowledge and capabilities of finding their way about society surroundings. These elements are used to the fullest of their potential, with the Stooges' absurdities emerging victorious at a society party where every guest begins slapping and kicking each other, stooge-style, in a nicely timed slapstick melee.

Disorder in the Court (1936) featured good dialogue and amusing performances. *Violent Is the Word for Curly* (1937) resembled a Marx Brothers–style film with very good results. Perhaps the Stooges' most fascinating effort was *You Natzy Spy* (1940), which casts Moe as a Hitleresque dictator similar to Chaplin's in *The Great Dictator* (1940).

While *You Natzy Spy* (and its followup, *I'll Never Heil Again*) is no *The Great Dictator*, it did manage to show the trio's capabilities in performing something other than their usual slapstick shenanigans. It is one of their best films.

Curly's off-screen drinking habits, reinforced by marital problems, began impairing his health during the forties. Eventually this deterioration began showing in his work and appearance on screen. It became rather evident in late 1945 releases (such as *Micro Phonies*) and early 1946 films that Curly was in serious trouble. His timing was off, his actions were slower and less deliberate, his speech was muddled, and his humor had diminished considerably.

Producer Jules White believed that "a major blood vessel broke in the man's head, and after that he just couldn't remember his lines." Director Edward Bernds recalled, "When we were making the film *Monkey Businessmen* (1946), Moe would be on the set coaching Curly as if he were a child."

A remake of *Hoi Polloi*, entitled *Half Wits Holiday*, (1946) turned out to be Curly's last film as one of the Stooges.

Character actor Emil Sitka, who played a butler in this picture, remembers, "I didn't quite know what was going on, but during the pie fight at the end of the picture I noticed that Curly wasn't there. It wasn't until I got home that night that I found out he had suffered a stroke."

Curly, after filming a previous scene, had left the shooting area and fallen victim to a stroke. Moe had him rushed to the hospital and finished the film with Larry without telling the other performers what had happened.

"I noticed that Curly was very quiet and shy while we were making the picture," recalled Sitka. "He would call me 'sir,' even though I was just a supporting player and he was the star.

"He would sit very quietly between takes waiting for his cue and instructions, but when the cameras rolled he'd cut up, and boy, he could really ad-lib."

As a replacement for Curly, Moe asked older brother Shemp to return to the group. By this time, Shemp had become quite successful on his own as both a character actor and star comic in features and short subjects. During the war years, Shemp was under contract to three studios simultaneously, and the shorts he did for Columbia as a soloist are said to have been more popular in their day than those featuring Moe, Larry, and Curly. While not as popular with today's stooge fans, Shemp was still every bit as talented a comic as his younger siblings.

Emil Sitka recalled that "even when Shemp walked through a restaurant everyone would be looking at him. He was the only stooge who was just as funny off-screen as on. When he would tell a joke or of some incident he'd have everybody laughing."

Edward Bernds agrees that Shemp was a capable comic: "Even when a scene would be completed he would keep clowning. Often I'd let the cameras roll just to see what he would do. Some of it we could use, and some we couldn't because it was too earthy."

When approaching the matter objectively with a critical viewpoint, one must acknowledge Shemp's comic talents. It's unfortunate that so few of his films were as well produced as Curly's. Shemp did not have the advantage of such talented directors as Charley Chase, who had died, and he was saddled with a great deal of bad material toward the end of his career.

At first the films with Shemp, often directed by Bernds and written by Bernds and Ellwood Ullman, would be on or above par. Curly made a brief appearance in Shemp's third stooge comedy, *Hold That Lion* (1947), which was to be his last screen appearance. He died in 1952.

Pardon My Clutch (1947) is among Shemp's best films with the Stooges, featuring some of their most inventive gags and funniest material. They fail at every simple task, such as Moe and Larry incompetently trying to care for an ailing Shemp, or all three boys trying to load a beat-up to auto with camping equipment. These scenes are performed with as much skill as shown in any of their earlier comedies.

Studio Stoops (1950) has Shemp hanging outside a building by a telephone a la Harold Lloyd (though not as skillfully), while *Spooks* and *Pardon My Backfire* were ill-fated experiments with the new 3-D process which was popular at the time.

Goof on the Roof (1953) is easily Shemp's best film with the Stooges and possibly the trio's finest effort. Resembling Laurel & Hardy's *Helpmates* and *Hog Wild* (two of that duo's finest short works), *Goof on the Roof*, though not in the same league as the Laurel and Hardy films, is quite an inventive little study in mounting frustrations.

Asked to clean up their pal's honeymoon cottage before he returns with his new bride, the Stooges manage to wreck furniture and walls, spill things, stain things, and engage in constant battle with assorted inanimate objects. Laurel and

Opposite: Moe, Curly, and Larry in "Micro-Phonies" (1946).

Shemp Howard (left) replaced Curly in 1946. Here, the Stooges point the finger at Emil Sitka in "Hold That Lion" (1947).

Hardy's attempts to straighten a messy house before the return of Ollie's nagging wife in *Helpmates* comes to mind as the Stooges stumble incompetently about.

Their frustration with the various household implements causes them to anthropomorphize the objects even to the point of attempting to punish them (e.g. Moe hitting himself in the face with a television's picture tube, then ripping the important fixture out of the set, shaking it, and grumbling, "Just for that you can't go in there!").

The most prominent "Man vs. Inanimate Object" battle occurs when Shemp tries to install a TV aerial on the roof (like Laurel and Hardy with their radio aerial in *Hog Wild*).

All of these ingredients are well structured, to the point where *Goof on the Roof* should perhaps get consideration as the major work by the trio.

Shemp Howard died suddenly in 1955. Jules White then decided to release four old films with new titles and a few new scenes with Moe, Larry, and Shemp's double, Joe Palma (whose face is never seen), to fullfill contractual requirements. Moe and Larry almost made films as the Two Stooges but ultimately decided to hire Joe Besser as a replacement for Shemp.

A friend of the Stooges from years back, Joe stated, "They asked me to join them and finish the remaining two years of their contract when Shemp passed away. So I did, willingly, because I liked the boys anyway, and I liked the fun."

Joe Besser (born 1907) was known as a character comedian who usually played the sissy as an obnoxious child-man. Supporting such players as Jack Benny, Milton Berle, Abbott and Costello, Joey Bishop, and Jerry Lewis, among others, Besser has enhanced the efforts of Hollywood's finest during his career.

The films made between 1956 and 1958 were of low quality, usually

Joe Besser joined the Stooges to replace Shemp, who died in 1955.

remakes of earlier films using scenes from the former, and all were directed by Jules White.

Besser was used to create differences between Moe and Larry in his Stooges comedies, and this showed a different facet of Moe and Larry's screen personalities. While not up to the earlier production standards, the trio's films with Besser were at times still amusing, mostly thanks to Joe's talents and presence. He fit in well and often outshone his two partners, who were beginning to look a little played out.

The Stooges made their last short, *Sappy Bullfighters*, in 1958. Shortly thereafter, Columbia's television subsidy, Screen Gems, packaged the Curly-Three Stooges films for television, intending them to be used as filler for films or sporting events which didn't run their fully allotted time. Instead they were used as children's entertainment, like cartoons, and caught on like wildfire. This unexpected explosion in mass appeal made the trio's popularity soar beyond its earlier reaches, and they planned to do a feature film and some personal appearances, but without Joe Besser.

"I was committed to do a picture at 20th Century Fox called *Say One for Me*," recalled Besser, "and that's why I couldn't go back with the boys."

He was replaced by Joe DeRita, a bland character actor who did some stage and television work. DeRita shaved his head and called himself Curly-Joe.

A rotund man with a slight physical resemblance to Curly, DeRita was not

in any way a good pick to fill Besser's shoes as third stooge. In features like *Have Rocket Will Travel* (1958), *The Three Stooges in Orbit* (1960), and *The Three Stooges Meet Hercules* (1961), DeRita's poor performance of the tried-and-true Stooges gags shows his profound incompetence. Moe and Larry have a great deal less vitality than in their short films, and coupled with DeRita's blandness, they are usually outdone by funnier character performers (like Emil Sitka in *The Three Stooges in Orbit*).

Because all 190 short films were still going strong on television, the Stooges' features were moneymakers and their personal appearances sellouts, despite lack of energy in Moe and Larry and a fifth-rate performance by DeRita. A series of cartoons with live-action footage of the Stooges shot in color was made in 1966, and the trio remained hot kiddie entertainers with records, comic books, and other items throughout that decade.

In 1970 the boys planned a TV series. The pilot, shot in 1969 and 1970 and planned for release the following year, featured the boys in a state of retirement out seeing the world. In 1971, Larry suffered a stroke which left him confined to a wheelchair, and thus the pilot, *Kook's Tour*, was shelved. Ultimately released to collectors in 1976, it has since been withdrawn from non-theatrical distribution.

Moe's grandson wrote a screenplay about the Stooges wreaking havoc in a concentration camp. Arrangements were being made for Emil Sitka to replace the ailing Larry and appear in the film with Moe and DeRita.

Sitka recalled, "A leading producer came out here from the Philippines, where the picture was to be shot, and at a meeting Moe asked me to bring up a few points concerning where the money would be deposited, whether or not the picture would be under the jurisdiction of the Screen Actors' Guild, and the possibility of doing future things.

"I was all gung-ho for the thing," Sitka continued, "but unfortunately the deal eventually fell through. Moe later told me it was all for the better."

Despite a valiant attempt at recovering, Larry died in January of 1975. Grief-stricken over the passing of his longtime partner, yet still undaunted, Moe negotiated another deal for himself, DeRita, and Sitka. The three were to appear as the Stooges in an independently produced feature entitled *The Jet Set*, which would feature Yvonne DeCarlo and Don "Red" Barry.

"Moe kept calling me and delaying things," said Sitka, "until finally I got the shocking call from his son. Moe had passed away."

Moe's death in May of 1975 put an end to the Three Stooges. *The Jet Set* was released as *Blazing Stewardesses* in 1976 with the two living Ritz Brothers, Harry and Jimmy, essaying the roles that were originally to be played by the Stooges.

Moe's autobiography, *I Stooged to Conquer* (retitled *Moe Howard & The*

Opposite: Larry, Joe DeRita (who replaced Joe Besser in 1958), and Moe with the late Tommy "Pops" Richards on Milwaukee's local kiddie show, "Pops' Theater."

Three Stooges), was published the following year with the help of his widow (who died the following October) and children.

"I frequently marvel at the popularity the Stooges pictures have attained," said Edward Bernds. "It's ironic that these humble little two-reelers the studio heads ignored have had a longer life and greater acceptance than many of their pretentious epics."

Unlike comedians who had pretentions beyond mere laughter, the Stooges' sole objective was to be funny, and they succeeded admirably. It is unlikely that their popularity will ever diminish.

Three Stooges Filmography

The Columbia Shorts
All two reels in length.

With Curly:

Woman Haters. (1934) ° With Marjorie White, Monty Collins, Bud Jamison, Tiny Sanford, Walter Brennan. Directed by Archie Gottler.

Punch Drunks. (1934) *** With Dorothy Granger, Tiny Lipson, Arthur Housman, Billy Blectcher, Al Hill. Original story by the Stooges. Directed by Lou Breslow.

Men in Black. (1934) *** With Dell Henderson, Jeanie Roberts, Ruth Hiatt, Billy Gilbert, Bud Jamison. Nominated for an Academy Award. Directed by Raymond McCarey.

Three Little Pigskins. (1934) ** With Walter Long, Lucille Ball, Joseph Young, Phyllis Crane, Gertie Green. Directed by Raymond McCarey.

Horse's Collars. (1935) ** With Dorothy Kent, Fred Kelsey, Fred Kohler, Hank Mann, June Gittleson. Directed by Clyde Bruckman.

Restless Knights. (1935) ° With Walter Brennan, Geneva Mitchell, Jack Duffy, Stanley Blystone. Directed by Charles Lamont.

Pop Goes the Easel. (1935) *** With Bobby Burns, Jack Duffy, Leo White, Geneva Mitchell. Directed by Del Lord.

Uncivil Warriors. (1935) *** With Bud Jamison, Phyllis Crane, Theodore Lorch, Marvin Loback. Directed by Del Lord.

Pardon My Scotch. (1935) ** With James C. Morton, Billy Gilbert, Grace Goodall, Nathan Carr. Directed by Del Lord.

Hoi Polloi. (1935) *** With Harry Holmes, Robert Graves, Grace Goodhall, Betty McMahon, Bud Jamison. Based on a story by Moe's wife, Helen. Directed by Del Lord.

Three Little Beers. (1935) ** With Bud Jamison, Tiny Lipson, Bobby Burns. Directed by Del Lord.

Ants in the Pantry. (1935) *** With Clara Kimball Young, Jack Duffy, Bud Jamison, James C. Morton. Directed by Preston Black.

Movie Maniacs. (1936) ** With Bud Jamison, Mildred Harris, Jack Kenney, Lois Lindsey. Directed by Del Lord.

Half-Shot Shooters. (1936) ** With Stanley Blystone, Vernon Dent, John Kascier. Directed by Preston Black.

Disorder in the Court. (1936) *** With Bud Jamison, Susan Karaan, Tiny Jones, Bill O'Brien. Directed by Preston Black.

A Pain in the Pullman. (1936) * With Bud Jamison, James C. Morton, Eve Reynolds. A remake of the Thelma Todd–ZaSu Pitts comedy *Show Business*, which was again remade as *Training for Trouble* by Gus Schilling and Dick Lane. Directed by Preston Black.

False Alarms. (1936) *** With Stanley Blystone, June Gittleson. Directed by Del Lord.

Whoops I'm an Indian. (1936) ° With Bud Jamison. Directed by Del Lord.

Slippery Silks. (1937) ** With Vernon Dent, Symona Boniface, Robert Williams, Judy Gittleson. Directed by Preston Black.

Grips, Grunts, and Groans. (1937) ** With Harrisson Greene, Casey Columbo, Herb Stagman. Directed by Preston Black.

Dizzy Doctors. (1937) ** With June Gittleson, Vernon Dent, Bud Jamison, Wilfred Lucas. Directed by Del Lord.

Three Dumb Clucks. (1937) ** With Lynton Brent, Frank Austin, Eva Murray. Curly plays two roles—himself and his own father. Directed by Del Lord.

Back to the Woods. (1937) ° With Bud Jamison, Vernon Dent. Directed by Preston Black.

Goofs and Saddles. (1937) ** With Stanley Blystone, Hank Mann, Sam Lufkin. Directed by Del Lord.

Cash and Carry. (1937) * With Lester Dorr, Cy Schindell. Directed by Del Lord.

Playing the Ponies. (1937) ** With Tiny Lipson, Bill Irving, Ted Toones. Directed by Charles Lamont.

The Sitter Downers. (1937) ** With June Gittleson, James C. Morton, Marcia Healy, Betty Mack. Reminiscent of Keaton's *One Week* (1920). Directed by Del Lord.

Termites of 1938. (1938) ** With Dorothy Granger, Bud Jamison, Bess Flowers, Michael Mahnke. Directed by Del Lord.

Wee Wee Monsieur. (1938) * With Bud Jamison, Vernon Dent, Grant "Poncho" Rex. Directed by Del Lord.

Tassels in the Air. (1938) *** With Bud Jamison, Bess Flowers, Vernon Dent, Dorothy Granger. Directed by Charley Chase (based on Chase's own comedy *Luncheon at Twelve*).

Flat Foot Stooges. (1938) ** With Dick Curtis, Chester Conklin, Lola Jensen. Directed by Charley Chase.

Healthy, Wealthy, and Dumb. (1938) *** With Bud Jamison, James C. Morton, Lucille Lund, Bobby Burns. Directed by Del Lord.

Violent Is the Word for Curly. (1938) *** With Gladys Gale, Marjorie Dean, Bud Jamison, Pat Gleason. Directed by Charley Chase.

Three Missing Links. (1938) * With Jane Hamilton, James C. Morton, Monty Collins, Grant "Poncho" Rex. Directed by Jules White.

Mutts to You. (1938) *** With Bess Flowers, Dick Curtis, Vernon Dent, Bud Jamison, Lane Chandler. Directed by Charley Chase.

Three Little Sew and Sews. (1939) * With James C. Morton, Vernon Dent, Bud Jamison, Phyllis Barry. Directed by Del Lord.

We Want Our Mummy. (1939) ** With Bud Jamison, James C. Morton, Dick Curtis. Directed by Del Lord.

A-Ducking They Did Go. (1939) *** With Vernon Dent, Bud Jamison, Lane Chandler. Directed by Del Lord.

Yes We Have No Bonanza. (1939) *** With Vernon Dent, Dick Curtis, Lynton Brent. Directed by Del Lord.

Saved By the Belle. (1939) ** With Carmen LaRue, LeRoy Mason, Richard Fiske. Directed by Charley Chase (his last work with them).

Calling All Curs. (1939) *** With Lynton Brent, Cy Schindell. Directed by Jules White.

Oily to Bed, Oily to Rise. (1939) *** With Dick Curtis, Eva McKenzie, Eddie Laughton, Richard Fiske. Directed by Jules White.

Three Sappy People. (1939) *** With Lorna Gray, Don Beddoe, Bud Jamison, Ann Doran, Richard Fiske. Directed by Jules White.

You Natzy Spy. (1940) *** With Dick Curtis, Don Beddoe. Directed by Jules White.

Rockin' Through the Rockies. (1940) *** With Kathryn Sheldon, Dorothy Appelby, Linda Winters, Lorna Gray. Directed by Jules White.

A-Plumbing We Will Go. (1940) *** With Symona Boniface, Bud Jamison, Bess Flowers, Dudley Dickerson. Directed by Del Lord.

Nutty But Nice. (1940) *** Vernon Dent, John Tyrell. Directed by Jules White.

How High Is Up. (1940) ** With Vernon Dent, Bruce Bennett, Edmund Cobb. Directed by Del Lord.

From Nurse to Worse. (1940) *** With Vernon Dent, Cy Schindell, Dorothy Appelby. Directed by Jules White.

No Census, No Feeling. (1940) *** With Vernon Dent, Symona Boniface, Max Davidson, Babe Kane. Directed by Del Lord.

Cuckoo Cavaliers. (1940) ** With Jack O'Shea, Dorothy Appelby. Directed by Jules White.

Boobs in Arms. (1940) * With Richard Fiske, Evelyn Young, Phil Van Zandt. Directed by Jules White.

So Long Mr. Chumps. (1941) * With Bruce Bennett, Eddie Laughton, Dorothy Appelby, Vernon Dent. Directed by Jules White.

Dutiful But Dumb. (1941) *** With Vernon Dent, Bud Jamison, James C. Morton, Bruce Bennett. Directed by Del Lord.

All the World's a Stooge. (1941) ** With Lelah Tyler, Emroy Parnell, Symona Boniface, Richard Fiske. Directed by Del Lord.

I'll Never Heil Again. (1941) ** With Mary Ainslee, Vernon Dent, Bud Jamison, Duncan Renaldo. Directed by Jules White.

An Ache in Every Stake. (1941) *** With Vernon Dent, Gino Corrado, Bud Jamison, Bess Flowers, Symona Boniface. Directed by Del Lord.

In the Sweet Pie and Pie. (1941) *** With Dorothy Appelby, Mary Ainslee, Eddie Laughton, John Tyrell, Vernon Dent. Directed by Jules White.

Some More of Samoa. (1941) ** With Louise Carver, Monty Collins. Often not run on television due to racial slurs. Directed by Del Lord.

Loco Boy Makes Good. (1942) ** With Dorothy Appelby, Vernon Dent, Bruce Bennett, Robert Williams. Directed by Jules White.

Cactus Makes Perfect. (1942) ** With Monty Collins, Vernon Dent, Ernie Adams. Directed by Del Lord.

What's the Matador. (1942) ** With Suzanne Karaan, Harry Burns, Dorothy Appelby, Eddie Laughton. Directed by Jules White.

Matri-phony. (1942) * With Vernon Dent, Marjorie Dean, Cy Schindell. Directed by Harry Edwards.

Three Smart Saps. (1942) ** With Bud Jamison, Vernon Dent, John Tyrell. Directed by Jules White.

Even As I.O.U. (1942) *** With Ruth Skinner, Stanley Blystone, Vernon Dent, Bud Jamison. Directed by Del Lord.

Sock-a-Bye-Baby. (1942) *** With Julie Gibson, Clarence Straight, Bud Jamison. Directed by Jules White.

They Stooge to Conga. (1943) ** With Vernon Dent, Dudley Dickerson. Overtly violent sequence involving a climbing spike driven into Moe's eye is often edited out of TV prints. Directed by Del Lord.

Dizzy Detectives. (1943) ** With Bud Jamison, John Tyrell, Cy Schindell. Directed by Jules White.

Spook Louder. (1943) ** With Stanley Blystone, Bill Kelly, Symona Boniface. Directed by Del Lord.

Back from the Front. (1943) ** With Vernon Dent, Bud Jamison. Directed by Jules White.

Three Little Twerps. (1943) * With Stanley Blystone, Bud Jamison, Chester Conklin. Directed by Harry Edwards.

Higher Than a Kite. (1943) ** With Vernon Dent, Dick Curtis. Directed by Del Lord.

I Can Hardly Wait. (1943) ° With Bud Jamison, Vernon Dent. Semi-remake of Laurel and Hardy's *Leave 'Em Laughing* (1928). Directed by Jules White.

Dizzy Pilots. (1943) * With Richard Fiske, Robert Williams. Directed by Jules White. Includes footage from *Boobs in Arms.*

Phoney Express. (1943) ** With Bud Jamison, Snub Pollard, Chester Conklin. Directed by Del Lord.

A Gem of a Jam. (1943) ** With Bud Jamison, Dudley Dickerson. Directed by Del Lord.

Crash Goes the Hash. (1944) ** With Vernon Dent, Bud Jamison, Symona Boniface, Dick Curtis. Directed by Jules White.

Busy Buddies. (1944) *** With Vernon Dent, Fred Kelsey. Directed by Del Lord.

The Yoke's on Me. (1944) ° With Bob McKenzie. WWII-oriented short which is rarely revived on TV. In one awful sequence, Moe pulls Curly by the eyelid! Directed by Jules White.

Idle Roomers. (1944) ** With Christine McIntyre, Vernon Dent, Duke York. Directed by Del Lord.

Gents Without Gents. (1944) ** With Lindsay, Laverne, and Betty; Eddie Laughton. The boys perform the old burlesque sketch "Slowly I Turned" (aka

"Niagra Falls"). Originally intended as footage for feature *Good Luck Mr. Yates*. Directed by Jules White.

No Dough Boys. (1944) *** Vernon Dent, Christine McIntyre. WWII-oriented short which is rarely revived on TV. Directed by Jules White.

Three Pests in a Mess. (1945) ** With Christine McIntyre, Vernon Dent, Snub Pollard, Stanley Blystone. This one has Curly shooting a gun which knocks down a manikin, leading him to believe (throughout the entire film) that he has committed murder. Perhaps the trio's most morbid short. Directed by Del Lord.

Booby Dupes. (1945) ** With Vernon Dent, Rebel Randall. The last short in which Curly looks and performs with his usual vitality. In all subsequent films his health is noticeably impaired. Directed by Del Lord.

Idiot's Deluxe. (1945) * With Vernon Dent, Paul Krueger. Directed by Jules White.

If a Body Meets a Body. (1945) * With Fred Kelsey. A remake of *The Laurel & Hardy Murder Case* (1930). Directed by Jules White.

Micro-Phonies. (1945) ** With Symona Boniface, Christine McIntyre, Gino Corrado. Directed by Edward Bernds.

Beer Barrel Polecats. (1946) ° With Vernon Dent, Eddie Laughton. Contains large extracts from *So Long Mr. Chumps* (1941). Directed by Jules White.

A Bird in the Head. (1946) ° With Vernon Dent, Robert Williams. Directed by Edward Bernds.

Uncivil War Birds. (1946) ° With Faye Williams, Marilyn Johnson, Eleanor Counts. Directed by Jules White.

Three Troubledoers. (1946) * With Dick Curtis, Christine McIntyre. Directed by Edward Bernds.

Monkey Businessmen. (1946) * With Kenneth McDonald, Fred Kelsey, Snub Pollard, Cy Schindell. Directed by Edward Bernds.

Three Loan Wolves. (1946) * With Harold Brauer, Joe Palma. Directed by Jules White.

G.I. Wanna Home. (1946) ° With Symona Boniface, Judy Malcomb. Directed by Jules White.

Rhythm & Weep. (1946) ° With Jack Norton, Ruth Godfrey. Directed by Jules White.

Three Little Pirates. (1946) * With Christine McIntyre, Vernon Dent. The Stooges perform their Maharaja routine. Directed by Edward Bernds.

Half Wits Holiday. (1946) ** With Symona Boniface, Vernon Dent, Emil Sitka, Barbara Slater, Ted Lorch, Helen Dickson. Curly's last film as one of the Stooges. A remake of *Hoi Polloi* (1935). Directed by Jules White.

With Shemp:

Fright Night. (1946) ** With Harold Brauer, Dick Wessel, Cy Schindell. Directed by Edward Bernds.

Out West. (1946) *** With Jock Mahoney, Christine McIntyre, Vernon Dent. Directed by Edward Bernds.

Hold That Lion. (1947) * With Kenneth McDonald, Emil Sitka, Dudley Dickerson. Directed by Jules White.

Brideless Groom. (1947) *** With Emil Sitka, Dee Green, Christine McIntyre. Directed by Edward Bernds.

Sing a Song of Six Pants. (1947) *** With Harold Brauer, Vernon Dent, Dee Green, Virginia Hunter. Directed by Jules White.

All Gummed Up. (1947) ** With Emil Sitka, Christine McIntyre. Directed by Jules White.

Shivering Sherlocks. (1948) ** With Christine McIntyre, Duke York. Directed by Del Lord.

Pardon My Clutch. (1948) *** With Matt McHugh, Emil Sitka, Virginia Hunter. Directed by Edward Bernds.

Squareheads of the Round Table. (1948) *** With Jock Mahoney, Christine McIntyre, Vernon Dent. Directed by Edward Bernds.

Fiddlers Three. (1948) * With Vernon Dent, Phil Van Zandt, Joe Palma. Directed by Jules White.

Heavenly Daze. (1948) ** With Vernon Dent, Symona Boniface, Sam McDaniel. Directed by Jules White.

Hot Scots. (1948) * With Herbert Evans, Christine McIntyre, Ted Lorch, Charles Knight. Directed by Edward Bernds.

I'm a Monkey's Uncle. (1948) ** With Dee Green, Cy Schindell, Virginia Hunter. Directed by Jules White.

Crime on Their Hands. (1948) *** With Emil Sitka, Kenneth MacDonald, Christine McIntyre, Cy Schindell. Directed by Edward Bernds.

The Ghost Talks. (1948) ° Directed by Jules White.

Who Done It. (1949) ** With Emil Sitka, Christine McIntyre, Duke York, Dudley Dickerson. Directed by Edward Bernds.

Hocus Pocus. (1949) ** With Jimmy Lloyd, Mary Ainslee, Vernon Dent. Directed by Jules White.

Fuelin' Around. (1949) * With Christine McIntyre, Emil Sitka, Jock Mahoney. Directed by Edward Bernds.

Malice in the Palace. (1949) ° With Vernon Dent, Frank Lackteen. Directed by Jules White.

Vagabond Loafers. (1949) ** With Kenneth McDonald, Christine McIntyre, Emil Sitka, Symona Boniface, Dudley Dickerson. A remake of Curly's *A-Plumbing We Will Go*, using some stock footage. Directed by Edward Bernds.

Dunked in the Deep. (1949) ° With Gene Roth. Directed by Jules White.

Punchy Cowpunchers. (1950) *** With Jock Mahoney, Christine McIntyre, Emil Sitka, Vernon Dent, Dick Wessel. Directed by Edward Bernds.

Hugs & Mugs. (1950) ° With Christine McIntyre, Nanette Bourdeaux, Emil Sitka. Directed by Jules White.

Dopey Dicks. (1950) ** With Phil Van Zandt, Stanley Price, Christine McIntyre. Directed by Edward Bernds.

Love at First Bite. (1950) ° With Christine McIntyre, Yvette Reynard, Marie Montiel. Directed by Jules White.

Selfmade Maids. (1950) ° All parts played by the Stooges. Directed by Hugh McCollum.

Three Hams on Rye. (1950) ** With Emil Sitka, Christine McIntyre. Directed by Jules White.

Studio Stoops. (1950) *** With Vernon Dent, Christine McIntyre, Kenneth MacDonald, Stanley Price. Directed by Edward Bernds.

Slap Happy Sleuths. (1950) ** With Kenneth MacDonald, Stanley Price, Vernon Dent, Emil Sitka. Directed by Hugh McCollum.

A Snitch in Time. (1950) ** With Henry Kulky, Jean Willes, Stanley Price. Directed by Edward Bernds.

Three Arabian Nuts. (1951) ** With Vernon Dent, Wesley Blye, Dick Curtis, Phil Van Zandt. Directed by Edward Bernds.

Baby Sitters Jitters. (1951) ** With Lynn Davis, Dave Windsor. Directed by Jules White.

Don't Throw That Knife. (1951) * With Dick Curtis, Jean Willes. Directed by Jules White.

Scrambled Brains. (1951) *** Emil Sitka, Babe London, Vernon Dent. Directed by Jules White.

Merry Mavericks. (1951) ** With Dan Harvey, Mary Martin, Paul Campbell. Directed by Edward Bernds.

The Tooth Will Out. (1951) * With Vernon Dent, Margie Listz. Directed by Edward Bernds.

Hula La La. (1951) ** With Emil Sitka, Kenneth McDonald, Jean Willes. Directed by Hugh McCollum.

The Pest Man Wins. (1951) ** With Nanette Bourdeaux, Emil Sitka, Vernon Dent, Helen Dickson. A remake of Curly's *Ants in the Pantry* (1934), with footage from *Half Wits Holiday* (1946). Directed by Jules White.

A Missed Fortune. (1952) ** With Nanette Bourdeaux, Vernon Dent. Directed by Jules White.

Listen Judge. (1952) *** With Vernon Dent, John Hamilton, Emil Sitka, Kitty McHugh. A partial remake of Curly's *An Ache in Every Stake* (1941). Directed by Edward Bernds.

Corny Casanovas. (1952) * With Connie Cezan. Directed by Jules White.

He Cooked His Goose. (1952) * With Mary Ainslee, Angela Stevens. Directed by Jules White.

Gents in a Jam. (1952) *** With Emil Sitka, Mickey Simpson, Kitty McHugh, Mary Ainslee. Directed by Edward Bernds.

Three Dark Horses. (1952) ** With Kenneth McDonald, Ben Welden. Directed by Jules White.

Cuckoo on a Choo Choo. (1952) * With Patricia Wright, Victoria Horne. Directed by Jules White.

Up In Daisy's Penthouse. (1953) * With Connie Cezan. A remake of Curly's *Three Dumb Clucks* (1937), with stock footage. Directed by Jules White.

Booty & the Beast. (1953) * With Kenneth MacDonald. A remake using stock footage from *Hold That Lion* (1947), including Curly's cameo (Curly had, by now, passed away). Directed by Jules White.

Loose Loot. (1953) * With Kenneth MacDonald, Tom Kennedy, Nanette Bourdeaux; footage from *Hold That Lion* (1947). Directed by Jules White.

Tricky Dicks. (1953) ** With Benny Rubin, Connie Cezan. Directed by Jules White.

Spooks. (1953) * With Phil Van Zandt, Tom Kennedy, Norma Randall. In 3-D. Directed by Jules White.

Pardon My Backfire. (1953) * With Benny Rubin, Frank Sully, Phil Arnold, Fred Kelsey. In 3-D. Directed by Jules White.

Rip, Sew, and Stitch. (1953) ** Virtually the same film as *Sing a Song of Six Pants* (1947) with only two brief new scenes. Directed by Jules White.

Bubble Trouble. (1953) ** This is *All Gummed Up* (1947) with a new ending shot. Directed by Jules White.

Goof on the Roof. (1953) *** With Phil Arnold, Maxine Gates. Arguably the finest Stooge film. Directed by Jules White.

Income Tax Sappy. (1954) ** With Benny Rubin, Nanette Bourdeaux. Directed by Jules White.

Musty Musketeers. (1954) * This is *Fiddlers Three* (1948) with a new beginning and a new ending. Directed by Jules White.

Pals and Gals. (1954) ** With Christine McIntyre, Vernon Dent. Footage from Curly's *Goofs & Saddles* (1937) and Shemp's *Out West* (1946). Directed by Jules White.

Knutzy Knights. (1954) *** This is *Squareheads of the Round Table* (1948) with a new beginning. Directed by Jules White.

Shot in the Frontier. (1954) ° Directed by Jules White.

Scotched in Scotland. (1954) * This is *Hot Scots* (1948) with some brief new scenes. Directed by Jules White.

Fling in the Ring. (1954) * This is *Fright Night* (1946) with a new beginning and some brief new scenes. Viewed years later by Edward Bernds, who directed the original *Fright Night* footage, this film prompted a lawsuit. "I won a little bit of money from Columbia for that," Bernds remembers. Directed by Jules White.

Of Cash and Hash. (1954) ** This is *Shivering Sherlocks* (1948) with a few brief new scenes. Directed by Jules White.

Gypped in the Penthouse. (1955) ** With Jean Willes, Emil Sitka. Directed by Jules White.

Bedlam in Paradise. (1955) ** A remake of *Heavenly Daze* (1948), with stock footage. Directed by Jules White.

Stone Age Romeos. (1955) ** With Emil Sitka, Cy Schindell, Dee Green. New opening and closing framework for *I'm a Monkey's Uncle* (1948) footage. Directed by Jules White.

Wham Bam Slam. (1955) ** Inferior new footage mars old *Pardon My Clutch* (1948) footage. Directed by Jules White.

Hot Ice. (1955) ** This is *Crime on Their Hands* (1948) with beginning from *Hot Scots* (1948) and a new ending. Directed by Jules White.

Blunder Boys. (1955) ° With Benny Rubin, Kenneth MacDonald, Angela Stevens. Directed by Jules White.

Husbands Beware. (1956) *** This is *Brideless Groom* (1947) with a new beginning and brief new ending. Directed by Jules White.

Creeps. (1956) ° This is *The Ghost Talks* (1949) with a new beginning and ending. Directed by Jules White.

Flagpole Jitters. (1956) ** This is *Hocus Pocus* (1949) with brief new footage. Directed by Jules White.

For Crimin' Out Loud. (1956) ** This is *Who Done It* (1949) with some brief new scenes. This was to be the last film to contain new footage of Shemp, who died after its completion. The next four films only featured him in stock footage, with the new footage limited to brief scenes of Moe, Larry, and Shemp's double, Joe Palma. Directed by Jules White.

Rumpus in the Harem. (1956) ° This is *Malice in the Palace* (1949) with a new beginning and brief new scenes. Directed by Jules White.

Hot Stuff. (1956) ** This is *Fuelin' Around* (1949) with a new beginning and brief new scenes. Directed by Jules White.

Scheming Schemers. (1956) *** This is *Vagabond Loafers* (1949) with a new ending; footage from *Half Wits Holiday* (1946). Directed by Jules White.

Commotion on the Ocean. (1956) ** This is *Dunked in the Deep* (1949), edited to vast improvement with a few brief new scenes. Directed by Jules White.

With Joe Besser:

Hoofs and Goofs. (1957) * With Harriette Tarler, Benny Rubin. Directed by Jules White.

Muscle Up a Little Closer. (1957) ** With Frank Sully, Maxine Gates. Directed by Jules White.

A Merry Mix-Up. (1957) ** With Nanette Bourdeaux, Frank Sully, Harriette Tarler. Directed by Jules White.

Space Ship Sappy. (1957) * With Benny Rubin, Harriette Tarler, Emil Sitka, Lorraine Crawford. Directed by Jules White.

Guns A-Poppin'. (1957) * With Frank Sully, Joe Palma, Vernon Dent (in stock footage). A remake of Curly's *Idiot's Deluxe* (1946), with stock footage. Directed by Jules White.

Horsing Around. (1957) ° Pointless sequel to *Hoofs and Goofs* (1957). Directed by Jules White.

Rusty Romeos. (1957) * With Connie Cezan. A remake of *Corny Casanovas* (1952), with stock footage. Directed by Jules White.

Outer Space Jitters. (1957) * With Dan Blocker, Emil Sitka, Gene Roth. Directed by Jules White.

Quiz Whizz. (1958) ** With Gene Roth, Greta Thyssen. Directed by Jules White.

Fifi Blows Her Top. (1958) * With Phil Van Zandt, Vanda Dupre. Some stock footage from *Love at First Bite* (1950) is used. Directed by Jules White.

Pies and Guys. (1958) ** With Emil Sitka, Gene Roth, Milton Fromme. A remake of Curly's *Half Wits Holiday* (1946). Directed by Jules White.

Sweet and Hot. (1958) ° With Muriel Landers. Pointless musical with the Stooges in separate roles. Besser comes off best. Directed by Jules White.

Flying Saucer Daffy. (1958) ** With Harriette Tarler, Emil Sitka. Directed by Jules White.

Oil's Well That Ends Well. (1958) * Remake of Curly's *Oily to Bed Oily to Rise*, with very little stock footage. Directed by Jules White.

Triple Crossed. (1958) ** Remake of Shemp's *He Cooked His Goose* (1952), with stock footage. Directed by Jules White.

Sappy Bullfighters. (1958) ° This last and worst Stooge short is a remake, with stock footage, of Curly's *What's the Matador* (1942). Besser's last film as one of the Stooges. Directed by Jules White.

With Joe DeRita (or Curly-Joe). All these are features:

Have Rocket Will Travel. (1959) * With Jerome Cowan, Anna-Lisa, Bob Colbert, Marjorie Bennett, Don Lamond. Directed by Harry Romm and David Lowell Rich. 76 minutes.

Snow White and the Three Stooges. (1960) * With Carol Heiss, Edson Stroll, Patricia Medina, Guy Rolfe, Michael David. Directed by Walter Lang. 107 minutes. Color.

The Three Stooges Meet Hercules. (1961) * With Samson Burke, Vicki Trickett, Quinn Redecker, Emil Sitka. Directed by Edward Bernds. 90 minutes.

The Three Stooges in Orbit. (1962) * With Emil Sitka, Carol Christianson, Edson Stroll, Rayford Barnes. Directed by Edward Bernds. 90 minutes.

The Three Stooges Go Around the World in a Daze. (1963) * With Jay Sheffield, Joan Freeman, Walter Burke, Peter Forster, Richard Devon. Directed by Norman Maurer. 95 minutes.

The Outlaws Is Comin'. (1965) * With Adam West, Nancy Kovack, Joe Bolton, Emil Sitka, Henry Gibson. Directed by Norman Maurer. 90 minutes.

Kook's Tour. (1970) * With Emil Sitka, Moose The Wonder Dog. Directed by Norman Maurer. 60 minutes.

Moe, Larry, and Joe DeRita also appeared in 40 color live-action sequences as introductions to a series of 156 color Three Stooges Cartoons for Normandy Productions in 1966 and 1967. Emil Sitka appeared in many of these sequences, and the Stooges provided their own voices for the animated films. One 30-minute color TV film, *The Three Stooges Scrapbook* (1960) was never run, but a one-reel version was issued to theaters. Moe, Larry, and DeRita also did about a half-dozen appearances in TV commercials during the sixties, not to mention live and TV appearances, children's records, and posing for the front covers of several Three Stooges comics during the sixties.

The Stooges had supporting roles in the following films:
With Curly for Ted Healy films:

Nertsrey Rhymes. (1933) Directed by Jack Cummings. Two reels. Color.

Beer and Pretzels. (1933) Directed by Jack Cummings. Two reels.

Hello Pop. (1933) Directed by Jack Cummings. Two reels. Color.

Plane Nuts. (1933) Directed by Jack Cummings. Two reels.

Turn Back the Clock. (1933) Directed by Edgar Selwyn. 80 minutes.

Meet the Baron. (1933) Directed by Walter Lang. 68 minutes.

Dancing Lady. (1933) Directed by Robert Leonard. 94 minutes.

Myrt and Marge. (1933) Directed by Al Boasberg. 65 minutes.

The Big Idea. (1934) Directed by William Crowley. Two reels.

Fugitive Lovers. (1934) Directed by Richard Boleslavsky. 85 minutes.

Hollywood Party. (1934) Directed by Richard Boleslavsky and others. 70 minutes.

Also with Curly:

The Captain Hates the Sea. (1934) Directed by Lewis Milestone. 90 minutes.

Start Cheering. (1938) Directed by Albert Rogell. 80 minutes.

Time Out for Rhythm. (1941) Directed by Sidney Salkow. 75 minutes.

My Sister Eileen. (1942) Directed by Alexander Hall. 95 minutes.

Rocking in the Rockies. (1945) Directed by Vernon Keays. 67 minutes.

Swing Parade of 1946. (1946) Directed by Phil Karlson. 75 minutes.

With Shemp:

The Gold Raiders. (1951) Directed by Edward Bernds. 55 minutes.

With Joe DeRita: (all in color)

It's A Mad Mad Mad Mad World. (1962) Directed by Stanley Kramer. 162 minutes.

Four for Texas. (1964) Directed by Robert Aldrich. 125 minutes.

Star Spangled Salesman. (1968) Directed by Norman Maurer. Two reels.

The Stooges made no supporting appearances while Besser was a member of the act.

Anthologies Containing the Stooges' Work

Three Stooges Fun-O-Rama. (1960) Directed by Jules White. (Joe Besser)

MGM's Big Parade of Laughs. (1965) Produced by Robert Youngson. (Curly)

Stop Look and Laugh. (1965) Directed by Jules White. (Curly)

Three Stooges Follies. (1974) Directed by Jules White. (Curly and Shemp)

The Stooges' likenesses have also appeared in several animated cartoons for Hanna-Barbera over the past few years.

Solo Appearances:

Moe

Jailbirds of Paradise. (1934) Directed by Al Boasberg. Two reels. Color.

Space Master X-7. (1958) Directed by Ed Bernds. 70 minutes.

Don't Worry We'll Think of a Title. (1966) Directed by Harmon Jones. 80 min. Color.

Doctor Death: Seeker of Souls. (1973) Directed by Eddie Saeta. 90 minutes. Color.

Curly

Roast Beef and Movies. (1934) Directed by Samuel Baerwitz. Two reels. Color.

Jailbirds of Paradise. (1934) Directed by Al Boasberg. Two reels. Color.

Shemp

Vitaphone Shorts (1933–1937), all two reels.

Salt Water Daffy, In The Dough, Close Relations, Here Comes Flossie, How'd Ya Like That, Mushrooms, Pugs and Kisses, Very Close Veins, Corn on the Cop, I Scream, Art Trouble, My Mummy's Arms, Smoked Hams, Dizzy & Daffy, A Peach of a Pair, His First Flame, Why Pay Rent, Serves Your Right, On the Wagon, Officer's Mess, While the Cat's Away, For the Love of Pete, Absorbin Junior, Here's Howe, Punch and Beauty, The Choke's on You, The Blonde Bomber, Kick Me Again, Henry the Ache (1934; RKO), The Knife of the Party (1934; RKO)

Columbia Shorts (1938–1947), all two reels.

Home on the Range, Glove Slingers, Money Squawks, Boobs in the Woods, Pleased to Mitt You, Farmer for the Day, Pick a Peck of Plumbers, Open Season for Saps, Off Again on Again, Where the Pests Begin, A Hit with a Miss, Mr. Noisy, Jiggers My Wife, Society Mugs, Bride and Gloom.

Feature Film Appearances

Millionares in Prison (1940), Leatherpushers (1940), The Bank Dick (1940), Give Us Wings (1940), Six Lessons From Madame Lazonga (1941), Buck Privates (1941), Meet the Chump (1941), Mr. Dynamite (1941), Too Many Blondes (1941), In the Navy (1941), Tight Shoes (1941), San Antonio Rose (1941), Hit the Road (1941), Hold That Ghost (1941), Hellzapoppin (1941), The Invisible Woman (1941), Butch Minds Baby (1942), Mississippi Gambler (1942), The Strange Case of Dr. Rey (1942), Private Buckaroo (1942), Pittsburgh (1942), Arabian Nights (1942), Hw's About It (1943), It Ain't Hay (1943), Keep 'Em Slugging (1943), Crazyhouse (1943), Strictly in the Groove (1943), Three of a Kind (Cooking Up Trouble) (1944), Moonlight & Cactus (1944), Strange Affair (1944), Crazy Knights (Ghost Crazy) (1944), Trouble Chasers (1945), Gentlemen Misbehaves (1946), One Exciting Week (1946), Dangerous Business (1946), Blondie Knows Best (1946), Africa Screams (1949).

Joe Besser
Columbia Shorts (1949–1956) with Jimmy Hawthorne, all two reels.

Waiting in the Lurch, Dizzy Yardbirds, Fraidy Cats, Aim Fire & Scoot, Caught on the Bounce, Spies and Guys, Fire Chasers, G.I. Dood It, Hook a Crook, Army Daze.

Features

Hey Rookie (1944), Eadie Was A Lady (1945), Talk About a Lady (1946), Feudin' Fussin' & Fightin' (1948), Africa Screams (1949), Woman in Hiding (1950), Joe Palooka Meets Humphrey (1950), Outside the Wall (1950), The Desert Hawk (1950), I the Jury (1953), Sins of Jezebel (1953), Abbott and Costello Meet the Keystone Cops (1955), Headline Hunters (1955), Two Gun Lady (1956), Plunderers of Painted Flats (1959), Say One For Me (1959), Woodcutter's House (1959), The Rookie (1959), Story on Page One (1959), Let's Make Love (1960), The Silent Call (1961), The Errand Boy (1961), The Hand of Death (1961), With Six You Get Eggroll (1968), The Comeback (1969), Which Way to the Front (1970), Hey Abbott (1976).

Besser also did voice-overs for many cartoons throughout the sixties, seventies, and eighties and appeared on TV as a regular on the Joey Bishop show, and The Abbott & Costello show.

Joe DeRita
Columbia Shorts (1946–1948) all two reels.

Slappily Married, The Good Bad Egg, Wedlock Deadlock, Jitter Bughouse.

Features

The Doughgirls (1944), Sailor Takes a Wife (1945), People Are Funny (1946), Coroner Creek (1948), The Bravados (1958).

DeRita also appeared several times on TV's "Bachelor Father" in the fifties. He formed a New Three Stooges stage act with Frank Mitchell and Paul "Mousie" Garner in the early seventies. It was reportedly as bad as it sounds.

11

Abbott and Costello

Abbott and Costello are a rather difficult piece of comedy development to discuss. Not leading comedians in the sense that Chaplin and Keaton were, Bud and Lou are, nevertheless, highly important figures in the evolution of the movie comedians.

First we must acknowledge the fact that they were highly skilled vaudeville and burlesque comics, coming into prominence during the thirties on the strength of routines which had been floating around since the 1880s. This fact makes it safe to assume that Abbott and Costello's rendition of these routines was about the best one could expect. The era of burlesque and vaudeville humor (or many of its most important elements) may have been lost forever had Bud and Lou not preserved these classic sketches (including the immortal "Who's On First") on film.

Next we must make mention of the fact that in their day, Abbott and Costello were more popular than Laurel and Hardy, Fields, the Marx Brothers, or Buster Keaton at their respective peaks. They reached the number one spot among the top box office draws in 1942 (beating out folks like Jimmy Cagney, Cary Grant, Humphrey Bogart, Mickey Rooney, and Spencer Tracy), and always succeeded in pleasing the contemporary screen critics.

Their films were filled with comedy routines that were ancient, yet performed with a freshness moviegoers were just becoming familiar with; romantic sub-plots with attractive co-stars; and period pop songs from musical personalities of the day like The Andrews Sisters, Ella Fitzgerald, and Dick Powell.

But, today, their films have dated a bit. The routines hold up and remain wonderfully timeless examples of an essential factor in the development of American humor, but the scripts are rife with corny dialogue from the routine players, and the music hardly holds up at all.

During the war years, when the team was at their peak, their rat-a-tat delivery and music and romance was just what America needed to take its mind off what was happening overseas. This was coupled with the fact that Abbott and Costello were about the only leading comedians around. The talents of Laurel and Hardy and Buster Keaton were being wasted in cheap vehicles. Chaplin did nothing between 1940 and 1947, Lloyd nothing from 1938 to 1947. The Marx Brothers were off-screen from 1942 until 1946. W.C. Fields made his last starring

Bud Abbott, the consummate straight man, and Lou Costello, the perfect patsy.

film in 1941. Fatty Arbuckle died in 1933, Charley Chase in 1940, Harry Langdon in 1944, and their work had definitely been behind them.

The time had come for a new crop of comedians, a new comic breed that relied on smart patter instead of carefully built, perfectly structured physical gags, and Abbott and Costello were leading the pack.

William "Bud" Abbott was an amazing straight man, one who would bully and belittle his partner to the point where the viewer would have even more sympathy for the comic. His timing and delivery reached a perfection that no other straight man in show business history could match.

Louis Francis Cristillo was the perfect patsy: short, chubby, and baby-faced, with good (albeit often overplayed) reactions and a nice sense of slapstick.

Bud was ten years older than Lou and had more experience. This shows in many of their films, for although Lou has most of the payoff lines in the routines, it's Bud's pacing and masterful execution that makes them work as well as they do.

Bud and Lou had already made it on stage and radio when they entered films in 1940, taking supporting roles in the tired musical *One Night in the Tropics*. Whenever they were on screen, the boys would go into one of their classic routines in sessions that seemed too hurried to be wholly successful. All of the bits they did in *Tropics* were performed better once the team began starring in their own films.

Buck Privates (1941) was their first starring film and the essential example of the Abbott and Costello films of the war years. Period music by the Andrews Sisters and an obtrusive romantic triangle involving studio players Lee Bowman, Alan Curtis, and Jane Frazee surrounded the comedy of Bud and Lou in the army.

Today the music has dated and the romantic subplot is unendurable. The final third of this film, dealing with war game maneuvers (entering around the romantic subplot), is just plain boring. Much of it is done instructively, something that may have had some appeal during the war, but now it's just a lousy way to kill time.

On the positive side, *Buck Privates* shows Abbott and Costello in peak form doing some very funny burlesque-derived routines on army life. Their timing is great, and they seem to have more energy than in virtually any of their other pictures. This exuberance and talent makes *Buck Privates* worthwhile in spite of the intrusions one has to bear.

Two other service comedies, *In the Navy* (1941) and *Keep 'Em Flying* (1942), were like *Buck Privates* in that they were hampered by the music and romantic subplot, but abetted by the energy and excitement of the team.

Hold That Ghost (1941) looks like another tired haunted house comedy at first glance, but emerges as a fast, fresh approach to the timeworn gags, and thus is one of their greatest films. It showed that the boys didn't need music and romantic subplots (both of which were there, but toned down) and also proved that even the oldest, most familiar comic ideas looked fresh when performed by the talented and energetic Bud and Lou.

Costello's scare take is indescribably funny, and his comic dance with co-star Joan Davis is excruciatingly hilarious. Abbott is there to provide the necessary straight-man badgering of his buddy, arriving too late to see the supernatural goings-on witnessed by his bewildered pal only moments before.

Throughout the war, Bud and Lou made many popular comedies that all relied on the same formula: good routines and energy, surrounded by musical and romantic interludes that just got in the way. *The Naughty Nineties* (1945), however, was the last use of this formula for a while, because times had changed and audiences were looking for something more substantial in movies . . . even in low comedy.

Two experiments had the boys working separate roles rather than as a team. While *Little Giant* (1946) and *The Time of Their Lives* (1946) were both good films (the latter among their all-time best), they didn't click with period movie-goers.

The duo returned to the old formula with *Buck Privates Come Home* (1947), a sequel rather late in coming, and *The Wistful Widow of Wagon Gap* (1947), a western satire with Marjorie Main.

In 1948, the boys made the film which remains their most popular. With *Abbott & Costello Meet Frankenstein*, Bud and Lou had found their new formula: blending their comedy with horror movie elements.

Abbott & Costello Meet Frankenstein is easily the best example of this formula. It is an expert blend of comedy and horror, with fine performances all around by Bela Lugosi, Lon Chaney, Jr., and Glenn Strange in the familiar roles of Dracula, the Wolf Man, and Frankenstein's monster, respectively. Not only is the comedy very funny, but the horror scenes are very exciting and the two styles blend perfectly.

Bud and Lou had used milder elements of terror in earlier films like *Hold That Ghost* and *Who Done It* (both among their very best works), but they went to the limit with this one, the results being so glorious that *Abbott & Costello Meet Frankenstein* is only a very slight notch below many of screen comedy's top achievements. The film was also popular enough to get the boys back among the top ten box office draws.

Unfortunately, the subsequent "meet" pictures were not on this level. In rapid succession they met *The Killer* (1949), *The Invisible Man* (1951), *Captain Kidd* (1952), *Dr. Jekyll & Mr. Hyde* (1953), *The Keystone Cops* (1955), and *The Mummy* (1955) in films that were anywhere from childishly amusing to downright bad. The major problem wasn't only uneventful scripts and lackluster direction. Bud and Lou just didn't have the old energy anymore.

Other than the "meet" pictures, the boys made *Abbott & Costello in the Foreign Legion* (1950), *Abbott & Costello Go to Mars* (1955), *Lost in Alaska* (1952), *Mexican Hayride* (1948), and *Africa Screams* (1949), all of which were fair at best, unendurable at worst.

They did a syndicated television show during the early fifties, but, despite the presence of Joe Besser in the cast, "The Abbott & Costello Show" consisted basically of the old routines they had done with more zest in their earlier feature films.

Shortly after making their last movie, *Dance with Me Henry* (1956), Abbott and Costello split up. Abbott retired from show business. Costello worked as a single in both dramatic and comedy roles on television, and in one film, *The Thirty-Foot Bride of Candy Rock*, which was made in 1959 but released two years later. Costello died a few months after completing this film. Abbott died in 1974.

While they never made a brilliant picture from fade in to fade out and weren't filmmakers in the same sense as geniuses like Chaplin, Keaton, Lloyd, Chase, and Laurel and Hardy, Abbott and Costello should not be dismissed as the banal equivalent of, say, the Three Stooges. Bud and Lou preserved some of America's greatest and most valid examples of humor. Their renditions of these routines had such energy that they have given some of the oldest jokes the longest lives and the biggest laughs.

No, they weren't responsible for any of the screen's most brilliant contributions, but Abbott and Costello were two very talented and funny men. The musical and romantic intrusions in their films have hampered the movies, causing them to become dated, but the duo's routines will always be surefire.

Phil Silvers once said, "Nobody knows where 'Who's On First' came from. Everybody used to do it. I did it myself with Rags Ragland. But Bud and Lou had the first crack at the big time audiences with it, and nobody performed it quite like they did. It's a piece of Americana."

It definitely is a piece of Americana. And, in many ways, so are Bud Abbott and Lou Costello.

Abbott and Costello Filmography

One Night in the Tropics. (1940) * With Allan Jones, Robert Cummings, Nancy Kelly, Mary Boland, Peggy Moran, William Frawley. Directed by Eddie Sutherland. 82 minutes.

Buck Privates. (1941) *** With the Andrews Sisters, Nat Pendelton, Lee Bowman, Jane Frazee, Alan Curtis, Shemp Howard. Directed by Arthur Lubin. 83 minutes.

In the Navy. (1941) ** With the Andrews Sisters, Dick Powell, Dick Foran, Claire Dodd, Shemp Howard. Directed by Arthur Lubin. 85 minutes.

Hold That Ghost. (1941) **** With Joan Davis, Richard Carlson, Evelyn Ankers, the Andrews Sisters, Ted Lewis, Shemp Howard. Directed by Arthur Lubin. 86 minutes.

Keep 'Em Flying. (1941) *** With Martha Raye, William Gargan, Dick Foran, Carol Bruce, Charles Lang. Directed by Arthur Lubin. 86 minutes.

Ride 'Em Cowboy. (1941) *** With Anne Gwynne, Dick Foran, Ella Fitzgerald,

Johnny Mack Browne, Dick Lane, Douglas Dumbrille. Directed by Arthur Lubin. 82 minutes.

Rio Rita. (1942) *** With Kathryn Grayson, John Carrol, Tom Conway, Arthur Space, Barry Nelson, Patricia Dane. Directed by S. Sylvan Simon. 90 min.

Pardon My Sarong. (1942) ** With Virginia Bruce, Robert Paige, Lionel Atwill, Leif Erickson, William Demarest. This one is severely hampered by a disturbing scene where Bud tries to talk Lou into committing suicide. Directed by Erle C. Kenton. 84 minutes.

Who Done It. (1942) **** With William Bendix, William Gargan, Mary Wickes, Patric Knowles, Louise Albritton. Directed by Erle C. Kenton. 77 minutes.

It Ain't Hay. (1943) *** With Eugene Pallette, Patsy O'Connor, Shemp Howard, Richard Lane, Mike Mazurki. Directed by Erle C. Kenton. 80 minutes.

Hit the Ice. (1943) *** With Patric Knowles, Ginny Simms, Sheldon Leonard, Elyse Knox. Directed by Charles Lamont. 80 minutes.

In Society. (1944) *** With Marion Hutton "Sky King" Grant, Arthur "Fish 'n Chips" Treacher. Directed by Jean Yarbrough. 75 minutes.

Lost in a Harem. (1944) *** With Marilyn Maxwell, Douglas Dumbrille, John Conte, Jimmy Dorsey, Ralph Sanford. Directed by Charles "Chuck" Reisner. 90 minutes.

Here Come the Coeds. (1945) *** With Peggy Ryan, Lon Chaney, Jr., Donald Cook, Richard Lane, Martha O'Driscoll. Directed by Jean Yarbrough. 87 minutes.

Abbott & Costello in Hollywood. (1945) *** With Frances Rafferty, Jean Porter, Rags Ragland, Lucille Ball, Preston Foster, Butch Jenkins. Directed by S. Sylvan Simon. 85 minutes.

The Naughty Nineties. (1945) *** With Alan Curtis, Rita Johnson, Henry Travers, Joe Sawyer, Jack Norton, John Hamilton. Directed by Jean Yarbrough. 75 minutes.

Little Giant. (1946) *** With Elena Verdugo, Brenda Joyce, Donald MacBride, Victor Kilian, Margaret Dumont. Directed by William Seiter. 90 minutes.

The Time of Their Lives. (1946) **** With Marjorie Reynolds, Binnie Barnes, John Shelton, Donald MacBride. Directed by Charles Barton. 80 minutes.

Abbott and Costello in "Rio Rita" (1942).

Buck Privates Come Home. (1947) *** With Tom Brown, Joan Shawlee, Nat Pendelton, Beverly Simmons, Donald MacBride. Directed by Charles Barton. 77 minutes.

The Wistful Widow of Wagon Gap. (1947) *** With Marjorie Main, Audrey Young, George Cleveland, Gordon Jones, Jimmy Bates. Directed by Charles Barton. 78 minutes.

The Noose Hangs High. (1948) ** With Leon Errol, Cathy Downs, Joseph Calleia, Mike Mazurki, Fritz Feld. Directed by Charles Barton. 77 minutes.

Abbott & Costello Meet Frankenstein. (1948) **** Bela Lugosi, Glenn Strange, Lon Chaney, Jr., Lenore Aubert, Frank Ferguson. Directed by Charles Barton. 83 minutes.

Mexican Hayride. (1948) * With Virginia Grey, Luba Malina, John Hubbard, Fritz Feld, Sid Fields. Directed by Charles Barton. 77 minutes.

Abbott & Costello Meet the Killer, Boris Karloff. (1949) *** With Boris Karloff, Lenore Aubert, Gary Moore, Donna Martell, Percy Helton. Directed by Charles Barton. 95 minutes.

Africa Screams. (1949) * With Shemp Howard, Hilary Brooke, Joe Besser, Max Baer, Clyde Beatty, Frank Buck. Directed by Charles Barton. 80 minutes.

Abbott & Costello in the Foreign Legion. (1950) ** With Patricia Medina, Walter Slezak, Douglas Dumbrille, Tor Johnson. Directed by Charles Lamont. 79 minutes.

Abbott & Costello Meet the Invisible Man. (1951) *** With Arthur Franz, Nancy Guild, Sheldon Leonard, Adele Jergens, Sid Saylor, Bobby Barber. Directed by Charles Lamont. 84 minutes.

Comin' Round the Mountain. (1951) * With Dorothy Shay, Kirby "Sky King" Grant, Glenn Strange, Margaret Hamilton, Joe Sawyer. Directed by Charles Lamont. 77 minutes.

Jack & the Beanstalk. (1952) ** With Buddy Baer, Dorothy Ford, Barbara Brown, William Farnum. Warner Brothers; part color, à la *The Wizard of Oz*. Directed by Jean Yarbrough. 78 minutes.

Abbott & Costello Meet Captain Kidd. (1952) ** With Charles Laughton, Hilary Brooke, Fran Warren, Bill Shirley, Rex Lease. Warner Brothers; color. Directed by Charles Lamont. 70 minutes.

Lost in Alaska. (1952) * With Tom Ewell, Mitzi Green, Bruce Cabot, Rex Lease, Joe Kirk. Directed by Jean Yarbrough. 76 minutes.

Abbott & Costello Go to Mars. (1953) * With Robert Paige, Mari Blanchard, Martha Hyer, Horace McMahon, Anita Ekbert. Directed by Charles Lamont. 77 minutes.

Abbott & Costello Meet Dr. Jekyll & Mr. Hyde. (1953) * With Boris Karloff, Craig Stevens, Helen Westcott, Reginald Denny, Lucille Lamarr. Directed by Charles Lamont. 76 minutes.

Abbott & Costello Meet the Keystone Cops. (1955) * With Fred Clark, Lynn Bari, Maxie Rosenbloom, Frank Wilcox, Mack Sennett, Henry Kulky. Directed by Charles Lamont. 79 minutes.

Abbott & Costello Meet the Mummy. (1956) ** With Marie Windsor, Michael Ansara, Dan Seymour, Richard Deacon, Peggy King. Directed by Charles Lamont. 79 minutes.

Dance with Me Henry. (1956) * With Rusty Hamer, Gigi Perreau, Mary Wickes, Ted DeCorsia, Frank Wilcox. Directed by Charles Barton. 80 minutes.

Anthologies containing the work of Abbott and Costello:

MGM's Big Parade of Comedy (1965). Produced by Robert Youngson.

The World of Abbott & Costello (1965). Produced by Max Rosenberg.

Hey Abbott (1976). Directed by Jim Gates.

-Lou Costello appeared alone in the posthumously released The Thirty-Foot Bride of Candy Rock *(1959), directed by Sidney Miller.*

12

Bob Hope

Bob Hope exemplifies the type of comedian that came into prominence during the forties, when the original screen comics had all but vanished.

Relying on quips and wisecracks rather than slapstick, Hope was more of a popular personality in show business than a screen comic. However, because he was responsible for some good film work, and because he is one of America's greatest entertainers, his contribution to motion pictures is worth special mention.

Success in nightclubs and on radio led Hope to a film career which began with seven rather standard short subjects which even Hope today dismisses as insignificant. His first feature appearance was in Paramount's *The Big Broadcast of 1938* in which he sang "Thanks For The Memory," which was to become his theme song.

He made a lot of features, and his vitality and knowhow suited them well. But it was in 1940 that he finally developed a more substantial screen persona in *The Road to Singapore*, the first of many similar ventures with Bing Crosby and Dorothy Lamour.

Bob was the wisecracking, lecherous coward who would get money by any means, just as long as it wasn't honest. This characterization played beautifully off of suave crooner Crosby as the two battled for the attention of Miss Lamour in seven "Road" pictures, all the way up to 1963.

Bob used this characterization in his subsequent non–"Road" pictures as well, including *Caught in the Draft* (1941), *My Favorite Blonde* (1942), *My Favorite Brunette* (1947), and two funny western satires, *The Paleface* (1948) and its sequel, *Son of Paleface* (1952), both of which featured Jane Russell.

All of Hope's films were worthwhile entertainment vehicles, and some rose even higher, helping to build his image as one of our greatest entertainers.

Aside from movies, Hope did some entertainment work overseas during three wars: World War II, the Korean conflict, and the Viet Nam catastrophe. His annual Christmas shows with many top names are still fondly remembered as some of the most commendable achievements in the field of entertainment.

Two attempts at dramatic work (with inevitable comic touches) in *The Seven Little Foys* (1955) and *Beau James* (1957) also were rather successful, but his con-

146

Bob Hope, a show business personality and screen comic.

centration on live shows and, by now, television specials caused him to decelerate his big screen activities. He made nothing up to par after *Alias Jesse James* in 1959, although he remained semi-active in movies until *Cancel My Reservation* in 1972.

Hope is not one to retire, and still commanded the entertainment industry past his eightieth birthday. His television specials continue to be ratings boosters for the NBC network and his live appearances are always sellouts.

And as for his films, they remain popular items on television, for they show yet another facet of a legendary showman's talents, making them important contributions to the development of screen comedy.

Hope Filmography

Feature Films
All Paramount releases unless otherwise noted.

The Big Broadcast of 1938. (1938) *** With W.C. Fields, Martha Raye, Ben Blue, Dorothy Lamour. Directed by Mitchell Leisen. 90 minutes.

College Swing. (1938) *** With George Burns & Gracie Allen, Martha Raye, Edward Everett Horton, Ben Blue. Directed by Raoul Walsh. 84 minutes.

Give Me a Sailor. (1938) *** With Martha Raye, Betty Grable, Jack Whiting, Clarence Kolb. Directed by Elliott Nugent. 80 minutes.

Thanks for the Memory. (1938) ** With Shirley Ross. Directed by Elliott Nugent. 77 minutes.

Never Say Die. (1939) *** With Martha Raye, Andy Devine, Sig Ruman, Alan Mowbray, Gale Sondergaard, Monte Wooley. Directed by Elliott Nugent. 80 minutes.

Some Like It Hot. (1939) *** With Shirley Ross, Una Merkel, Gene Krupa, Richard Denning. (Alternate title: *Rhythm Romance*) Directed by George Archainbaud. 65 minutes.

The Cat and the Canary. (1939) *** With Gale Sondergaard. Directed by George Marshall. 80 minutes.

Road to Singapore. (1940) *** With Bing Crosby, Dorothy Lamour, Charles Coburn, Judith Barrett, Anthony Quinn. Directed by Victor Schirtzinger. 84 minutes.

The Ghost Breakers. (1940) *** With Paulette Goddard, Anthony Quinn, Willie Best, Richard Carlson, Paul Lukas. Directed by George Marshall. 82 minutes.

Caught in the Draft. (1940) *** With Dorothy Lamour, Eddie Bracken, Lynne Overman, Willis Tracy. Directed by David Butler. 83 minutes.

The Road to Zanzibar. (1941) *** With Dorothy Lamour, Bing Crosby, Una Merkel, Eric Blore. Directed by Victor Schirtzinger. 92 minutes.

Louisiana Purchase. (1941) *** With Vera Zorina, Victor Moore, Irene Bordoni, Dona Drake. Directed by Irving Cummings. 98 minutes. Color.

My Favorite Blonde. (1942) *** With Madeline Carrol, Gale Sondergaard, George Zucco, Victor Varconi. Directed by Sidney Landfield. 78 minutes.

Road to Morocco. (1942) *** With Bing Crosby, Dorothy Lamour, Anthony Quinn, Vladimir Sokoloff, Monte Blue, Dona Drake. Directed by David Butler. 83 minutes.

Star Spangled Rhythm. (1942) *** With Bing Crosby, Ray Milland, Veronica Lake, Dorothy Lamour, Susan Hayward, Dick Powell, Alan Ladd, Paulette Goddard, Cecil B. DeMille, Arthur Treacher, William Bendix, Rochester. Directed by George Marshall. 100 minutes.

They Got Me Covered. (1943) ** With Paulette Goddard, Lenore Aubert, Otto Preminger, Marion Martin, Donald Meek. Directed by David Butler. 95 minutes.

Let's Face It. (1943) *** With Betty Hutton, ZaSu Pitts, Eve Arden. Directed by Sidney Landfield. 76 minutes.

The Princess & the Pirate. (1944) *** With Virginia Mayo, Walter Slezak, Walter Brennan, Victor McLaglan. Directed by David Butler. 94 minutes. Color.

Road to Utopia. (1945) *** With Bing Crosby, Dorothy Lamour, Hilary Brooke, Douglas Dumbrille, Jack LaRue, Robert Benchley. Directed by Hal Walker. 90 minutes.

Monsieur Beaucaire. (1946) *** With Joan Caufield, Patric Knowles, Cecil Kellaway, Reginald Owen. Directed by George Marshall. 93 minutes.

My Favorite Brunette. (1947) *** With Dorothy Lamour, Peter Lorre, Lon Chaney, Jr., Alan Ladd, Bing Crosby. Directed by David Butler. 90 minutes.

Where There's Life. (1947) *** With William Bendix, Signe Hasso. Directed by Sidney Landfield. 75 minutes.

Road to Rio. (1948) *** With Bing Crosby, Dorothy Lamour, Frank Faylen, Gale Sondergaard, The Wierre Brothers. Directed by Norman McLeod. 100 minutes.

The Paleface. (1948) *** With Jane Russell, Robert Armstrong, Iris Adrian, Robert Watson, Jackie Searle. Directed by Norman McLeod. 90 minutes. Color.

Sorrowful Jones. (1949) *** With Mary Jane Saunders, Lucille Ball, William Demarest, Bruce Cabot, Thomas Gomez, Ben Welden. Sidney Landfield. 88 minutes.

The Great Lover. (1949) *** With Rhonda Fleming, Roland Young, Roland Culver, Richard Lyon, Gary Gray, Jerry Hunter, Jim Backus. Directed by Alexander Hall. 80 minutes.

Fancy Pants. (1950) ** With Lucille Ball, Bruce Cabot, Jack Kirkwood, Eric Blore. Directed by George Marshall. 94 minutes. Color.

The Lemon Drop Kid. (1951) *** With Marilyn Maxwell, Lloyd Nolan, Jane Darwell, William Frawley. Directed by Sidney Landfield. 90 minutes.

My Favorite Spy. (1951) ** With Hedy LaMarr, Francis L. Sullivan, John Archer, Iris Adrian. Directed by Norman McLeod. 90 minutes.

Son of Paleface. (1952) *** With Jane Russell, Roy Rogers, Bill Williams, Harry Von Zell, Iron Eyes Cody. Directed by Frank Tashlin. 95 minutes. Color.

Road to Bali. (1953) *** With Bing Crosby, Dorothy Lamour, Murvin Vye, Ralph Moody, Dean Martin & Jerry Lewis (cameo). Directed by Hal Walker. 90 minutes. Color.

Off Limits. (1953) *** With Mickey Rooney, Marilyn Maxwell, Marvin Miller. Directed by George Marshall. 90 minutes.

Here Come the Girls. (1953) *** With Fred Clark, Rosemary Clooney, Arlene Dahl, Tony Martin. Directed by Claude Binyon. 78 minutes. Color.

Casanova's Big Night. (1954) *** With Joan Fontaine, Audrey Dalton, Raymond Burr, Vincent Price, Basil Rathbone. Directed by Norman McLeod. 87 minutes. Color.

Seven Little Boys. (1955) *** With Milly Vitale, Billy Gray, George Tobias, Jimmy Cagney, Eddie Foy, Jr. Directed by Melville Shavelson. 95 minutes. Color.

That Certain Feeling. (1956) *** With Pearl Bailey, Jerry "Beaver" Mathers, Eva Marie Saint, George Sanders. Directed by Norman Panama. 100 minutes. Color.

Opposite: Dorothy Lamour, Bing Crosby, and Bob Hope on the road to Morocco (1942).

The Iron Petticoat. (1956, MGM.) ** With Katherine Hepburn, James Robertson Justice, Robert Helpmann, David Kossoff. Directed by Ralph Thomas. 87 minutes. Color.

Beau James. (1957) *** Vera Miles, Paul Douglas, Alexis Smith, Darren McGavin. Directed by Melville Shavelson. 105 minutes. Color.

Paris Holiday. (1958) ** With Fernandel, Vera Miles, Martha Hyer, Anita Ekberg, Preston Sturges. Directed by Gerd Oswald. 100 minutes. Color.

Alias Jesse James. (1959) *** With Rhonda Fleming, Wendell Corey, Jim Davis, Gloria Talbott. Directed by Norman McLeod. 92 minutes. Color.

The Facts of Life. (1960) ** With Lucille Ball, Ruth Hussey, Don DeFore. Directed by Melvyn Frank. 103 minutes.

Bachelor in Paradise. (1961) ** With Lana Turner, Janis Paige, Jim Hutton, Paula Prentiss. Directed by Jack Arnold. 109 minutes.

The Road to Hong Kong. (1962) *** With Bing Crosby, Dorothy Lamour, Peter Sellers, Joan Collins, Robert Morley. Directed by Norman Panama. 93 minutes.

Critics Choice. (1963) ** With Lucille Ball, Marilyn Maxwell, Rip Torn, Marie Windsor. Directed by Don Weis. 100 minutes. Color.

Call Me Bwana. (1963) ** With Yvonne DeCarlo, Robert Sterling, John McGiver, Lilo Pulver. Directed by Jack Arnold. 84 minutes.

A Global Affair. (1964) ** With Yvonne DeCarlo, Robert Sterling, John McGiver, Lilo Pulver. Directed by Jack Arnold. 84 minutes.

I'll Take Sweden. (1965) ° With Tuesday Weld, Frankie Avalon, Dina Merrill, Jeremy Slate. Directed by Freddie DeCordova. 96 minutes. Color.

Boy Did I Get a Wrong Number. (1966) * With Phyllis Diller, Elke Sommer, Cesare Danova, Marjorie Lord. Directed by George Marshall. 99 minutes. Color.

Eight on the Lam (1967) * With Phyllis Diller, Jonathan Winters, Jill St. John, Shirley Eaton. Directed by George Marshall. 106 minutes. Color.

The Private Navy of Sergeant O'Farrel. (1968) ° With Phyllis Diller, Jeffrey Hunter, Gina Lollobrigida, John Myhers, Mako. Directed by Frank Tashlin. 93 minutes. Color.

How to Commit Marriage. (1969) ° With Jackie Gleason, Jane Wyman, Maureen Arthur, Leslie Nielson, Tina Louise, Irwin Corey. Directed by Norman Panama. 95 minutes. Color.

Cancel My Reservation. (1972) ° With Eva Marie Saint, Ralph Bellamy, Forrest Tucker, Keenan Wynn. Directed by Paul Bogart. 99 minutes. Color.

Hope also starred in the following two-reel shorts:

Going Spanish (1934; Educational Pictures), *Paree* (1935; Warner Bros), *The Old Gray Mayor* (1935; Warner), *Watch the Birdie* (1935; Warner), *Double Exposure* (1935; Warner), *Calling All Tars* (1936; Warner), *Shop Talk* (1936; Warner).

He made guest appearances in the following features:

Variety Girl. (1947) Directed by George Marshall. 75 minutes.

The Greatest Show on Earth. (1952) Directed by Cecil B. DeMille. 152 minutes.

Scared Stiff. (1955) Directed by George Marshall. 108 minutes.

The Five Pennies. (1959) Directed by Melville Shavelson. 117 minutes.

The Oscar. (1966) Directed by Russell Rouse. 120 minutes.

13

Red Skelton

Richard "Red" Skelton is one of the most beloved comedians in show biz history, but mostly on the strength of his classic television series. What people don't realize is that Skelton made a number of excellent comedy movies, and with proper management, he could have become one of our most important screen clowns.

When under the supervision of silent great Buster Keaton (as with the 1948 classic *A Southern Yankee*), Skelton could match the best, but when thrown into a vehicle that didn't suit him, he just couldn't rise above the material.

All in all, Skelton is the most important screen comic who came into major prominence during the forties, with better films than Abbott and Costello, Danny Kaye, or Bob Hope.

With an extremely likeable personality akin to Joe E. Brown's, Red made the audience love him, not as a figure of sympathy but as a friend, by seducing them with his sincerity. His routines were priceless, his performing gags excellent, and his overall skills beyond what was usual in screen comedy by this time.

Skelton wasn't limited to comedy, however. In a reworking of *The Champ* entitled *The Clown*, Red surprised all of us with his stirring dramatic performance. Such a performance was something his contemporaries didn't seem capable of.

Red developed most of his characterization and best routines in vaudeville during the thirties before landing minor screen work in the late thirties and early forties. When he was a victim of material that didn't suit his comic style (as with the 1944 *Bathing Beauty*) he had no chance, but in his starring films, like *Whistling in Dixie* (1942), *The Fuller Brush Man* (1948), and *The Yellow Cab Man* (1950); he shone like no comic since the thirties.

He made fewer films than the other leading screen comics, and most of these were mere supporting roles. Nevertheless, the few starring classics Red Skelton did made earn him a spot among the most important movie comedians of the era.

While Skelton is, along with Jackie Gleason, Steve Allen, Lucille Ball, and Johnny Carson, among television's most important and influential comedy figures, his work in movies also deserves special mention as a major contribution to screen comedy of the forties and fifties.

Best known for his television series, Red Skelton also shone in comic films.

Skelton Filmography

The Starring Features

Whistling in the Dark. (1941) **** With Ann Rutheford, Rags Ragland, Virginia
  Grey, Conrad Veidt, Eve Arden. Directed by S. Sylvan Simon. 77 minutes.

Whistling in Dixie. (1942) **** With Ann Rutheford, Rags Ragland, George
  Bancroft, Guy Kibbee. Directed by S. Sylvan Simon. 74 minutes.

I Dood It. (1943) *** With Eleanor Powell, Richard Ainley, Lena Horne, Jimmy
  Dorsey and his Orchestra. Directed by Vincente Minelli. 102 minutes.

Whistling in Brooklyn. (1944) **** With Ann Rutheford, Rags Ragland, Jean
  Rogers, Ray Collins, William Frawley. Directed by S. Sylvan Simon. 87
  minutes.

The Fuller Brush Man. (1948) ***** With Janet Blair, Don McGuire, Adele Jergens, Ross Ford, Hilary Brooke. Directed by S. Sylvan Simon. 93 minutes.

A Southern Yankee. (1948) ***** With Brian Donlevy, Arlene Dahl, John Ireland, Joyce Compton. Directed by Edward Sedgwick and Buster Keaton. 90 minutes.

Neptune's Daughter. (1949) *** With Esther Williams, Ricardo Montalban, Keenan Wynn, Betty Garrett, Mel Blanc. Directed by Edward Buzzell. 93 minutes. Color.

The Yellow Cab Man. (1950) **** With Gloria DeHaven, Walter Slezak, Edward Arnold, Polly Moran, Al Kaiser. Directed by Jack Donahue. 85 minutes.

Three Little Words. (1950) ** With Fred Astaire, Vera Ellen, Arlene Dahl, Keenan Wynn. Directed by Richard Thorpe. 102 minutes. Color.

Watch the Birdie. (1950) **** With Arlene Dahl, Ann Miller, Leon Ames, Pamela Britton, Mike Mazurki. Directed by Jack Donahue. 70 minutes.

Excuse My Dust. (1951) *** With MacDonald Carey, Sally Forrest, Monica Lewis, William Demarest. Directed by Roy Rowland. 82 minutes. Color.

The Clown. (1953) ***** With Jane Greer, Tim Considine, Steve Forrest. Directed by Robert Z. Leonard. 93 minutes.

Half a Hero. (1953) ** With Jean Hagen, Charles Dingle, Willard Waterman, Mary Wickes, Polly Bergen. Directed by Don Weis. 70 minutes.

Great Diamond Robbery. (1953) *** With Cara Williams, James Whitmore, Gloria Stickney, Steven Geray. Directed by Robert Z. Leonard. 70 minutes.

Public Pigeon Number One. (1957) **** With Vivien Blaine, Janet Blair, Jay C. Flippen, Allyn Joslyn. Directed by Norman McLeod. 79 minutes. Color.

Red Skelton also starred in the following two-reel shorts:

The Broadway Buckaroo (1939; Warner Bros.), *Seeing Red* (1939; Warner Bros.).

He made appearances in the following features:

Flight Command. (1940) Directed by Frank Borzage. 110 minutes.

The People Vs. Dr. Kildare. (1941) Directed by Harold Bucquet. 79 minutes.

Dr. Kildare's Wedding Day. (1942) Directed by Harold Bucquet. 74 minutes.

Lady Be Good. (1941) Directed by Norman McLeod. 77 minutes.

Ship Ahoy. (1942) Directed by Edward Buzzell. 95 minutes.

Maisie Get Her Man. (1942) Directed by Roy Del Ruth. 85 minutes.

Panama Hattie. (1942) Directed by Norman McLeod. 77 minutes.

Thousands Cheer. (1943) Directed by George Sidney. 126 minutes.

Bathing Beauty. (1944) Directed by George Sidney. 110 minutes.

Ziegfeld Follies. (1946) Directed by Vincente Minelli. 110 minutes.

Duchess of Idaho. (1950) Directed by Robert Z. Leonard. 95 minutes.

The Fuller Brush Girl. (1950) Directed by Lloyd Bacon. 85 minutes.

Susan Slept Here. (1954) Directed by Frank Tashlin. 95 minutes.

Oceans Eleven. (1960) Directed by Lewis Milestone. 127 minutes.

Those Magnificient Men in Their Flying Machines. (1965) Directed by Ken Annakin. 132 minutes.

14

Danny Kaye

Danny Kaye is one of America's most beloved musical comedy entertainers. His popularity is due to many things, including his work in television, nightclubs, the stage, and motion pictures.

Danny was much like Harold Lloyd, a youthful go-getter who never gave up; but with more of a bumbling sense about him. Aside from comedies which employed this characterization, Danny was also capable of playing it straight in such delightful musicals as *Hans Christian Andersen* (1952) and *White Christmas* (1954).

Although he did only seventeen features, Kaye's contribution to screen comedy deserves special mention because he was talented, popular, and unique. He was the only comic to blend song with his characterization, and the only performer to retain his youthful vitality to its very fullest throughout his twenty-five year film career.

On the serious side, Kaye has been active with UNICEF for many years, and is noted for his unselfish contribution to this worthy cause.

Danny didn't tell jokes, do slapstick, or make with the smart quips; Danny played a character, did

Danny Kaye, star of musical comedy.

158

double-talk, novelty numbers, danced, and filled the screen with energy and excitement. He reportedly didn't like to make pictures, however, and this is why we have so little to say about his film work. But the examples he did give us prove him to be an important factor in screen comedy's development, and an essential example of the type of entertainer that was popular in the forties and fifties.

Kaye Filmography

The Starring Features
All color unless noted.

Up in Arms. (1944) *** With Dinah Shore, Virginia Mayor, Dana Andrews, Constance Dowling. Directed by Elliott Nugent. 106 minutes.

Wonder Man. (1945) **** With Virginia Mayo, Vera Ellen, Donald Woods, S.Z. "Cuddles" Sakall. Directed by Bruce Humberstone. 98 minutes.

The Kid from Brooklyn. (1946) **** With Virginia Mayo, Vera Ellen, Steve Cochran, Eve Arden, Walter Abel, Lionel Stander. Directed by Norman McLeod. 103 minutes.

The Secret Life of Walter Mitty. (1947) *** With Virginia Mayo, Boris Karloff, Fay Bainter, Ann Rutherford. Directed by Norman McLeod. 105 minutes.

A Song Is Born. (1948) *** With Virginia Mayo, Steve Cochran, Louis Armstrong, Benny Goodman, Tommy Dorsey. Directed by Howard Hawks. 113 minutes.

Inspector General. (1949) **** With Walter Slezak, Barbara Bates, Elsa Lanchester, Gene Lochart, Alan Hale, Walter Catlett. Directed by Henry Koster. 102 minutes.

On the Riviera. (1951) *** With Gene Tierney, Corrine Cavet, Marcel Dalio, Jean Murat. Directed by Walter Lang. 90 minutes.

Hans Christian Andersen. (1952) *** With Farley Granger, Jean Marie, Roland Pettet, John Qualen. Directed by Charles Vidor. 105 minutes.

Knock on Wood. (1954) **** With Mai Zetterling, Torin Thatcher, David Burns, Leon Askin. Directed by Norman Panama. 103 minutes.

White Christmas. (1954) *** With Bing Crosby, Rosemary Clooney, Vera Ellen, Dean Jagger. Directed by Michael Curtiz. 120 minutes.

The Court Jester. (1956) ***** With Glynis Johns, Basil Rathbone, Angela Lansbury, Cecil Parker, Mildred Natwick. Directed by Norman Panama. 101 minutes.

Merry Andrew. (1958) *** With Pier Angeli, Baccaloni, Robert Coote. Directed by Micahel Kidd. 103 minutes.

Me & the Colonel. (1958) ** With Curt Jurgens, Nicole Maurey, Frances Rosay. Directed by Peter Glenville. 109 minutes.

The Five Pennies. (1959) ** With Barbara Bel Geddes, Tuesday Weld, Bob Crosby, Louis Armstrong. Directed by Melville Shavelson. 117 minutes.

On the Double. (1961) *** With Dana Winter, Wilfred Hyde-White, Margaret Rutherford, Diana Dors. Directed by Melville Shavelson. 92 minutes.

The Man from the Diner's Club. (1963) *** With Martha Hyer, Cara Williams, Telly Savalas, Everet Sloane, George Kennedy. Directed by Frank Tashlin. 96 minutes.

The Madwoman of Chaillot. (1969) ** With Katherine Hepburn, Charles Boyer, Claude Doulphine, Edith Evans, John Gavin. Directed by Bryan Forbes. 132 minutes.

Kaye also did the following two-reel shorts:

Dime a Dance (1937; Educational), *Getting an Eyeful* (1938; Educational), *Cupid Takes a Holiday* (1938; Educational), *Assignment Children* (1955; Paramount, for UNICEF).

15

Significant Minor Comedians of the Thirties and Forties

The 1930s and 1940s were very prolific years for movie comedians, and aside from the aforementioned entertainers there were some less exciting yet still significant screen humorists.

Many of these performers were radio and vaudeville comedians who came into pictures with the advent of talkies to capitalize on their verbal skills. While physical comedy was still in use, verbal humor crept in more and more as each decade went on.

Those comedians who carried feature films were usually naive bumpkins with pleasant personalities. Others who did feature work, but only in a smaller capacity, were those who relied on routines they had established after years of stage work. Finally, there were many short-subject comics who did their schtick in two reels.

While these clowns did not reach the artistic or commercial heights of those mentioned in previous chapters, they did contribute significantly enough to warrant acknowledgment some forty to fifty years after their product's initial release. It would be virtually impossible to cover *all* of the comedians who popped up in motion pictures, especially since there are so many really insignificant ones (Amos and Andy, Moran and Mack, Mitchell and Durant, Chic Sale, El Brendel, etc.). Others (Billy Gilbert, Bert Lahr, ZaSu Pitts, Patsy Kelly, Ben Blue, Margaret Dumont, etc.) are supporting players. Both groups are listed in the first appendix to this text.

Those included here are significant in at least a minor way for having had some type of impact on the development of screen comedy, even if only for the fact that their work is still funny today after all these years.

Joe E. Brown

Brown was one of the most pleasant screen personalities of the thirties and forties. Although he lacked a strong characterization and a general comic focus,

Joe E. Brown with Judy Garland.

Brown's sincerity and amusingly amiable personality won audiences over in his time, and still succeed in doing so when his pictures are revived today.

An avid sports fan, Joe included athletic themes in nearly all of his features. Best at the baseball-oriented comedies like *Elmer the Great* (1933), *Alibi Ike* (1935), and *Earthworm Tractors* (1936), Joe also appeared as a boxer in *When's Your Birthday* (1937), a wrestler and football player in *The Gladiator* (1938), and a bowler in *The Daring Young Man* (1943).

Joe also did straight roles convincingly in pictures like *Circus Clown* (1932) and *The Tender Years* (1955) but always was best loved for his comedies.

The Gladiator is perhaps his best film. Daffy science professor Lucien Littlefield concocts a potion that, when consumed by Brown, transforms the meek college student into a veritable superman, bringing him to reign as the university football star. Later, in an attempt to prove himself, Joe takes on three-hundred-pound pro wrestling champ Man Mountain Dean, in a two-out-of-three fall match, only to have his powers wear off during the second fall!

Brown remained active into the fifties, with Billy Wilder's wonderful *Some Like It Hot* (1959) the best of his later work. He died in 1975.

While none of his pictures had the artistry of any major comedy releases, Joe E. Brown will always be remembered with great fondness as a warm, loveable movie clown.

Wheeler & Woolsey

Bert Wheeler and Robert Woolsey were vaudeville comics who scored in movies with the filmed Broadway hit *Rio Rita* (1929; later reworked by Abbott & Costello).

In early films, the duo comes off as corny, the routines stagey, and the music very dated. In later comedies like *Cockeyed Cavaliers* (1934), *Hips Hips Hooray* (1934), *Hold 'Em Jail* (1932), *Kentucky Kernels* (1934), and *Caught Plastered* (1936), Wheeler and Woolsey are quite funny.

Their humor is a combination of Marx Brothers–style zaniness and Abbott & Costello–type burlesque routines. Wheeler is the shy dimwit, while Woolsey is the cigar-chomping wiseacre.

The team's success was cut short by Woolsey's death in 1938, after which Wheeler worked alone in Broadway revues and in some films. He died in 1968.

Clark & McCollugh

Clark and McCollugh were very similar to Wheeler and Woolsey. Bobby Clark teamed with Paul McCollugh in burlesque, and the stage success of the duo landed them a film series of short subjects at RKO studios. Zany burlesque routines touched with slapstick in films like *False Roomers* (1932) and *Odor in the Court* (1933) made the team very appealing, but their career (like Wheeler and Woolsey's) was cut short by death.

In 1936, Paul McCollugh committed suicide, forcing Bobby Clark to go it alone in films and Broadway revues. Clark died in 1960.

Edgar Kennedy

Edgar Kennedy has one of the most impressive careers in the history of screen comedy, spanning all of the genre's most important years (the teens, twenties, thirties, and forties).

He began as a contract player at the Keystone studios (he's one of the original Keystone Cops) during the teens, then began work at the Hal Roach studios as a character in films like Laurel and Hardy's *The Finishing Touch* (1928) or Charley Chase's *Limousine Love* (1928), as well as directing under the name E. Livingstone Kennedy such films as Laurel and Hardy's classic *You're Darn Tootin'* (1928), which bore similarites to Edgar's own starring short *A Pair of Tights* (1929).

During the thirties Kennedy made supporting appearances in films with Laurel and Hardy, the Marx Brothers (unforgettable in their 1933 *Duck Soup*), and in more prestigious films like David O. Selznick's original *A Star Is Born* (1937) with Fredric March and Janet Gaynor.

The thirties also saw the beginning of Edgar's short subject series of domestic comedies at RKO. These two-reelers featured Kennedy as "Mr. Average Man" beset by a nagging wife (Vivien Oakland) or daffy wife (Florence Lake or Sally Payne), an overbearing mother-in-law (Dot Farley), and a sponging brother-in-law (William Eugene or Jack Rice). These shorts were brilliant comedies which were instrumental in the development of the domestic sitcom. Later TV shows like "The Honeymooners" and "I Love Lucy" would have been inconceivable without the Edgar Kennedy short subjects.

Kennedy is one of the great character players in comedy history, his starring short films among the most important of their kind. He remained very active and popular until his death in 1948, the night before a party which was to be given in his honor.

Leon Errol

Leon Errol was a vaudeville headliner who entered films during the twenties, playing various character roles in both dramatic and comedy films. After some early talkies like *Her Majesty Love* (1931) with W.C. Fields, Leon became active in two series.

One was a series of short films at RKO. These were domestic sitcoms like that studio's Edgar Kennedy comedies. While not as good as Kennedy's, the Errol shorts are still amusing little items, most of which center around Leon's getting caught in the company of an attractive blonde by his jealous wife. The best efforts were made from 1944–1951 with Dorothy Granger as the wife.

Leon also appeared in the Joe Palooka features at Monogram studios. These prizefighter programmers were action films with comic touches (like that studio's East Side Kids efforts). By this time, Errol was quite a powerful man in screen comedy.

Emil Sitka recalls; "Nobody told Errol what to do, not the director, nobody! He was the boss!

"I remember in a Joe Palooka picture I did with him, a group of us were playing reporters. We were supposed to fire questions at Leon, who, as manager Knobby Walsh, was announcing to the press that Joe Palooka was retiring from the ring. Now the next reporter was supposed to interrupt Leon with another question before he was able to answer the previous one, and he insisted on split-second timing from us. Well I was on time with my question, but the others weren't, and every time one of them wasn't quick enough for Leon, he asked him to leave. It ended up with me doing the whole scene with Errol alone, asking *all* the questions. After this he requested my services often for roles in the Joe Palookas and the short films at RKO. This helped my career greatly."

Errol remained a powerful and popular man in movie comedies until his death in 1951.

Leon Errol (center) is accosted by roughnecks (Ralph Peters, left, and Emil Sitka, right) in "Cactus Cut-up" (1949).

Our Gang

"Gosh, you're pretty, Miss Crabtree. You're even prettier 'n Miss McGilicutty!"

Here it is, folks, the bottom of the barrel. As you can see by the nauseating dialogue above, we have now come to the section on Our Gang, a series of Hal

Roach-produced short subjects featuring a group of "typical" children. They were, in a word, terrible.

It started back in the early twenties when Roach got the idea to take a black kid, a fat kid, a freckle-face, a cute little girl, a rich kid, a snob, a tomboy, et al., and put them together for a series of two-reelers.

The first group included Joe Cobb, Mickey Daniels, Mary Kornman, Sunshine Sammy Morrison, and Donald Haines.

The second group included Cobb, Allen Clayton "Farina" Hoskins, Norman "Chubby" Chaney, Jackie Cooper, Mary Ann Jackson, Dorothy DeBorba, and Bobby "Wheezer" Hutchins among the principals.

The third group consisted of George "Spanky" McFarland, Carl "Alfalfa" Switzer, Matthew "Stymie" Beard, Scotty Becket, Darla Hood, Dickie Moore, and Sidney Kilbrick.

The fourth group had Spanky, Alfalfa, Darla, Tommy "Butch" Bond, Leonard "Woim" Kilbrick, Billy "Buckwheat" Thomas, and Gordon "Porky" Lee.

The fifth and final group included Spanky, Alfalfa, Buckwheat, Porky, Darla, Butch, Woim, Janet Burston, Billy "Froggy" Laughlin, and Mickey Gubitosi (later known as Bobby Blake, and then Robert Blake).

These kids weren't actors or comics, but just typical children pushed in front of rolling cameras by overbearing stage mothers or lazy parents who wanted their child to support them. Not in every case, of course, but in many cases.

The Our Gang comedies benefited early on from amusing performances by adult supporting players like Edgar Kennedy in *When the Wind Blows* and Dell Henderson in *Choo Choo*, but for the most part these comedies have about as much to do with the development of screen comedy as Alvin and the Chipmunks have to do with the development of rock and roll.

Most of the more popular kids — Spanky, Alfalfa, etc. — were basically overbearing pests, barely tolerable. When Alfalfa would sing, it would be more grating than cute and when in later entries they went for the "Gee whiz golly swell" stuff that made Andy Hardy movies, they were lost completely.

All films were shorts except an attempt at one feature, *General Spanky* (1936), which bombed. Spanky claimed that this film's Civil War setting was "a stilted situation that just didn't fly." Roach sold the series to MGM in 1938, including the Our Gang name, which is why the Roach efforts are now known as The Little Rascals. I guess it should be mentioned that one Roach effort, the awful *Bored of Education* (1936), won an Oscar.

Of the fates of the kids, Spanky became a salesman, Tommy Bond a TV broadcaster, Mickey Daniels a construction worker, while the whereabouts of the other living members are unknown (many, when located, refuse to discuss Our Gang; others who will talk about it often state it was a bad trip).

Opposite: Our Gang, circa 1934. L-r: Harold Switzer, Carl "Alfalfa" Switzer, Darla Hood, George "Spanky" McFarland, Billy "Buckwheat" Thomas, Pete the Dog, Scotty Becket, unknown.

Spanky (center) with Pete the Dog and other Gang members, including Matthew "Stymie" Beard (in derby).

Froggy was killed in 1948, Alfalfa shot to death in 1959, Chubby died in 1936, Darla in 1979, Buckwheat & Stymie in 1980, Mary Kornman in 1973, and Wheezer was killed in a World War Two training mishap.

Robert Blake grew up to be a very good, and very charismatic, film & TV performer, while Jackie Cooper not only improved as an actor with each passing year, but also became one of the television industry's most respected directors.

Andy Clyde

Clyde (see photo p. 170) was a former Keystone player who acted as a Keystone Cop and was teamed with Billy Bevan in films like *Circus Today* (1922) and *The Railroad Stowaways* (1923). He did some short films for Sennett during the early talkie years, but hit his stride more strongly when joining Columbia's short subject department in 1934, remaining there until 1956.

Andy played a flustered old man who usually stumbled innocently into trou-

predictable and only fairly amusing, but he still deserves respect for having worked successfully in the medium for so many years.

Andy Clyde also worked in Hopalong Cassidy westerns as California, and then went into TV on the series "The Real McCoys" with Walter Brennan. Clyde remained active until his death in 1967.

Character actor Emil Sitka remembers Andy Clyde as a thorough professional. "He was an utterly sincere guy, and totally immersed in his role," Emil recalled. "Even off the set he was constantly mumbling his lines to himself."

Some of Andy's best comedies at Columbia include *It Always Happens* (1935), *Boobs in the Woods* (1940) with Shemp Howard, and *Wife to Spare* (1947) with Emil Sitka.

Burns & Allen

George Burns and Gracie Allen (see photo p. 171) were a vaudeville and radio team who did some short subject work at Paramount as well as throwing in a routine or two in that studio's musical pictures with stars like Fred Astaire and Eleanor Powell.

The duo's best screen work would be two films which also featured W.C. Fields: *International House* (1933) and *Six of a Kind* (1934). They left motion pictures to concentrate more on radio and the stage in 1939, and hit it even bigger on television during the fifties.

Burns was a terrific straight man, ranking with Bud Abbott for top timing and delivery, with excellent reactions to what the daffy Gracie had to say. Gracie was a loveable crackpot whose craziness actually sounded logical after a while, thanks mostly to her incomparable sincerity when delivering the punch lines.

When Gracie died in 1964, Burns went on alone with continued success, really scoring in 1975 with his Oscar-winning performance in Neil Simon's *The Sunshine Boys* (which also featured Walter Matthau and Richard Benjamin). Subsequent films like *Oh God* (1976) and *Going in Style* (1979) as well as stage appearances and record albums have kept him on top in the entertainment world well past his 85th birthday.

While responsible for only minor screen work, George Burns and Gracie Allen remain among show business's most endearing and enduring legends.

Jack Benny

Another great vaudeville and radio personality who did pictures and later television was Jack Benny (see photo p. 172), the perennial tightwad who never admitted to being older than 39, despite the fact that he remained active until 80.

His tightwad personality was the very centerpiece of his stage, radio, and later TV work. In movies, however it, emerged only when Jack was playing himself,

George Burns and Gracie Allen, famous for their radio and television work, also appeared in films.

as in *Buck Benny Rides Again* (1940) and *It's in the Bag* (1945), both of which also featured Jack's radio rival Fred Allen.

Benny really came off best in straight seriocomic roles where he actually did play a character rather than his usual persona. This was especially true in two very funny pictures, *To Be Or Not to Be* (1942), which was sadly Carole Lombard's last film, and *The Horn Blows at Midnight* (1945).

While Benny really didn't fare as well in pictures as he did in the other media, his screen work was still very commendable, and he certainly deserves a space in the development of American humor. Jack remained beloved by both colleagues and fans until his death in 1974, when America lost one of its most prized entertainers.

The Ritz Brothers

Al, Harry, and Jimmy Ritz (see photo p. 173) were a marginally interesting link between the Three Stooges and the Marx Brothers during the thirties and forties in pictures like *The Gorilla* (1939) and *Behind the Eight Ball* (1941).

While a few routines hold up, their lack of characterization makes it hard to know which brother is which (Harry makes the funny faces).

Opposite: Andy Clyde hides from lawyer Emil Sitka as Christine McIntyre and Dick Wessell look on in "Wife to Spare" (1947).

Jack Benny (left) with Edgar Bergen (right) and Charlie McCarthy.

Al Ritz died in 1963, but Harry and Jimmy remained active years afterward, doing little screen work, but still appearing in nightclubs. Respected by their colleagues and remembered fondly by many, the Ritz Brothers' wild undisciplined style was perhaps not utilized properly in the film medium, and thus they had only a minor impact on the development of screen comedy. Jimmy Ritz died in 1985.

Olsen and Johnson

Ole Olsen and Chic Johnson were very similar to Abbott and Costello, and this may be the reason for their lack of prestige today. They weren't copiers (they entered films a few years before Bud and Lou), but did have the vaudeville-duo style of laughmaking similar to the more successful Abbott and Costello.

Olsen and Johnson were quite talented, with the all-star *Crazy House* (1942) and the filmed version of the Broadway hit *Hellzapoppin* (1943) the best examples of their work. The team's other films concentrated on timeworn cliché plots (haunted houses, etc.) and thus are less exciting. Johnson died in 1962 and Olsen in 1965.

Brown and Carney

The Ritz Brothers: Jimmy (kissing woman), Harry, and Al.

Like Olsen and Johnson, Brown and Carney were a vaudeville-based duo overshadowed by the popularity of Abbott and Costello. Their performances in pictures like *Step Lively* (1944) with Frank Sinatra and *The Girl Rush* (1944) with Robert Mitchum added a nice comic zest and were good examples of the duo's work, but cheapies like *Zombies on Broadway* (1945) are conventional. Wally Brown died in 1960, Alan Carney in 1973.

Arthur Lake

Arthur Lake (born, Arthur Silverlake, 1905) is famous even today as the movies' Dagwood Bumstead in what was the most engaging of all film series of the period.

Based on Chic Young's comic strip, the Blondie films were lightly entertaining sitcoms about domestic life. Penny Singleton starred as Blondie, Larry Simms as Baby Dumpling (Alexander), Marjorie Kent as Cookie, and Jonathan Hale as Mr. Dithers (replaced in 1947 by Jerome Cowan as Mr. Radcliffe) in a series which spanned a dozen years (1938–1950) and 28 titles.

Lake, as Dagwood, was the epitome of the fidgety bumbler who seasoned his sincere performance with a variety of comic skills including slapstick, verbal timing and delivery, gag execution, and a special nervous reaction from a timid character, which could evolve into an all-out animalistic he-man reaction when his self or family was threatened.

Arthur was typecast, but content to play Dagwood for all those years in movies, radio, and later on television in a series of episodes opposite the late Pamela Britton. The Blondie movies remain important contributions to screen comedy if only for the fact that Lake's portrayal of Dagwood may have been the

Ole Olsen and Chic Johnson.

most perfect piece of comedy character acting in the dozen years of the series' existence.

With the end of this chapter we come to the end of an era. Screen comedy's greatest contributors all worked during the twenties, thirties, and forties. By the fifties, those who were still active from the previous eras were either dwindling by mid-decade, or had vanished altogether.

The fifties saw a deadness in screen comedy due to the impact of a little box found in the corner of your living room. Television had virtually all of the best comedians at this time, and during the next three to four decades, Jerry Lewis, Jacques Tati, Woody Allen, and, to a lesser extent, Mel Brooks were the only genuinely innovative comedians in motion pictures.

The fifties and sixties didn't even have many significant minor names, these few that were active being very minor indeed. Comedy in motion pictures boasted more comedians into the seventies and eighties, but none have proven as remarkable as the old masters.

16

Jacques Tati

Jacques Tati is one of the most inventive comics in screen history. A Frenchman who rivals some of the screen's greatest clowns and most respected filmmakers, Tati's work has been very poorly distributed in the States, and thus few comedy fans have seen any examples.

Tati did not make films that were limited to French tastes. Like any of the screen greats, his motion pictures were universally appealing. With the exception of Jerry Lewis, Tati was the only true genius of comedy doing movies during the fifties and sixties.

Jacques Tati first gained prominence in France during the thirties when he wrote and starred in a series of short films which were not released in the States. After the war, he did some bit roles in features, finally writing and starring in his own feature, *Jour de fête (The Day of the Festival)*, in 1949.

The film received limited release in America in 1952 and garnered good reviews among the critics, but, as with the remainder of Tati's films, *Jour de fête* was poorly distributed and thus did not achieve the commercial success with which American film distributors (of domestic or foreign product) are so preoccupied.

It's the same old story. Because such lame dreck as *Smoky and the Bandit* on film, *The Dukes of Hazzard* on television, and Michael Jackson or Olivia Newton-John in music manage to achieve commercial success in the States (due to packaging and distribution, certainly not to artistic value), a motion picture as brilliant as *Jour de fête* (or any of Tati's starring features) is overlooked as unsuccessful at the box office, and dismissed as insignificant.

This feature was a throwback to the Mack Sennett style of silent screen slapstick, done with as much finesse as any of the major silent clowns. It has a simple structure and inventive gags.

In 1952 Tati introduced his Mr. Hulot character. *Les vacances de Monsieur Hulot (Mr. Hulot's Holiday)* is another good excursion into slapstick gags and general pandemonium silent film–style, the sound being limited to specifically scored music and nonverbal effects. Some of the gags in *Les vacances* compare favorably to Keaton's best work in classics like *The General* and *Sherlock, Jr.* The film was released to enthusiastic response in America around 1954, but its popularity today is yet restricted to cult status.

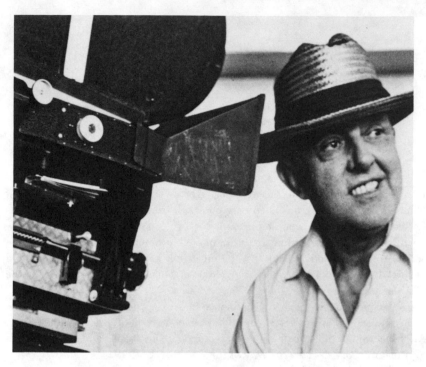

The talented Jacques Tati behind the camera.

Mon oncle (1958; known here as *My Uncle*) is one hundred percent Tati, not a throwback to silent comedy as were the other features. There's something a bit Chaplinesque about Tati's centering gags around an uncle (Hulot) and his adoring nephew (à la Chaplin's *The Kid*), but the reality of the proceedings differs from the fantasy of *Les vacances de Monsieur Hulot*, while still concentrating on some very innovative gags.

Like Chaplin, Tati needed time to make his creative ideas come to life the way he wanted to see them on film. After *Mon oncle*, Tati hibernated for nearly a decade before lining up the cast and crew for his next picture, commissioning these persons for one year, so that he was sure to have enough time to bring his ideas to life via the cinema.

Playtime (1967) was shot in 70 millimeter with stereophonic sound, thus limiting its run in many commercial theatres. Although Tati made another feature (and a television film in Sweden) afterward, it is best to consider *Playtime* the culmination of his work.

The great thing about *Playtime* is that Tati, though working with a large budget, did not sell out. Rather than cave in to commercialism, he retained his artistry and came up with yet another magnificent piece of work. He did not release it in 35mm until it saw its way to American theaters in 1973, a year after the American release of Tati's following film, *Trafic*. This worked out in such a way that Americans saw the films in the order Tati perferred: *Trafic* first, then *Playtime*.

Trafic (or *Traffic*, 1969) has the Hulot character racing to meet an auto show deadline, with hundreds of gags strewn throughout. The film bears strong similarities to *Les vacances* and *Mon oncle* in its overall construction. It is no wonder that Tati prefers it to be shown in festivals before the earlier *Playtime*, as *Playtime* represents the culmination of theme and production value.

Tati made one more film, a videotaped feature called *Parade* which he wrote and directed for Swedish television in 1973. It has never been released in the United States. Tati died in 1982.

Some of the most brilliant screen work of all time should be better represented in our country, a country noted for its motion pictures. While *Mon oncle* did receive an Oscar as Best Foreign Film, Tati's internationally appealing features should all receive both better recognition and better distribution here.

Tati Filmography

The Starring Features
All written and directed by Tati.

Jour de fête. (1949) **** With Guy Decomble, Paul Frankeur, Santa Relli, Maine Vallee. (American title: *Day of the Festival.*)

Les vacances de Monsieur Hulot. (1953) **** With Louis Perrault, Nathalie Pescaud, Andre Dubois, Lucien Fregis. (American title: *Mr. Hulot's Holiday.*) B/W.

Mon oncle. (1958) ***** With Jean-Pierre Zola, Adrienne Servanti, Alain Becourt, Lucien Fregis. (American title: *My Uncle.*)

Playtime. (1967) **** With Barbara Dennek, Jacqueline Lecomte, Valerie Camille, France Rummilly.

Trafic. (1971) **** With Maria Kimberly, Marcel Fraval, Honore Bostel, Francois Maisongrosse.

Tati wrote and starred in the following short films:

Oscar, champion de tennis. (1932)
On demande une brute. (1934)
Gai dimanche. (1935)

Soigne ton gauche. (1936)
Retour à la terre. (1938)
L'école des facteurs. (1947)

Tati did guest appearances in the following features:

Sylvie et le fantôme. (1945) as a ghost.

Le diable au corps. (1946) as a soldier.

Tati wrote, directed and starred in Parade *(1973) for Swedish television and was preparing an American made film known as* Confusion, *which was never made.*

Awards and Prizes

L'école des facteurs: Max Linder Award for Best Short Comedy, 1949.

Jour de fête: Best Scenario at Venice Film Festival, 1949, and French Grand Prix du Cinema, 1950.

Les vacances de Monsieur Hulot: International Critics' Prize at Cannes, 1953; the Femina Prize and the Louis Delluc Award, 1953.

Mon oncle: Special Jury Prize at Cannes, 1958; New York Film Critic's Award, 1959; and Academy Award for Best Foreign Film, 1959.

Playtime: Grand Prix de l'Academie du Cinema, Etoile de Cristal, 1968; Danish Academy Award for Best European Film, 1969; and the Prix d'Argent at the Moscow Film Festival, 1969.

17

Jerry Lewis

With Jacques Tati's work achieving such limited recognition here and virtually all of the creative screen comics of the past either dead or inactive, the fifties were a bleak time for movie comedy. There were some great things happening in television, and some minor junk occupying the big screen.

Then Dean Martin and Jerry Lewis, an exciting new comedy team full of energy and youthful vitality, burst onto the scene. Already a hit in the nightclubs, Dean and Jerry soon found their way into movies and became one of the hottest acts in a long time.

Their films were conventional, no greater in merit than the work of Abbott and Costello a decade before, and relied on the old formulas (army life, haunted houses, racetracks, etc.). But like Bud and Lou, Martin and Lewis were very funny and had a talent for timing and delivery. Also like Abbott and Costello, they had some great supporting players to act as foils in their pictures, Robert Strauss, Raymond Burr, Mike Kellin, and Donald McBride among them.

Unlike Bud and Lou, Martin and Lewis did not hire bad second leads to handle the inevitable romantic and musical interludes. That was left up to handsome straight man Martin, with Jerry tagging along like a pesky twelve-year-old.

While the Martin and Lewis comedies *Sailor Beware* (1951), *The Stooge* (1953), and their best film, *You're Never Too Young* (1955), all have their moments, none is among the screen's greatest comic contributions. Fact is, both Dean and Jerry fared better after their parting in 1956. Martin emerged to eventually deserve a place alongside Al Jolson, Frank Sinatra, and Elvis Presley as one of America's greatest musical entertainers, while Jerry Lewis became one of the screen's most important comedians since Charlie Chaplin himself.

With the erratic *Delicate Delinquent* (1957), *The Sad Sack* (1958), *Don't Give Up the Ship* (1959), and *Rock-a-Bye-Baby* (1959), Jerry was just getting his feet wet as a solo performer. While all of these efforts have moments to recommend them, they don't test the limits of Lewis's comic potential.

The Geisha Boy (1958), one of his earlier works, was a bit of a triumph for Jerry Lewis the performer. He displays both excellent comic skills and important emotional skills as an actor in scenes which call for pathos.

But his real breakthrough was *The Bellboy* (1960), the first film which Lewis

179

Dean Martin (left) and Jerry Lewis with Janet Leigh.

wrote and directed himself. A plotless comedy feature centering around an inept bellboy working at a plush Miami resort, *The Bellboy* is Jerry's testament to the nameless faces of the world working in small-time jobs with little thanks (no matter how difficult the tasks they must perform). It is also his testament to screen comedy, displaying virtually every facet of his genius as a comedian and filmmaker.

The Errand Boy (1961), a satirical look at filmmaking at a major studio, was another brilliant Lewis film which the comedian wrote and directed as well as starred in. The satirical elements of this film further displayed the intelligence behind Jerry's gags and bits of pantomime. There were messages as clear as those Chaplin had used in *Modern Times*, though these, too, were camouflaged by the amusements.

The Nutty Professor (1963) is as fascinating a comic film as one could ever expect. Pre-dating Woody Allen's brilliant *Annie Hall*, Lewis goes beyond the gags and gets inside himself as a meek college professor who creates a liquid concoction which, when consumed, transforms him into an aggressive, lecherous creep.

The film makes the ultimate statement that each of us is both a human and a monster, and we should all attempt to control whatever evil lurks within us.

With *The Nutty Professor*, Lewis clearly proved he was one of the screen's most original and brilliant comedy performers. Yet despite the artistically important aspects of his works and the commercial success they achieved, the Jerry Lewis pictures were relegated to a Three Stooges level of silliness by American critics.

It has never been clearly understood why American critics took such a dislike to these obviously essential works, especially when in France, where Jacques Tati was making some landmark comedies, Lewis was (and is) considered tantamount to Chaplin in comic ingenuity. In his own country, Lewis never won praise from many critics, but he did garner a huge fan following of comedy aficionados who saw past the silliness and into the profundity of his work. Aside from being funny on a gut level, the Jerry Lewis comedies have all of the intelligence-beyond-gags facets of any major comedian's screen work.

Jerry concentrated more on funny business with two Frank Tashlin-directed features, *The Disorderly Orderly* (1964) and *Who's Minding the Store* (1963). These films added the comedian's Chaplinesque talents for pantomime and pathos to a Marx Brothers style of lunacy with a Mack Sennett-styled slapstick backdrop. In terms of laughs, these are probably Jerry's funniest pictures, with comedy's traditional "authority-gets-it-in-the-end-from-sympathetic-victim" formula.

The Family Jewels (1965) has Lewis playing seven parts, all potential guardians for an orphaned girl. In this construction, Lewis displays a fascinating versatility found in few performers (Peter Sellers in *Dr. Strangelove*, Tony Randall in *The Seven Faces of Doctor Lao*).

Lewis runs the full gamut of emotions, with sincerity, humor, stupidity, rudeness, and zaniness all played in one aspect or another. The pathos remains convincing and not overplayed, the gags as amusing as ever. *The Family Jewels* is one of Jerry's most enchanting films.

The Big Mouth (1967) is a James Bond spoof with a wildly uninhibited performance by Lewis and supporting player Charlie Callas (in his first major screen role). Unfortunately, it was Lewis's last really top rate film for some time.

The late sixties were bizarre, experimental years in movies, and Jerry's experimenting (quieter, less physical, more reserved comedy in *Way Way Out, Three on a Couch,* and *Don't Raise the Bridge, Lower the River*), was for naught. Two more films, *Hook Line & Sinker* (1969) and *Which Way to the Front* (1970), were more in the old style, but made with apparent haste and lack of motivation.

Jerry then tried one more experiment, a dramatic story (or tragedy) entitled *The Day the Clown Cried*, in 1971. This film was never released due to financial matters regarding its production that remain unresolved over a decade later. After this film, Lewis left movies, not to return for some years. He concentrated instead on personal appearance tours and working with the Muscular Dystrophy Association, for which he held nationally televised telethons each Labor Day weekend.

He was nominated for the Nobel Peace Prize in America, and in France received an honor which is tantamount to our Congressional Medal, having previously been awarded to such luminaries as Louis Pasteur and Charles Chaplin.

Jerry returned to movies in 1979 with *Hardly Working* (released in America in 1981), which did great box office but was not among his best films. Lewis as an inept mailman was funny, and the comedian did explore the full comic potential

Jerry Lewis played it straight and very effectively in Martin Scorcese's "The King of Comedy" (1982) with Robert DeNiro (right).

of the situations, but the film's lack of focus and apparent indecisiveness about the point its humor was trying to make hampered its overall feel.

After a critically acclaimed dramatic performance opposite Robert DeNiro in Martin Scorcese's haunting *The King of Comedy* (1982), Lewis made *Smorgasboard* (1983), which was released under the title *Cracking Up* in 1984. As a bumbler who is incapable of everything from jobs to suicide, Jerry shines as in no film since *The Big Mouth* with great gags abounding in this plotless farce. The only real "message" in *Smorgasboard* was a "these-things-happen-to-everybody-don't-they?" spirit surrounding the proceedings. The film exaggerates (in both satirical and slapstick terms) man's petty problems in accomplishing the smallest tasks.

Another possible message found in *Smorgasboard* was that, after over thirty years in comedy, Jerry Lewis is still capable of some of the funniest schtick and most energetic comic acting that the screen has ever known. Despite American critics' blindness to his talents and capabilities in the fields of comedy and film-making, Jerry Lewis remains one of the most essential comedians in screen history.

Lewis Filmography

With Dean Martin:

My Friend Irma. (1949) ** With Marie Wilson, John Lund, Diana Lynn, Don DeFore. Directed by George Marshall. 103 minutes.

My Friend Irma Goes West. (1950) ** With Marie Wilson, John Lund, Corrine Calvet. Directed by Hal Walker. 90 minutes.

At War with the Army. (1950) *** With Polly Bergen, Angela Greene, Mike Kellin. Directed by Hal Walker. 93 minutes.

That's My Boy. (1951) ** With Eddie Maychoff, Marion Marshall, Ruth Hussey, Polly Bergen. Directed by Hal Walker. 98 minutes.

Sailor Beware. (1951) *** With Corrine Calvet, Robert Strauss, Marion Marshall, Betty Hutton. Directed by Hal Walker. 108 minutes.

Jumping Jacks. (1952) *** With Robert Strauss, Don DeFore, Mona Freeman. Directed by Norman Taurog. 96 minutes.

The Stooge. (1953) *** With Polly Bergen, Eddie Mayehoff, Marion Marshall, Frances Bavier, Percy Helton. Directed by Norman Taurog. 100 minutes.

Scared Stiff. (1953) *** With Lizabeth Scott, Carmen Miranda, Dorothy Malone. Reworking of Bob Hope comedy *The Ghost Breakers.* Directed by George Marshall. 108 minutes.

The Caddy. (1953) *** With Donna Reed, Fred Clark, Barbara Bates, Joseph Calleia, Nancy Kulp. Directed by Norman Taurog. 95 minutes.

Money from Home. (1954) ** With Robert Strauss, Pat Crowley, Jack Kruschen. Directed by George Marshall. 100 minutes. Color.

Living It Up. (1954) ** With Janet Leigh, Edward Arnold, Fred Clark, Sherrie North. Remake of Carole Lombard feature *Nothing Sacred.* Directed by Norman Taurog. 95 minutes. Color.

Three Ring Circus. (1954) *** With Zsa Zsa Gabor, Wallace Ford, Joanne Dru, Elsa Lanchester. Directed by Joseph Pevney. 103 minutes. Color.

You're Never Too Young. (1955) **** With Raymond Burr, Diana Lynn, Nina Foch, Veda Ann Borg, Milton Fromme. Remake of the Ray Milland-Ginger Rogers starrer *The Major & the Minor*. Directed by Norman Taurog. 102 minutes. Color.

Artists and Models. (1955) *** Shirley MacLaine (her film debut), Dorothy Malone, Eva Gabor, Anita Ekberg. Not a remake of the similarily titled Jack Benny feature. Directed by Frank Tashlin. 109 minutes. Color.

Pardners. (1956) ** With Lori Nelson, Jack Loughery, John Baragrey, Jeff Morrow, Agnes Moorehead, Lon Chaney, Jr. Directed by Norman Taurog. 90 minutes. Color.

Hollywood or Bust. (1956) ** With Anita Ekberg, Pat Crowley, Maxie Rosenbloom. Directed by Frank Tashlin. 95 minutes. Color.

Solo Films:

Delicate Delinquent. (1957) *** With Darren McGavin, Martha Hyer, Horace McMahon. Directed by Don McGuire. 100 minutes.

The Sad Sack. (1958) *** With Phyllis Kirk, Peter Lorre, David Wayne, Gene Evans, Mary Treen. Directed by George Marshall. 98 minutes.

Rock-a-Bye Baby. (1958) ** With Marilyn Maxwell, Reginald Gardener, Connie Stevens, Baccaloni. Directed by Frank Tashlin. 103 minutes. Color.

The Geisha Boy. (1958) **** With Suzanne Pleshette, Sessue Hayakawa, Nobu McCarthy, Marie McDonald, Barton MacLaine. Directed by Frank Tashlin. 98 minutes. Color.

Don't Give Up the Ship. (1959) ** With Dina Merrill, Diana Spencer, Gale Gordon, Robert Middleton, Mickey Shaughnessy, Claude Akins. Directed by Norman Taurog. 99 minutes.

Visit to a Small Planet. (1960) ** With Gale Gordon, Fred Clark, Earl Holliman, Lee Patrick, Joan Blackman. Loosely based on Gore Vidal's satire. Directed by Norman Taurog. 85 minutes.

The Bellboy. (1960) ***** With Milton Berle, Walter Winchell, Maxie Bosenbloom, Alex Gerry, Bob Clayton, Sonny Sands. Written and directed by Jerry Lewis. 72 minutes.

Cinderfella. (1960) ** With Ed Wynn, Judith Anderson, Anna Maria Alberghetti, Count Basie. Directed by Frank Tashlin. 91 minutes. Color.

The Ladies' Man. (1961) *** With Kathleen Freeman, Buddy Lester, George Raft, Helen Traubell, Doodles Weaver, Jack Kruschen. Written and directed by Lewis. 106 minutes. Color.

The Errand Boy. (1961) ***** With Brian Dunlevy, Howard McNear, Fritz Feld, Doodles Weaver, Sig Ruman, Kathleen Freeman, Iris Adrian, Joe Besser. Written and directed by Lewis. 92 minutes.

It's Only Money. (1962) ** With Zachary Scott, Joan O'Brien, Mae Questel, Jesse White, Jack Weston, Buddy Lester. Directed by Frank Tashlin. 84 minutes.

The Nutty Professor. (1963) ***** With Stella Stevens, Howard Morris, Elvia Allman, Del Moore, Kathleen Freeman. Written and directed by Lewis. 107 minutes. Color.

Who's Minding the Store. (1963) ***** With Agnes Moorehead, Jill St. John, John McGiver, Ray Walston, Francesca Bellini, Fritz Feld, Nancy Kulp. Directed by Frank Tashlin. 90 minutes. Color.

The Patsy. (1964) **** With Hans Conried, George Raft, Peter Lorre, Ina Balin, Everett Sloane, Keenan Wynn, John Carradine, Nancy Kulp. Written and directed by Lewis. 101 minutes. Color.

The Disorderly Orderly. (1964) ***** With Kathleen Freeman, Glenda Farrel, Susan Oliver, Everett Sloane, Jack E. Leonard, Alice Pearce, Barbara Nichols, Milton Fromme. Directed by Frank Tashlin. 90 minutes. Color.

The Family Jewels. (1965) ***** With Donna Butterworth, Sebastian Cabot, Milton Fromme, Robert Strauss. Written and directed by Lewis. 100 minutes. Color.

Boeing Boeing. (1965) *** With Tony Curtis, Thelma Ritter, Dany Savall, Christiane Shcmidtmer, Suzannah Leigh. Directed by John Rich. 102 minutes. Color.

Three on a Couch. (1965) * With Janet Leigh, Mary Ann Mobley, Leslie Parrish, Kathleen Freeman. Directed by Jerry Lewis. 109 minutes. Color.

Way Way Out. (1966) * With Connie Stevens, Dick Shawn, Anita Ekberg, Brian

Keith, Robert Morley, Dennis Weaver, Howard Morris. Directed by Gordon Douglas. 106 minutes. Color.

The Big Mouth. (1967) **** With Charlie Callas, Susan Bey, Harold J. Stone, Col. Harlan Sanders, Del Moore, Buddy Lester, Paul Lambert. Written and directed by Lewis. 107 minutes. Color.

Don't Raise the Bridge, Lower the River. (1968) * With Terry Thomas, Jacqueline Pearce, Bernard Cribbins. Directed by Jerry Paris. 109 minutes. Color.

Hook Line and Sinker. (1969) ** With Peter Marshall, Anne Francis, Pedro Gonzales-Gonzales, Jimmy Miller. Directed by George Marshall. 91 minutes. Color.

Which Way to the Front? (1970) * With Jan Murray, Kaye Ballard, Steve Franken, John Wood, Joe Besser. Directed by Lewis. 96 minutes. Color.

Hardly Working. (1981) *** With Susan Oliver, Roger C. Carmel, Steve Franken, Harold J. Stone. Written and directed by Lewis. 91 minutes.

The King of Comedy. (1982) ***** With Robert DeNiro, Sandra Bernhardt. Directed by Martin Scorcese. 101 minutes.

Slapstick of Another Kind. (1983) * With Madeline Kahn, Marty Feldman, Jim Backus. Directed by Steven Paul. 90 minutes.

Smorgasboard. (1983) **** With Herb Edelman, Zane Busby, Foster Brooks, Milton Berle, Sammy Davis, Jr., Buddy Lester. Released to cable television under the title *Cracking Up.* Written and directed by Lewis. 89 minutes.

Retenez-moi ou je fais un malheur. (1984) With Michel Blanc, Charlotte De Turckheim, Maurice Rasch, Phillipe Castelli, Laura Betti. Directed by Michel Gerard. (French production not released in U.S. English title: *To Catch a Cop.*)

Guest Appearances:

Road to Bali. (1952) Directed by Hal Walker. 90 minutes.

Li'l Abner. (1959) Directed by Melvin Frank. 113 minutes.

It's a Mad, Mad, Mad, Mad, World. (1962) Directed by Stanley Kramer. 154 minutes.

Lewis wrote, directed and starred in the unreleased film *The Day the Clown Cried* (based on Joan O'Brien's book) in 1971.

Lewis directed, but didn't appear in, *One More Time* (1970), featuring Sammy Davis, Jr.

18

Significant Minor Comedians
of the Fifties and Sixties

There were a few other comedians in film at this time, but none coming near to the magnitude of Jerry Lewis in America or Jacques Tati in France.

There were so few comics in film that we are forced to acknowledge series entries like "Francis the Talking Mule" as being among the comedy of the period. There just wasn't much of anything else.

Comedy was still big, but largely on television. That new invention in the corner of the living room boasted names like Milton Berle, Jack Benny, Burns and Allen, Phil Silvers, Red Skelton, Abbott and Costello, Jackie Gleason, Steve Allen, Lucille Ball, Joan Davis, and many others, week after week, in new episodes.

Movie comedies included Billy Wilder's *Some Like It Hot* (1959) with Jack Lemmon and Tony Curtis, and his *One Two Three* (1961) with James Cagney. These films, however, featured actors playing comedy and not movie comedians per se.

Jacques Tati was doing some amazing things in France that few Americans had the pleasure of knowing about, while Jerry Lewis continued to release essential material.

But the minor comedy of the period was minor indeed, with only brief moments of inspiration sprinkled over the two decades. It is these brief moments that we acknowledge in this chapter.

The Bowery Boys

These were situation comedy features similar to the Blondie, Henry Aldrich, or Andy Hardy films, but they didn't begin as comedies.

Billy Halop, Leo Gorcey, Huntz Hall, Bobby Jordan, Gabe Dell, and Bernard Punsly were cast as a group of juvenile toughs in Samuel Goldwyn's production of *Dead End* (1937). They made such an impact that they became known as The Dead End Kids in subsequent crime dramas at Warners, such as *Angels with Dirty Faces* (1938) with James Cagney. They also appeared in programmers

188

specifically suited for them, such as *Crime School, Hell's Kitchen,* and *Angels Wash Their Faces,* the latter two featuring a young Ronald Reagan.

Everyone except Gorcey went on to Universal in 1939 to appear as the Little Tough Guys in serials like *Junior G-Men* and features like *Give Us Wings, Mug Town, Call a Messenger,* and *Keep 'Em Slugging.* Gorcey stayed at Warners doing character role in features like *Destroyer* and *Invisible Stripes.*

In 1940 Gorcey and Bobby Jordan were cast as leading players in a low budget series at Monogram studios called *The East Side Kids.* Huntz Hall and Gabe Dell joined this group the following year, with Halop doing solo character roles in films, and Punsly leaving show business to study medicine.

The films of the Dead End Kids, Little Tough Guys, and East Side Kids were basically "B" action dramas about street kids who use their tough exteriors and streetwise savvy to thwart hoods, nazis, and other wrongdoers. The films were short (about an hour), simple, and rather exciting, thanks to a fast pace and excellent performances with a great deal of energy and charisma. The films were cheapies for Saturday matinees, but the kids were all rather accomplished actors, and their roles were a welcome relief from the bland Momma's-boy wholesomeness of Andy Hardy and Our Gang films.

Comedy began creeping into the films of the East Side Kids gradually, with Leo Gorcey as Muggs, the tough leader; Huntz Hall as the silly Glimpy; Bobby Jordan as Danny, the good kid; and Billy Benedict, Stanley Clements, Leo's brother David Gorcey, and Donald Haines popping up as incidental members with names like "Skinny" and "Whitey."

Gabe Dell alternated in playing a rival gang member and a member of the East Siders in these films, and Sunshine Sammy Morrison, the original black kid in the Our Gang pictures, was on hand in the somewhat stereotypical role of Scruno.

In 1946, Monogram changed the name of the series to the Bowery Boys, and the format changed to include more comedy.

Still playing delinquents (albeit grown-up delinquents by now), Gorcey was cast as Slip, the leader; Hall as Sach, the naive buffoon; Dell as Gabe Moreno, the newsman, or lawyer, or cop, or some other position, representing the kid who made good; and Billy Benedict played Sach's pal Whitey. David Gorcey, Bobby Jordan, and Bennie Bartlett were incidental members of the gang with very few lines per film. (Jordan left the group after a year.) In a character role, Leo cast his father, Bernard, as Louie, owner of the sweet shop the boys hung out in.

These 48 features were also cheapies, but remain enjoyable, moral, and energetic if only for the charisma of the performers. The quality slipped a bit when Bernard lost his life in a 1955 car crash, leaving son Leo so distraught that he left the act after one more film, *Crashing Las Vegas* (1956). Actor Emil Sitka, who was in that film, recalled, "Leo was drinking so heavily that at times he had to literally be carried on and off the set."

Stanley Clements replaced Gorcey as a character named Duke, and the boys continued to churn out features until 1958. Overall, the best entries include

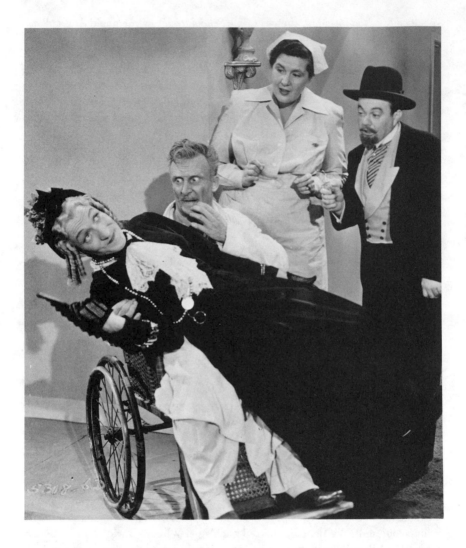

Bowery Boy Huntz Hall (in drag) flirts with patient Emil Sitka as a bearded Leo Gorcey looks on in "Private Eyes" (1953).

Fighting Fools, No Holds Barred, Private Eyes, and *Bowery Battalion,* all with Gorcey.

Leo Gorcey died in 1969, Stanley Clements in 1982, Billy Halop in 1976, and Bobby Jordan in 1965. Bernard Punsly is a doctor; Gabe Dell did some work with Steve Allen on television and some Tony-award winning Broadway work; and Huntz Hall and Billy Benedict have also remained active in show business.

Ma and Pa Kettle

This was a "folksy" series designed to combat television's popularity. It starred Marjorie Main and Percy Kilbride. These two talented film performers first enacted the roles in the 1947 Fred MacMurray-Claudette Colbert starrer *The Egg and I* and later appeared in a series which ran from 1949–1957.

The Kettles were ignorant country folks forever set upon by big city sharpies who were ultimately defeated by the Kettles' good-natured naivete.

Kilbride left the series in 1955. The last two entries feature either no Pa Kettle at all, or Parker Fennely in the Kilbride role.

The films remain popular to this day. Ten years after their demise, a TV show called *The Beverly Hillbillies* became remarkably successful with the same formula. Percy Kilbride died in 1964, and Marjorie Main died in 1975.

Francis the Talking Mule

This series of kid-oriented comedies was created by Arthur Lubin and starred Donald O'Connor as a good-natured oaf whose best friend is the title character. While interesting in their inclusion of up-and-comers like David Jannsen and Clint Eastwood in the cast, the pictures were no more than predictable corn.

O'Connor left the series in 1955, claiming the animal received more fan mail. Mickey Rooney tried his hand at one vehicle, *Francis in the Haunted House* (1956), when the animal died. Lubin went on to create a similar TV series entitled "Mr. Ed" about a talking horse.

Peter Sellers

Peter Sellers was a gifted comic in many British features as well as a regular on Britain's comedy TV series "The Goon Show" before being cast as the inept, bumbling detective Inspector Clouseau in Blake Edwards' *The Pink Panther* (1964). This characterization was so well received that it was repeated in a *Shot in the Dark* (1965), a minor comedy classic.

Sellers did slapstick with a remarkably fine execution and naturalness, seemingly stating that he belonged in the Sennett comedy of fifty years before. The style and grace he gave to basic pratfalls, and the new, innovative twists with which he accented the physical humor, make his contribution important. It is a pity he didn't concentrate more on that contribution rather than the scores of really awful films he was to make as time went on.

Three Panther revival films in the seventies—*Return of the Pink Panther* (1974), *The Pink Panther Strikes Again* (1976), and *Revenge of the Pink Panther* (1978)—were also amusing in the same vein as the sixties entries. More

Peter Sellers as Inspector Clouseau.

were planned, but Sellers' death in 1980 put a tragic halt to whatever progress could have been attained.

One posthumous release, *Trail of the Pink Panther* (1982), was haphazardly made up of outtakes and is an ill example of Sellers' work. His last great screen performance was in the seriocomic classic *Being There* (1979).

Don Knotts

A timid comic whose forte was nervousness to its furthest limits, Knotts had a starring series of screen comedies on the strength of his TV work with Steve Allen and Andy Griffith.

While best remembered as Barney Fife from the Griffith television series, Knotts scored rather substantially in his series of average family comedies.

His first was *The Incredible Mr. Limpit* (1964), which featured him as a meek fish lover who actually becomes a fish (via animation). It was a very basic kiddie flick.

The Ghost and Mr. Chicken (1966), albeit predictable, was the best setting for the Knotts character. As a timid reporter forced to spend the night in a house which is supposedly haunted, Knotts is able to use his full potential in nervous humor, with results one might expect.

Don Knotts with Betty Lynn of "The Andy Griffith Show."

The Reluctant Astronaut (1967) has Knotts as an astronaut who is deathly afraid of heights. This amusing premise is not sufficiently explored, and in fact is pretty much overlooked as the film progresses.

His next three films—*The Shakiest Gun in the West* (1968), a remake of Bob Hope's *The Paleface*; *The Love God* (1969), a worthless adult comedy; and *How to Frame a Figg* (1970)—were all completely dismissible.

Knotts stayed away from the big screen until 1975, when he did *The Apple Dumpling Gang* for Disney opposite Tim Conway, an overacting bumbler who achieved notoriety on TV's "McHales Navy" and "The Carol Burnett Show." The picture was bad, but successful enough for a 1979 sequel, *The Apple Dumpling Gang Rides Again*.

Other Disney vehicles included *No Deposit No Return* (1976) and *Hot Lead and Cold Feet* (1978) before Knotts teamed with Conway once again in two independent productions, *The Prize Fighter* (1979) and *Private Eyes* (1981). Both of these films were written by Conway and were embarassingly predictable. On TV, Knotts appeared as landlord Mr. Furley on the series "Three's Company" with John Ritter until 1984.

By the end of the sixties, the great movie comedians of the twenties, thirties, and forties were long gone, and even the innovative comedy that was happening on television during the fifties had petered out. Jerry Lewis took a leave from pictures by the beginning of the seventies, and Jacques Tati's work still wasn't recognized by the commercial masses in this country.

It seemed as though the development of the movie comedian had ceased, and the seventies held very little hope for progress.

Mel Brooks and Woody Allen did some work that merits attention, their success paving the way for a whole new wave of brash young comics from nightclubs and television to migrate onto the movie screen. Unfortunately, despite an occasional spark of comic inventiveness, the golden era of movie comedy was not recaptured.

19

Mel Brooks

Mel Brooks is not a movie comedian as much as a comedy film producer (he doesn't even appear in many of his own productions). Creator of the classic TV series "Get Smart" and a featured writer on Sid Caesar's wonderful series "Your Show of Shows," Brooks began making movies in the late sixties. His films through the early seventies showed great innovation, with wonderful comic ideas in satire and a blend of many early elements of screen comedy. His success is perhaps most responsible for the resurgence of popularity in screen comedy, with many new comic faces like Gene Wilder, Dom DeLuise, Marty Feldman, and Madeline Kahn entering films in the Brooks-produced comedies.

Mel's first motion picture, and one of his best, is *The Producers* (1968). This film features Zero Mostel and Gene Wilder as corrupt producers of a surefire Broadway flop (entitled *Springtime for Hitler*) who plan to skip town with the backers' money once the show flops. To their chagrin, the show is a hit.

The Twelve Chairs (1970) is straighter and more elaborate, but still very funny. Frank Langella, Ron Moody, and a hilarious Dom DeLuise battle to find twelve chairs, one of which contains priceless jewels. Brooks appears in this one as a two-thousand-year-old man, a character he had created in television sketches.

Blazing Saddles (1973) was Mel's greatest triumph. A perfect satire on movie westerns (aiming directly at the classic *Destry Rides Again*), Brooks hits every stock western bit and abuses it with the combined talents of Gene Wilder, Cleavon Little, Alex Karris, Slim Pickens, Harvey Korman, Madeline Kahn, and Brooks himself.

Prejudices, shootouts, outlaws, and even riding off into the sunset are given the Brooks treatment with a scenario that included Richard Pryor as one of its contributors. This R-rated film is totally destroyed by TV censors when run on the small screen, but pay TV and theatrical revivals will sustain its endurance as a classic screen satire.

Young Frankenstein (1974) was a satire on the Universal studios horror cycle of the thirties. It, too, is brilliantly constructed, but one must see *Frankenstein* (1931), *Bride of Frankenstein* (1933), and *Son of Frankenstein* (1935) first to fully appreciate most of the gags; thus it suffers in some minor respects.

Mel Brooks and Madeline Kahn in "High Anxiety" (1977).

Gene Wilder, Cloris Leachman, Teri Garr, Madeline Kahn, Kenneth Mars, and Gene Hackman all do wonderfully in *Young Frankenstein*, but it is Marty Feldman as Ygor and Peter Boyle as the monster who score the highest marks in sheer lunacy. Brooks made no appearance, but is said to have planned appearing as Ygor before deciding upon Feldman.

By this time the name Mel Brooks was associated with the most important screen names in the movie business, and was the new Mack Sennett (or king of comedy) as far as moviegoers were concerned (by now Woody Allen was the new Chaplin).

Silent Movie (1976) was exactly what its title suggests: a slapstick satire on the early days of movie making with only one moment of dialogue (aside from title cards). Guest appearances by Burt Reynolds, James Cahn, Paul Newman, and Marcel Marceau (an actual mime, he spoke the only dialogue) in a film starring Brooks, DeLuise, Marty Feldman, Sid Caesar, and Anne Bancroft (Mrs. Mel Brooks). The humor ranged from hilarious to sophomoric, and the film as a whole lacked the wit and excitement of any earlier Brooks productions.

High Anxiety (1978) was a botched attempted at a Hitchcock parody. Only a few important jokes on the great director's techniques rose above what was otherwise a rather silly vehicle starring Brooks, Madeline Kahn, Harvey Korman, Cloris Leachman, and Dick Van Patten.

History of the World (1981) was the only really bad film Brooks made. A disaster from beginning to end, *History* contained crude, offensive, and sacreligious moments to spice a meaningless screenplay with almost none of the Brooks magic. It died at the box office and was buried by the critics.

After gaining prominence in the Brooks films, Gene Wilder, Marty Feldman, and Dom DeLuise branched out into other vehicles.

Wilder was most successful, with his own *Sherlock Holmes' Smarter Brother* (1976) and *The World's Greatest Lover* (1978) as well as two vehicles opposite Richard Pryor—*Silver Streak* (1976) and *Stir Crazy* (1980). He also made *The Frisco Kid* (1979), *Hanky Panky* (1981), and *The Woman in Red* (1984).

DeLuise did *Smokey & The Bandit II* (1980) and *The Cannonball Run* (1981) opposite Burt Reynolds, as well as his own *Hot Stuff* (1979) and the seriocomic *Fatso* (1980), directed by Brooks' wife, Anne Bancroft.

Feldman appeared in the crude *Think Dirty* (1977), *Sex with a Smile* (1976), *The Last Remake of Beau Geste* (1978), *In God We Trust* (1980). Two films were released after his death in December of 1982: *Slapstick* (1984), with Jerry Lewis, and the all-star *Yellowbeard* (1983).

Mel Brooks is the closest thing we now have in the field of screen writing and directing to a Preston Sturges. His films are important examples of screen comedy of this period, and remain essential if only for their huge impact on the public and the medium at a time when innovative screen comedy was somewhat of a rarity.

Brooks Filmography

Brooks appeared only in those where his name is listed among players. All are in color unless otherwise noted.

The Producers. (1969) ***** With Zero Mostel, Gene Wilder, Dick Shawn, Kenneth Mars, Estelle Winwood. Directed by Mel Brooks. 98 minutes.

The Twelve Chairs. (1970) **** With Frank Langella, Ron Moody, Dom DeLuise, Mel Brooks. Directed by Mel Brooks. 94 minutes.

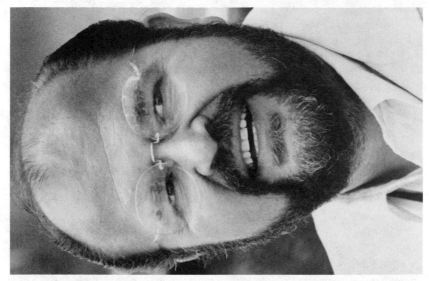

Blazing Saddles. (1973) ***** With Cleavon Little, Gene Wilder, Mel Brooks, Harvey Korman, Madeline Kahn. Directed by Mel Brooks. 93 minutes.

Young Frankenstein. (1974) **** With Marty Feldman, Gene Wilder, Madeline Kahn, Peter Boyle, Teri Garr, Cloris Leachman. Directed by Mel Brooks. 108 minutes. B/W.

Silent Movie. (1976) *** With Mel Brooks, Dom DeLuise, Marty Feldman, Anne Bancroft, Sid Caesar, Burt Reynolds, Paul Newman, James Cahn, Fritz Feld, Marcel Marceau. Directed by Mel Brooks. 86 minutes.

High Anxiety. (1978) * With Madeline Kahn, Cloris Leachman, Harvey Korman, Dick Van Patten, Mel Brooks. Directed by Mel Brooks. 94 minutes.

History of the World. (1981) ° With Mel Brooks, Anne Bancroft, Sid Caesar. Directed by Mel Brooks. 105 minutes.

To Be or Not to Be. (1983) ** With Mel Brooks, Anne Bancroft, Charles Durning, Tim Matheson. Directed by Mel Brooks. 93 minutes.

Opposite: Gene Wilder (left), Dom DeLuise, and Marty Feldman, all stars of Brooks' pictures, have also made films on their own.

20

Woody Allen

In a book on movie comedians, everything is comparable to Chaplin. Now that we have come to the chapter discussing Woody Allen, these comparisons will tend to assert themselves.

Allen is one of the most incredible, fascinating screen performers in the history of motion pictures. He ranks with Chaplin not only as a comic and filmmaker, but also as an innovator. Allen's comedies can master wit, satire, slapstick, and zaniness with new, intelligent twists which belie the fact that these elements were created years ago by the screen's most important comedians, then used and experimented with in various ways to develop screen comedy itself.

Allen has opened the doors to newer, more amazing uses of the original ways and traditions than one may expect. While he will often not play to the masses, it is absolutely undeniable that he is one of the major forces in screen comedy and his ideas and motivations are almost as essential to its development as even some of Chaplin's (which is really saying an awful lot for anybody).

What's New Pussycat? (1965) was an inauspicious start as Woody's first screen venture, his screenplay having been botched by production values and various hacks. It is best overlooked, as is *What's Up Tiger Lily?* (1966), a curio which has Woody overdubbing an old Japanese spy flick with his own dialogue.

Take the Money and Run (1968) is his first film of major importance and one of his best works. Originally planning to ask Jerry Lewis to direct, Allen directed the film himself when other projects prevented Lewis from taking the job.

In this comedy tracing the development of an inept street kid who rises to a life of crime, Allen toys with the film's potential by using a pseudo-documentary style and playing many scenes straight to enhance the comedy's subtlety. He is definitely the most unlikely street-kid-turned-hood ever found in a motion picture, and he uses this to his advantage in the comedy of the film.

Robbery-planning, the police force, family reaction, prison life, and American living in general are all given the bizarre, fascinating Allen treatment. Molded together, these elements emerge in one of the screen's most intelligent and hilarious comedies.

Bananas (1971) concentrated on gags and displayed Allen's active comedy imagination. *Play It Again Sam* (1972) casts Allen as a movie buff with a

Woody Allen, ingenious writer, director, and comedian.

Humphrey Bogart fixation so severe that it causes him actually to see Bogey giving him lovemaking tips during his various unsuccessful romantic endavors.

Play It Again Sam is also Allen's breakthrough film, for it was the first where he exhibited facets of his inner self. He used his own human characteristics and inadequacies to the furthest limits of their comic potential—a trick he would soon transform into a science.

The crudity of *Everything You Always Wanted to Know About Sex* (1972) detracted from its comic value, but there was still enough hilarity mixed with the offensive to warrant the film worthy of consideration.

Sleeper (1973) was Woody's example of doing straight comedy in the Bob Hope vein, with elements of the Marx Brothers, Keaton, Chaplin, and Oliver Hardy used to touch the highlight certain areas of comic execution. Remaining the best film on the strength of straight belly laughs that Allen has created, this story of a third-rate clarinet player frozen and brought back two hundred years later is every bit as fast, funny, and exciting as one would ever hope to find.

Love and Death (1975) continued the Bob Hope fixation with accents on the filmmaking style of Ingmar Bergman (most notably the classic *Seventh Seal*) to add further facets of intelligence and creativity to Allen's style. It was a perfect setup for his masterpiece, *Annie Hall*, which he released in 1977.

Annie Hall emerged after Woody's surprisingly good dramatic performance in *The Front* the previous year. All of the elements which marked the brilliance of Woody's earlier films were called upon to create *Annie Hall*, the first comedy to win a major Oscar in the Academy's fifty-year existence. Winning for Best Picture, Best Director (Allen), Best Screenplay (Allen), and Best Actress (Diane Keaton), *Annie Hall* ranks with Chaplin's *Limelight* as a work of screen perfection.

Woody Allen emerges victorious in a duel with Harold Gould in a scene from "Love and Death" (1975).

Woody uses all facets of his genius for comedy, blends them with the thought-provoking inner feelings the comedian shares with many, and succeeds in creating a motion picture with such depth and intelligence that it is unlikely any filmmaker, here or abroad, will ever match it.

    Manhattan (1979) almost reached the *Annie Hall* mark of brilliance, thanks to magnificent cinematography (in black and white) and some fine acting by Diane Keaton, Mariel Hemingway, and Meryl Streep in support of Allen. Allen's decision to use Gershwin's "Rhapsody in Blue," among others, as a score for the film only adds to its depth and screen value.

Stardust Memories (1981) strayed more toward pretention, but not far enough away from brilliance to make it more than a slight notch below the master filmmaker's steady stream of classics. *A Midsummer Night's Sex Comedy* (1982) was a rather unsuccessful (for Allen) combination of Shakespeare and *Everything You Always Wanted to Know About Sex* and emerged as his weakest film since *What's Up Tiger Lily?* His *Zelig* (1983) and *Broadway Danny Rose* (1984) were tremendous improvements.

The films of Woody Allen are among the screen's most definitive works, their importance to screen comedy beyond one's expectations. They show further development in a medium that most of us thought had run dry of innovation, and they have proven Allen to be the most gifted and fascinating screen comic since Chaplin himself.

Allen Filmography

All films are in color unless otherwise stated.
Many of Woody Allen's self-penned screenplays are co-written with Marshall Brickman.

What's New Pussycat? (1965) ** With Peter Sellers, Peter O'Toole, Romy Schneider, Paula Prentiss. Directed by Clive Donner. 108 minutes.

What's Up Tiger Lily? (1966) ** Japanese footage compiled and dubbed by Allen. 80 minutes.

Take the Money and Run. (1968) ***** With Janet Margolin, Marcel Milliare, Jacquelyn Hyde. Written and directed by Woody Allen. 85 minutes.

Bananas. (1971) *** With Louise Lasser, Carlos Montalban, Howard Cosell, Sly Stallone. Written and directed by Allen. 102 minutes.

Play It Again Sam. (1972) ***** With Diane Keaton, Tony Roberts, Jerry Lacy, Susan Anspach, Jennifer Salt, Joy Bang. Written and directed by Allen. 87 minutes.

Everything You Always Wanted to Know About Sex (But Were Afraid to Ask). (1972) *** With Gene Wilder, Tony Randall, Burt Reynolds, John Carradine, Louise Lasser, Lou Jacobi. Written and directed by Allen. 87 minutes.

Sleeper. (1973) ***** With Diane Keaton, John Beck, Mary Gregory, Don Keefer. Written and directed by Allen. 83 minutes.

Love and Death. (1975) ***** With Diane Keaton, Harold Gould, Alfred Lutter. Written and directed by Allen. 83 minutes.

The Front. (1976) ***** With Zero Mostel, Herschel Bernardi, Michael Murphy, Joshua Shelley. Directed by Martin Ritt. 93 minutes.

Annie Hall. (1977) ***** With Diane Keaton, Tony Roberts, Paul Simon, Shelly Duvall, Carol Kane. Written and directed by Allen. 94 minutes.

Manhattan. (1979) ***** Mariel Hemingway, Meryl Streep, Tony Roberts, Diane Keaton, Michael Murphey. Written and directed by Allen. 96 minutes. B/W.

Stardust Memories. (1981) **** Written and directed by Allen. 90 minutes. B/W.

A Midsummer Night's Sex Comedy. (1982) *** With Mia Farrow, Jose Ferrer, Mary Steenburgen. Written and directed by Allen. 87 minutes.

Zelig. (1983) ***** With Mia Farrow, Susan Sontag, Garrett Brown, John Rothman. Written and directed by Allen. 79 minutes. B/W.

Broadway Danny Rose. (1984) **** With Mia Farrow. Written and directed by Allen. 86 minutes. B/W.

Allen also made an appearance in Casino Royale *(1967), directed by John Huston. He directed, but did not appear in* Interiors *(1978), which featured Diane Keaton and* The Purple Rose of Cairo *(1984) which featured Mia Farrow.*

21

Significant Minor Comedians of the Seventies and Eighties

You may recall that earlier in our text, when discussing the teens and twenties, it was mentioned that along with greats like Chaplin and the various neargreats like Will Rogers or Harry Langdon, there were dozens of insignificant journeymen like Bud Duncan, Neil Burns, and Max Davidson.

Now, during the seventies and eighties, we have come full circle; Woody Allen and Mel Brooks represent the greats, and the comics in this chapter represent the near-greats. These near-greats do not, however, measure up to the talents of Langdon or Rogers. The very best of their work never rises beyond a Three Stooges level of childish nonsense (it is rather ironic that the trio's films have become very popular in these decades).

It seemed as though every brash young upstart who clicked in a TV comedy sketch was given his own starring comedy feature. Sometimes the results were tolerable; often they were embarrassing.

The many insignificant contributors, or character comics (those who fared better in support of others rather than as leading players) are duly represented in the first appendix of this text (listing supporting players and secondary clowns). Those comics mentioned within this chapter are significant contributors to the period due to popularity, and to comedy in general perhaps only for their mediocrity.

Rather than the meek, insecure, sympathetic clown types, we have brash, smug, rebellious upstarts. Taboo subjects like death, sex, religion, and disease are dealt with freely, but the fine line between good taste and crudity is often blatantly overlooked.

Woody Allen is a fine comedian and a brilliant filmmaker. The early work of Mel Brooks made groundbreaking discoveries into satire. The other leading comics of the period have proven no more than semi-skilled journeyman clowns.

All in all, the comedians in this chapter just don't seem as talented or as funny as those from the golden age. They are no better than the minor contributors of the fifties and sixties (and even that period's Bowery Boys cheapies often had more depth than what has been cranked out in recent years).

Steve Martin.

The seventies and eighties have shown a disregard for artistry in the face of commercialism. Many of the worst films have made money; it doesn't seem to matter that they aren't good movies.

The presumption is that good comedy has been so scarce and hard to come by in movies or television during recent years that even the weakest pictures have gotten laughs. When compared to the rest of the comedians of this period, someone like John Belushi is no better or worse. When compared to even the minor comics of the twenties, thirties, or forties, the efforts of any of these so-called comics are severely lacking in all facets of acting and production.

Steve Martin

Martin is an obnoxious, cloying character who relies mostly on catch phrases rather than humor. While about as important to screen comedy as Our Gang, he does deserve some mention due to a following he garnered in the mid- to late seventies on the strength of his TV and nightclub appearances. He began making films in 1979, and it is with this aspect of his career that we are concerned.

The Jerk (1979) was Steve's first film, which he co-wrote with Carl Reiner. It's a series of stupid, tired gags surrounding an inane plot about a white guy growing up in a black family. He later makes it in big business due to an accidental invention that later falters and lands him back in poverty. Martin's silliness is so undisciplined that it becomes disturbing, his character so stupid that he receives contempt from the viewer rather than sympathy.

After being embarrassingly miscast in the straight Cole Porter musical *Pennies from Heaven* (1981), Martin did *Dead Men Don't Wear Plaid* (1982), which he also wrote with Reiner. Its premise: a black and white detective satire, with clips from classic examples of film noir (*The Big Sleep, Double Indemnity*, etc.) interspliced within to make it look as though Martin were playing off such screen luminaries as Humphrey Bogart, Burt Lancaster, Fred MacMurray and James Cagney. The problem seemed to be that Martin and Reiner spent so much time with this idea, they forgot to write anything funny, as *Dead Men Don't Wear Plaid* contains virtually nothing in the way of humor. It should have been titled *Bad Films Won't Get Laughs*.

After his botched detective satire, Martin did a botched sci-fi satire. *The Man with Two Brains* (1983) didn't even amount to one. His subsequent films (*The Lonely Guy, All of Me*, etc.) have displayed no further progress, and thus Steve Martin remains the least interesting performer ever to achieve any notoriety in screen comedy.

Chevy Chase

Chase emerged in showbiz as a regular on NBC's "Saturday Night Live." He began making movies in 1978 with *Foul Play*, a comedy which also starred Goldie Hawn (former "Laugh-In" regular who had already made a name for herself in both dramatic and comedy films), and featured Dudley Moore in a small role. This one was followed by Neil Simon's *Seems Like Old Times* (1980), which also featured Chase with Hawn.

Both of these films tried to capture the thirties and forties romantic comedy "feel" (the works of Preston Sturges...*Palm Beach Story*, for instance), and they half-succeeded. While not a leading creator of brilliant comedy, Chase seemed capable of performing this type of role (sort of a poor man's modern-day Cary Grant or William Powell) a lot better than Burt Reynolds had done in similar films.

Chevy Chase and Goldie Hawn worked together in "Foul Play" (1978) and "Seems Like Old Times" (1980).

Then, Chase was rushed into a series of really bad pictures like *Caddyshack, Oh Heavenly Dog, Under the Rainbow, Modern Problems, Deal of the Century, National Lampoon's Vacation,* and *National Lampoon's European Vacation.*

Chevy Chase is a passable comic actor but is hopelessly at the mercy of his material.

Richard Pryor

Pryor is a black comedian who, like Lenny Bruce, engages in a series of slurs, curses, and offensive one-liners during his adults-only nightclub act (represented well by his "concert" films). His timing, delivery, and motivation are all good enough to give producers reason to make him into a movie comedian in everything from starring vehicles like *Which Way Is Up?* (1977), to team vehicles like *Silver Streak* (1976) and *Stir Crazy* (1980) with Gene Wilder, to character roles in *Superman III* (1983).

Pryor is important as the first black movie comic to achieve great fame and acceptance (as Bill Cosby was the first to do in television). Before Pryor, black com-

Richard Pryor

edians in movies were represented by the antics of Stepin Fetchit, Mantan Moreland, Willie Best, and the like, whose portrayals of lazy, shiftless, "nigger" stereotypes caused some furor among black American moviegoers.

In films like *Which Way Is Up?* (1977), Pryor showed the positive as well as the negative aspects of the black experience in a humorous way, almost immediately garnering a following among blacks, and gradually becoming popular with white audiences as well.

Richard Pryor is a capable performer and has quite a following, but does not represent any real, substantial importance in the development of screen comedy other than being the first black comedian to achieve recognition.

John Belushi

Belushi was another of the "Saturday Night Live" alumni to migrate onto the big screen, first in small roles (*Old Boyfriends, Going South*) and then in a pivotal character role in *National Lampoon's Animal House* (1978).

As a sloppy, anarchic fraternity brother in this silly campus comedy, Belushi garnered a following that surpassed his TV popularity. The film was only fair, sort of a modern-day Three Stooges, but was commercially successful.

Belushi then appeared in Steven Spielberg's expensive turkey *1941* (1979), then teamed with Dan Aykroyd for *The Blues Brothers* (1980), based on a sketch the two performed on "Saturday Night Live." The comedy relied more on special effects rather than any talent on the part of the actors (big gags like car chases through shopping malls further proving what Larry Semon discovered in the twenties . . . bigger doesn't mean better). What made this one so miserable was a combination of Dan Aykroyd's blandness and Belushi's ill-fated attempts at singing old rock classics like "Jailhouse Rock" and "Gimme Some Lovin' " both done better

Dan Aykroyd, John Belushi (shown at top in "The Blues Brothers," 1980) and Bill Murray (in "Razor's Edge," 1984) are all alumni of NBC's "Saturday Night Live."

by the artists who made them immortal (Elvis Presley, Steve Winwood and the Spencer Davis Group, respectively).

Aykroyd and Belushi teamed again for *Neighbors* (1981), which was even worse.

Continental Divide (1982) was Belushi's best film. A straight story with comic touches and a well-disciplined, sincere performance by Belushi combined to make a very likeable comedy-drama about a city-bred reporter who gets a taste of mountain life while covering a story. Whatever potential Belushi had to continue with equal success in films was left unfounded when the actor died tragically in 1982.

Bill Murray

Still another veteran of the "Saturday Night Live" program, Murray has a certain charisma which enhances his character in average films like *Meatballs* (1979), which features him as a summer camp counselor. *Meatballs* was his first starring film (he had also appeared in the awful *Loose Shoes* in 1978), and was well received.

Where the Buffalo Roam (1980) was a botched attempt at a story about writer Hunter Thompson. *Caddyshack* (1981) was an unbelievably bad film which should have ruined the careers of everyone associated with it. *Stripes* (1982) was yet another comedy on army life, with nothing that hadn't been done before by virtually every comic in pictures as far back as the teens.

But after three movies as bad as these, Murray appeared in a character role in Sydney Pollack's celebrated *Tootsie* (1983), which also featured Dustin Hoffman, Teri Garr, Jessica Lange, Charles Durning, and Dabney Coleman. Pollack allowed Murray to extend to his full comic potential while still keeping him from his limitations, and the results were excellent.

Bill then returned to mediocrity with *Ghostbusters* (1984) before taking a fling at dramatic acting in *The Razor's Edge* (1984).

Murray is capable of being funny to a better-than-average degree, but only if given a good script. When given a bad script, he has no chance but to languish within the banality of the proceedings.

Cheech & Chong

Richard "Cheech" Marin and Thomas Chong represent the comedy duo of this period, descendants of Laurel and Hardy, Abbott and Costello, and Martin and Lewis.

Cheech and Chong do drug-related humor, something that can be funny (even to the uninitiated) in the duo's routines (found on many of their record albums of the early seventies), but which can't always sustain an entire feature film.

Thomas Chong (left) and Richard "Cheech" Marin.

Their debut, *Up in Smoke* (1978), contained some mildly funny stuff. Their second film, appropriately titled *Cheech & Chong's Next Movie* (1980), also moved well (bogging down just a bit during its final third).

Their film career then spiraled downhill very quickly, with *Nice Dreams* (1981), *Things Are Tough All Over* (1982), *Still Smokin'* (1983), and *The Corsican Brothers* (1984) all representing very poor examples of the team's humor.

The one-joke drug premise employed by the team has a problem with dating badly and getting stretched too far in order to sustain a feature. The duo still deserves some credit for writing and directing their own films (a rarity during this period), even if they never rise above a level of harmless silliness.

Dudley Moore

A British comedian who first came into prominence as one half of the comedy team Derek and Clive (with Peter Cook) in films like *Bedazzled* (1968), Moore did a bit in *Foul Play* (1978) before becoming a household word on the strength of his performance in *10* (1979).

While Dudley was the only reason to sit through this silly Blake Edwards sex farce, his performance was attractive enough to make him a person to bear watching. He really proved himself with *Arthur* (1981), a comedy featuring Moore as a drunken, spoiled rich boy with a wild sense of humor. The energy and sincerity of his performance was the film's strong point, and his use of body movement would have been envied by any of Sennett's tumblers.

His screen career is erratic, with *Lovesick* (1982) and *Unfaithfully Yours* (1983) a waste of the man's talents. He also did *Mickey & Maude* (1984) and *Best Defense* (1984), the latter featuring Eddie Murphy.

Dudley Moore.

After eighty years, this is where we stand in screen comedy. There is much room for development, for new inventions. But whatever happens in the future, one of the great things about film is that the past never leaves us.

Afterword

It has now been eighty years, and screen humor most likely has not yet stopped developing. What we have thus far shows a very fascinating display of intelligence, emotion, hard work, creativity, and love.

For it is love along with laughter that stand as the most important of human emotions, and those people who invented new, exciting ways to bring out these emotions deserve the care and respect that this text has attempted.

Any book on the cinema will cite Chaplin as the leading comedy creator and will rank him as a filmmaker alongside such incredible geniuses as Griffith, Lang, Murnau, Melies, Renoir, Eisenstein, Rossellini, and Hitchcock, but is reading these statements really enough?

Actor Dustin Hoffman once stated during a salute to James Stewart that the film *It's a Wonderful Life* (1947) is a greater tribute to Stewart's acting skills than any awards ceremonies. This is correct, just as viewing *City Lights, Modern Times, The Gold Rush, Limelight, The Great Dictator*, or any one of dozens of short films will more substantially prove Chaplin's genius.

In viewing any films with major screen comedians, comparisons will tell the viewer quite clearly which films created what first, and which comedians make best use of what styles. Now, shouldn't these films be more open to public viewing than they presently are?

Many films are also neglected because they are older. While Woody Allen's *Annie Hall* is a screen triumph, it should not cause us to overlook *City Lights*, just as *Gone with the Wind* shouldn't obliterate our memories of *Birth of a Nation*, or Bruce Springsteen not cause us to forget Elvis Presley. No former creation should be overshadowed by the new one that comes along, especially when the latter entry has been so obviously influenced by the former.

Screen comedy is forever, as far back as it has gone and as far ahead as it shall go; later methods, no matter how outstanding, still would not have been conceivable without the earlier, original works.

Comedy has been unfairly neglected in many film circles, where it is dismissed as unworthy of serious consideration. Only *Annie Hall* and Laurel and Hardy's *The Music Box* have actually won Academy Awards, with few others even getting nominations, although many "special" awards are given to comedians, usually long after their careers are over. Many film institutions will opt for *Citizen Kane, Rules of the Game, Potemkin*, or even *Star Wars* in place of considering *City*

Lights, The General, Sons of the Desert, The Bank Dick, or *The Bellboy* in contention for a screen achievement award.

With love and laughter not only the most essential of human emotions, but the two major ingredients in screen comedy, isn't it a little ridiculous that so few people are giving comedy the appreciation and understanding that it deserves?

During a 1980 interview, former Dead End Kid Gabe Dell told me that "Laughter is the secret; the key to everything, really." I wonder if he realized just how intelligent a statement that was.

Thanks for reading!

Appendix A
Supporting Players
and Secondary Clowns

When a mountain climber is asked why he scales the mountain, his reply is, "Because it's there." There have been so many of the lesser movie comedians that a chapter covering each of them would be virtually impossible. I list them here despite the fact that they made little or no substantial contribution to the art with their efforts. They are listed here because, well, they were there! The list also includes the many important character actors and actresses who graced many a comic film in supporting roles. They, of course, deserve acknowledgment. Fair is fair, and everyone who tried his hand at movie comedy should be at least mentioned in a book on movie comedians that attempts at being comprehensive . . . even if they weren't particularly funny, as is often the case. Each person listed here is acknowledged for his or her contribution to the evolution of the movie comedian and the development of screen comedy, no matter how minor. Their credentials and merit are explained under their names, followed by the year they died, if deceased.

Again, these are strictly movie comedians and supporting players who appeared in a number of comedies. Although Cary Grant made comedies, he is not essentially a movie comedian, while a supporting player like Lionel Stander, who did comic and dramatic roles, *should* be included due to his having appeared in films with Harold Lloyd, Fatty Arbuckle, and others. And finally, somebody like Pier Angeli, although she appeared in Danny Kaye's *Merry Andrew*, would *not* be included because that is (I believe) the only comedy she appeared in, her brief career not encompassing a variety of different comic films. O.K.?

Frank "Fatty" Alexander. Comic heavy in Christie-produced films and many of Larry Semon's starring comedies. Died in 1937.

Fred Allen. Famous radio comedian. Appeared with Jack Benny in *Buck Benny Rides Again* (1940) and *It's In the Bag* (1945). Died in 1956.

Eddie "Rochester" Anderson. Black character actor in films like *Green Pastures*. Best known as Jack Benny's TV, movie, and radio valet. Died in 1977.

Phil Arnold. Appeared with the Three Stooges in some of their later short films with Shemp. Also made semi-regular appearances with Joan Davis on television. Died in 1968.

Johnny Arthur. Comic foil for Our Gang in *Anniversary Trouble* and *Feed 'Em and Weep*, both times as a whining, flustered father. Looked a little like a puny Charley Chase. Died in 1951.

Dan Aykroyd. "Saturday Night Live" alumnus. Teamed with John Belushi in *The Blues Brothers* (1980) and *Neighbors* (1982), appeared alone in *Doctor Detroit* (1982), teamed with Eddie Murphy in *Trading Places* (1983), and with Bill Murray and Harold Ramis in *Ghostbusters* (1984), which he co-wrote with Ramis. A very bland, unexciting performer.

Irving Bacon. The long-suffering mailman in many of the Blondie features with Arthur Lake. Also did character roles in other films. Died in 1965.

Lucille Ball. Appeared with the Stooges in *Three Little Pigskins* (1934), with the Marx Brothers in *Room Service* (1938), and in dozens of RKO features with everyone from Jack Oakie to Joe Penner. She didn't show her full potential for comedy until television happened along and transformed her into a legend.

Billy Barty. Midget actor for many years in comedies with Jerry Lewis, others. Also did extensive TV work.

Spencer Bell. Black comic in Christie comedies, appeared with Larry Semon, Louise Fazenda, others. Died in 1935.

Robert Benchley. Respected humorist and journalist. Appeared in his own short films for MGM and Paramount during the forties. Also did character roles in features at both studios, narrating the Hope-Crosby *Road to Utopia* (1945). Died in 1945.

William Bendix. Excellent, popular character actor in dramatic and comic films. Was so good in Abbott and Costello's *Who Done It* (1942) that Costello reportedly refused ever to work with him again. Also scored in his own *Kill the Umpire* (1950) and *The Life of Riley* (1949), which he also played on radio and later television. Died in 1964.

Edgar Bergen. Radio ventriloquist (?!) with dummies Charlie McCarthy and Mortimer Snerd who constantly rivaled W.C. Fields on radio. Appeared with

Fields in *You Can't Cheat an Honest Man* (1939) as well as other low-budget films at Universal and RKO. Did some TV work. Died in 1978.

Harry Bernard. Character actor in Roach films. Appeared often with Laurel and Hardy, Charley Chase, others. Died in 1940.

Willie "Sleep and Eat" Best. Black character comic in films and on television. Died in 1962.

Billy Bletcher. Did character roles and voice-overs in many features, shorts, and serials. Appeared often with Laurel and Hardy. Died in 1979.

Eric Blore. British-born character actor. Played upper-crust comic foil in RKO comedies and musicals, most notably *Top Hat* (1935). Died in 1959.

Ben Blue. Vaudeville comic. Was also in *Taxi Boys* series with Billy Gilbert at Roach studios during thirties. Active in movies and television. Died in 1975.

Stanley Blystone. Comic heavy and foil at Columbia and RKO during the thirties and forties. Rough Sergeant McGilicutty role in Stooges short *Half Wits Holiday* (1936) among his most remembered performances. Died in 1956.

Mary Boland. Dowager/foil in many comedies, most notably *If I Had a Million* (1932), *Six of a Kind* (1934), both with W.C. Fields, as well as *Ruggles of Red Gap* (1935), and Laurel and Hardy's *Nothing But Trouble* (1944). Died in 1965.

El Brendel. Philadelphia-born dialect comic (played a dumb Swede) in vaudeville and movies. Did short subjects at Columbia during the forties and fifties, some teamed with Harry Langdon. Died in 1964.

Ed Brophy. Character actor, usually as a dumb gangster, in Columbia and MGM films as well as some Warner Brothers efforts. Died in 1960.

Frank Brownlee. Character actor, mostly in silents. Did funny bit as drill instructor in Laurel and Hardy's talking feature *Pack Up Your Troubles* (1932), ("...and halt means to stop!"). Died in 1948.

Virginia Bruce. Universal stock actress. Appeared with Abbott and Costello in *Pardon My Sarong* (1942) as well as other comedies at that studio. Died in 1983.

Bilie Burke. In films like *Billie Gets Her Man* (1949) at Columbia, as well as more prestigious features like *Wizard of Oz* (1939) as the good witch. Died in 1970.

James Burke. Character actor at RKO and Warners. Appeared with many different comedians, usually as a befuddled detective. Died in 1968.

Carol Burnett. Television comedienne. Did some minor screen work as a character actress in films like *The Front Page* (1974) as well as some dramatic TV movies.

Neal Burns. Actor in Christie comedies during the teens and twenties. Died in 1969.

Mae Busch. Character actress at Roach and MGM. Appeared in many Laurel and Hardy comedies like *Come Clean* (1931), *Sons of the Desert* (1934), and *Bohemian Girl* (1936); the latter two as Mrs. Hardy. Died in 1946.

Sid Caesar. One of the best sketch comedians, appeared on television with his own "Your Show of Shows" which also featured Howard Morris, Imogene Coca, and Mel Brooks. Did some minor screen work in films like Brook's *Silent Movie* (1976).

Robert Callahan. Appeared with Curly Howard in *Roast Beef and Movies* (Curly's only film without Moe and Larry) and as an extra in some other things like Laurel and Hardy's *Helpmates* (1931). Died in 1938.

Godfrey Cambridge. Black comedy actor in films like the semi-classic *Watermelon Man* (1970). Died in 1976.

Eric Campbell. Comic heavy in Chaplin Mutual comedies. Killed in auto crash, 1918.

John Candy. Character actor in comedies, an alumnus of the Second City improvisational comedy group. Appeared in films like *Stripes* (1982), *National Lampoon's Vacation* (1983), and *Splash* (1984).

Eddie Cantor. Showbiz legend in comedy features with music. Films like *Kid Millions* (1937). Also did vaudeville, burlesque, and some television. Died in 1964.

Roger C. Carmel. Character actor in movies and TV. Appeared with Jerry Lewis in *Hardly Working* (1981).

Mary Carr. Character actress in Roach films with Charley Chase, Laurel and Hardy, Our Gang, usually as a kindly old lady. Died in 1973 at age 99!

Leo Carrillo. Pancho in Cisco Kid TV series opposite Duncan Renaldo, Carrillo was also a busy character actor at Universal and MGM, appearing in Abbott and Costello films at both studios. Died in 1961.

Walter Catlett. Appeared in some short comedies and did some character work in features at MGM, RKO, and Warners. Started as vaudeville headliner. Died in 1960.

Elise Cavannah. Foil in Sennett talkies, appeared in the censored sequence from W.C. Fields's *The Dentist* (1932). Died in 1963.

Nora Cecil. Ugly, mean old lady in Roach comedies like Laurel and Hardy's *Pack Up Your Troubles* (1932) and Charley Chase's *Girl Grief* (1932). Her last appearance of notoriety was in a 1940 Fields classic *The Bank Dick*. Died in 1954.

Lane Chandler. Actor in Columbia "B" detective and western films, also appeared in some short comedies. Died in 1972.

Lon Chaney, Jr. Horror film actor best known as The Wolf Man. Appeared in many Abbott and Costello films. Died in 1973.

Sydney Chaplin. Half-brother to Charlie. Was in many of Charlie's First National studio films. Also starred in his own comedies during the teens. An underrated comic who worked in the shadow of the much more talented and popular Charlie. Died in 1965.

Fred Clark. Character actor in hundreds of films and television shows from the forties through the sixties. Died in 1968.

Monty Collins. Vaudeville comic. Appeared in his own short subjects at Columbia, as well as those featuring Harry Langdon, Buster Keaton, Charley Chase, and the Three Stooges. Wrote many of these comedies as well. Died in 1951.

Chester Conklin. Actor at Keystone. One of the original Keystone Cops, appeared in hundreds of silents with Chaplin, Billy Bevan, Fatty Arbuckle, etc., joining Columbia during the talkies to appear with the Stooges, others. Remained semi-active right up until his death in 1971.

Jimmy Conlin. Little old man, fast talker. Appeared in nearly all of the Preston Sturges features including Harold Lloyd's *Sins of Harold Diddlebock* (1947) (aka *Mad Wednesday* (1951). Died in 1962.

Hans Conried. Gruff-voiced character actor in movies and television. *Blondie's Blessed Event* (1940) with Arthur Lake, and *The Patsy* (1964) with Jerry Lewis were among his appearances. Died in 1982.

Tim Conway. Overacting bumbler, undisciplined comic much like Steve Martin. Achieved notoriety on TV's *McHales Navy* and *Carol Burnett Show* as well as many lousy shows of his own which bombed (*Rango, Ace Crawford*, etc.). Starred in some really bad movies during the seventies and eighties with Don Knotts, Chuck McCann, others. More stupid and annoying than funny.

Clyde Cook. Australian-born character actor in silents and talkies. Appeared in many Roach-produced vehicles. A very minor comic. Died in 1984.

Baldwin Cooke. Roach stock player. Appeared with Chase, Laurel and Hardy, Our Gang, etc., usually in small roles. Died in 1953.

Charles Correll. "Andy" of "Amos and Andy" radio and early film group. Blackface bit called racist by the fifties, so their films have been rarely revived. Those which do exist are slow moving and weak. Later TV series featured actual blacks rather than white actors in blackface. Died in 1972.

Gino Corrado. Italian-born actor. Played hot tempered neopolitan types or drunks in films like *Micro Phonies* (1946) with the Three Stooges. Died in 1983.

Bill Cosby. Black comedy actor in television, in nightclubs, and films like *A Piece of the Action* and *Let's Do It Again*. Talented and funny, among TV's essential comedy actors.

Anthony "Pat" Costello. Brother of Lou, appeared in many Abbott and Costello films, radio, and TV shows. Also did some stunt work, and character acting at Monogram in "B" pictures with the East Side Kids, others.

Jerome Cowan. Character actor at virtually every film studio during the forties, fifties, and sixties. Played Mr. Radcliffe, Dithers's replacement, in the Blondie films at Columbia with Arthur Lake (1947–49), also appeared with Abbott and Costello in *Who Done It* (1942). Died in 1972.

Wally Cox. Meek character actor in movies and television. Voice of "Underdog" cartoon character and a regular on TV's "Hollywood Squares" game show. Appeared in films with Jerry Lewis, Don Knotts, others. Died in 1973.

Rychard Cramer. Heavy in westerns, appeared in Laurel and Hardy's *Scram* (1932) and *Saps at Sea* (1940). Also did other work at Roach studios. Died in 1960.

Bing Crosby. Actor/crooner who appeared with Bob Hope in Paramount's "Road" series. Died in 1977.

Alan Curtis. Universal stock player was in *Buck Privates* with Abbott & Costello. Died in 1953.

Dick Curtis. Western movie bad guy, appeared at Columbia with Stooges, others. Died in 1952.

Charlie Dale. One half of Smith and Dale comedy team in vaudeville, also in feature and short subject appearances. Died in 1971.

Rodney Dangerfield. Comedian in clubs, appeared on screen in comedies *Caddyshack, Easy Money.* A funny man at times doing standup bits, but on film he deserves "no respect."

Bebe Daniels. Ingenue in Harold Lloyd's *Lonesome Luke* silents. Died in 1971.

Frankie Darro. Juvenile character actor. Starred in many low-budget action dramas at Monogram. Appeared often with the Bowery Boys. Died in 1976.

Marion Davies. Girlfriend of William Randolph Hearst, aunt of Arthur Lake's wife, and actress in silent comedies at Roach, elsewhere. Died in 1961.

Joan Davis. Marvelously funny comedienne in films with Leon Errol, Abbott and Costello, Shemp Howard, many others. Also did TV work, with *I Married Joan* among the staples of fifties sitcoms. Died in 1961.

Richard Deacon. Character actor in many films and TV shows, best remembered from the "Dick Van Dyke" and "Leave It To Beaver" television programs. Also did *Abbott & Costello Meet the Mummy* (1955), others. Died in 1984.

Carter DeHaven. Father of Gloria, did acting and directorial work in some Chaplin silents. Died in 1977.

William Demarest. Character actor in many Preston Sturges features, as well as with Abbott and Costello, Olsen and Johnson, Jerry Lewis, others. Best remembered as Uncle Charley on the "My Three Sons" TV show. Died in 1983.

Vernon Dent. Comic heavy at Sennett's with Harry Langdon, Billy Bevan, etc. He migrated to Columbia to appear in talkies with the Three Stooges, Buster Keaton, others. Died in 1963.

Andy Devine. Character actor in many features and television shows. Died in 1977.

Dorothy Devore. Comedienne in early Christie-produced comedies. Died in 1977.

Billy DeWolfe. Worked as character actor in many films with Bob Hope, Jerry Lewis, others. Died in 1974.

Dudley Dickerson. Black character comic in many films, best known for work with the Three Stooges in films like *A-Plumbing We Will Go* and *A Gem of a Jam.* Died in 1968.

Donald Dillaway. In Christie comedies during the thirties. Best remembered for playing Eddie Smith in Laurel and Hardy's *Pack Up Your Troubles.* Died in 1982.

Ann Doran. Character actress in many Columbia comedies with Three Stooges, Charley Chase, Buster Keaton, Harry Langdon, Andy Clyde, Roscoe Karns, others. Played James Dean's mother in *Rebel Without a Cause.*

Marie Dressler. Actress in classics *Min & Bill, Tugboat Annie, Anna Christie,* and *Dinner at Eight* at MGM. Also appeared with Chaplin in Sennett feature *Tillie's Punctured Romance* and in several Christie comedies, usually teamed with Polly Moran. Died in 1934.

Jack Duffy. Silent comic actor for Christie, played gruff oldster with scraggly beard. Appeared in some early Stooges comedies like *Pop Goes the Easel* ("Is this the clay department?"). Died in 1939.

Douglas Dumbrille. Veteran character actor in many Hollywood films. Appeared with the Marx Brothers in *A Day at the Races* and with Abbott and Costello in *Lost in a Harem.* Died in 1974.

Margaret Dumont. Unforgettable dowager/foil in films with Laurel & Hardy, Abbott & Costello, W.C. Fields, and most notably the Marx Brothers. Her scenes with Groucho in *Monkey Business, Coconuts, Animal Crackers, Duck Soup, A Night at the Opera, A Day at the Races,* even *At the Circus* and *The Big Store* are among the screen's most delightful moments. Died in 1965.

Bud Duncan. One half of the team in the Ham and Bud series at Christie's during the teens (with Lloyd Hamilton), also appeared as Snuffy Smith in a low-budget series of quickie comedy features during the thirties. Died in 1960.

Bobby Dunn. Cross-eyed character comic in Laurel and Hardy films like *Me & My Pal, Bohemian Girl.* Died in 1937.

Jimmy Durante. Legendary entertainer, appeared in some comedies opposite Buster Keaton, as well as other films. Died in 1980.

Minita Durfee. Character actress at Keystone, was once married to Fatty Arbuckle. Died in 1975.

Charles Durning. Popular character actor during the seventies and eighties in films like *Dog Day Afternoon, Tootsie, The Best Little Whorehouse in Texas, To Be or Not To Be.*

Mary Eaton. Bland actress who appeared in two Marx Brothers films, *Coconuts* and *Animal Crackers*. Died in 1948.

Patricia Ellis. Appeared with Joe E. Brown in *Elmer the Great*, with Laurel & Hardy in *Blockheads*, and in many other films. Died in 1970.

Stuart Erwin. Comedy actor in many films, including *International House* (1933), which also featured W.C. Fields and Burns and Allen. Had his own TV show, *The Trouble with Father*, during the fifties at Roach. Died in 1967.

Dot Farley. Mother-in-law in the Edgar Kennedy short comedies at RKO. Died in 1971.

Jessylyn Fax. Little old lady character actress in many films during the fifties. Died in 1975.

Louise Fazenda. Important comedienne for Christie, quite popular during the twenties. Appeared in Christie remake of Sennett's milestone *Tillie's Punctured Romance*, which also featured W.C. Fields. Married to producer Hal Wallis. Died in 1962.

Fritz Feld. German character actor who makes the "pop" sound by slapping his mouth. In films with Abbott and Costello, Jerry Lewis, Mel Brooks, Jack Benny, Danny Kaye, others.

Frank Ferguson. Character actor in many films, most notable as MacDougle in *Abbott & Costello Meet Frankenstein*. Died in 1978.

Fernandel. Great French movie clown. Died in 1971.

Stepin Fetchit. Black comic actor. Played the lazy, shiftless stereotype that became a target for black militants during the sixties. His image made him a million-dollar star during the thirties and forties. Died in 1985.

Sidney Fields. Vaudeville, film, and TV actor, best noted as landlord in Abbott & Costello TV shows. Died in 1975.

Stanley Fields. Character actor in features like *Little Caesar* with Edward G. Robinson, deserves special mention for his portrayal of the sheriff in Laurel & Hardy's classic *Way Out West*. Died in 1941.

Flora Finch. Comedienne opposite John Bunny in many films until Bunny's death, when Flora was relegated to bit roles and extra work. Died in 1940.

James Finlayson. Master of the double-take reaction with one squinted eye and one raised eyebrow in films with Charley Chase, Our Gang, and most notably in Laurel and Hardy's *Big Business* and *Way Out West*. Died in 1953.

Richard Fiske. Comic foil in Stooges comedies, most notably *Boobs in Arms* as the bad tempered sergeant. Killed during WWII in 1944.

Joe Flynn. Remembered as Binghamton on TV's "McHales Navy," also did many Disney features and character roles in comedies. Died in 1974.

Eddie Foy, Jr. One of the Seven Little Foys in vaudeville, also did screen work. Died in 1983.

Billy Franey. Comedian in silent comedies. Died in 1940.

William Frawley. Character actor with Abbott and Costello, Arthur Lake, others. Best known as Fred Mertz on "I Love Lucy" television program. Died in 1966.

Kathleen Freeman. Character actress in many comedies with Jerry Lewis, most notably *The Disorderly Orderly*. Also appeared in *The Blues Brothers*.

Otto Fries. Bit comic actor at Roach. Appeared with Laurel and Hardy, Charley Chase, others. Died in 1938.

Stephen Furst. Comedy actor in teen cheapies like *Animal House* (as Flounder), *Gas, Swim Team, Take Down*.

Billy Gilbert. Busy character actor. Appeared with Laurel and Hardy (most notably in *The Music Box*), Charley Chase, Our Gang, the Marx Brothers, the Three Stooges, the Bowery Boys, in literally hundreds of comedies, always shining in whatever role. One of the top rank. Died in 1972.

James Gleason. Wisecracking character actor in many top Hollywood films. Died in 1959.

Paulette Goddard. Once married to Chaplin, appeared in his *Modern Times* and *The Great Dictator*, also with Bob Hope in *The Ghost Breakers*.

Norris Goff. Appeared as Abner in the "Lum 'n Abner" radio series and in the film *Dreaming Out Loud*. Chester Lauck was Lum. Died in 1978.

Minna Gombell. Hardy's nagging wife in *Blockheads*. Died in 1973.

Bert Gordon. Known as the Mad Russian ("How do you do?") in radio and films. Died in 1974.

Mitzi Green. Child actress in films like *Tom Sawyer, Huckleberry Finn*, and *Little Orphan Annie* during the early thirties. Retired at end of that decade but came out in 1950s to do Abbott & Costello's awful *Lost in Alaska*, then went right back into retirement. Died in 1969.

Charlotte Greenwood. Big tall gal in many comedies, most notably Buster Keaton's *Parlor, Bedroom, and Bath*. Died in 1978.

Eddie Gribbon. Character comic for Sennett, Monogram, RKO. Died in 1965.

Harry Gribbon. Comic for Sennett. One of the Keystone Cops, also played a villain. Died in 1961.

Raymond Griffith. Silent screen comic, a favorite among students of film comedy. Did films like the semi-classic *Hands Up*, as well as being active as a producer. Last appearance was in the movie classic *All Quiet on the Western Front*. Died in 1957.

Buddy Hackett. Nightclub and television comedian, did some screen work in pictures like *Fireman Save My Child* (where he substituted for an ailing Lou Costello), *All Hands on Deck, Everything's Ducky, It's a Mad Mad Mad Mad World*, and *God's Little Acre*, among others.

Raymond Hackett. Comic in Christie films like *Key Taxi, Take the Next Car*. Died in 1958.

Jonathan Hale. Mr. Dithers in the Blondie and Dagwood films from 1937–1946. Was typecast thereafter and became increasingly despondent, especially when his health began failing. Committed to the Motion Picture Home and Hospital, where he shot himself to death February 28, 1966.

Charley Hall. Comic foil at Roach in many Laurel and Hardy films including *Them Thar Hills, Tit for Tat, Angora Love, Laughing Gravy, Busy Bodies*, and many Charley Chase vehicles as well. Active into the fifties. Died in 1959.

Thurston Hall. Character actor in many films at virtually all of the studios, especially during the forties. Appeared in *You Can't Cheat an Honest Man* with W.C. Fields, *In Society* with Abbott and Costello, and many other comedies. Died in 1958.

John Hamilton. Perry White on the "Superman" television show with George Reeves. Hamilton also appeared in films with Abbott and Costello, the Three Stooges, the Bowery Boys, others. Died in 1958.

Jean Harlow. Famous actress of the thirties, got her start in Laurel and Hardy comedies *Double Whoopee* and *Bacon Grabbers*. Died in 1937.

Percy Helton. Soft-spoken character actor in films and on television, appeared in *Abbott & Costello Meet the Killer*. Died in 1973.

Dell Henderson. Character actor, foil in Roach comedies with Laurel and Hardy, Charley Chase, and most notably in *Choo Choo* with Our Gang. Died in 1956.

Gale Henry. Silent screen comedienne during teens and twenties. Died in 1972.

Hugh Herbert. The "WooWoo" man in several films, had his own series of features at Universal, and later his own series of short subjects at Columbia. Died in 1952.

Thelma Hill. Blonde flirt in Laurel and Hardy's *Two Tars*. Died in 1938.

Sterling Holloway. Character actor in many films with Joe E. Brown, W.C. Fields, others. Also did television.

Arthur Housman. Drunk in several Roach films with Laurel and Hardy, Charley Chase, others. Also played sober characters with Edgar Kennedy, the Three Stooges. Died in 1942.

Kathleen Howard. Character actress, Fields's nagging wife in *It's a Gift* and *Man on the Flying Trapeze*. Died in 1956.

Alice Howell. Actress at Essanay with Chaplin and in many other films. Died in 1961.

Bud Jamison. Comic heavy in Chaplin Essanays like *The Tramp* and *Champion*, as well as supporting player at Columbia for Keaton, Andy Clyde, Harry Langdon, and the Three Stooges, appearing in virtually all of the trio's films until his death in 1944.

Gordon Jones. Character actor. Appeared as the cop on Abbott & Costello's TV show. Died in 1961.

Eddie Kane. Character actor at Sennett, Christie, and Republic studios, appearing with virtually all of the comics playing at any of these. Died in 1969.

Babe Kane. Actress at Sennett's and Christie's, appeared in Fields' *The Dentist*, *The Pharmacist*. Died in 1966.

Roscoe Karns. Wise-guy comedian in films like *It Happened One Night*, also did short films at Columbia. Usually played an obnoxious pest. Died in 1970.

Joseph Kearns. Television character actor, also did much screen work during the fifties. Died in 1962.

Larry Keating. Character actor on TV's "Mr. Ed" and "Burns and Allen" shows, also did screen work with Don Knotts, others. Died in 1963.

Diane Keaton. Character actress who played the girlfriend in most of Woody Allen's best films.

Richard Keene. Soft-spoken actor in many Hollywood films, especially during the forties. Did several comedies. Died in 1971.

Patsy Kelly. Wisecracking comedienne in many films, starred in shorts with Thelma Todd at Roach. Died in 1982.

Fred Kelsey. Comic heavy in Laurel and Hardy's *Murder Case* and its remake, *If a Body Meets a Body*, featuring the Three Stooges. In many other films, mostly at Columbia. Died in 1961.

Pert Kelton. Opposite Patsy Kelly in short film after Thelma Todd's death. Also did other films and TV shows. Died in 1968.

Merna Kennedy. Ingenue in Chaplin's *The Circus*, also appeared in westerns with Tom Keene. Died in 1944.

Tom Kennedy. Former Keystone player. Did work in many features as dumb cop or witless crook. Died in 1965.

Guy Kibbee. Versatile. Starred in own RKO features like *The Big Shot*, also character roles, like *The Horn Blows at Midnight* with Jack Benny. Died in 1956.

Joe Kirk. Actor in many Abbott & Costello films (Lou's brother-in-law), was Mr. Baggagalupe on the duo's TV series. Died in 1975.

Harvey Korman. Character actor in Mel Brooks films like *Blazing Saddles* and *High Anxiety*. Appeared on television with Carol Burnett.

Bert Lahr. Cowardly lion in *The Wizard of Oz* at MGM. Also did his own short films like *Off the Horses, Henry the Ache*, and features including *Flying Wild*. One of the best. Died in 1967.

Florence Lake. Edgar Kennedy's daffy wife in most of his RKO short subjects. Arthur Lake's sister. Died in 1981.

Charles Lane. Gruff character actor in hundreds of films with just about everybody. Always played a rat, but a favorite nonetheless. Did TV too.

Richard Lane. Character actor with Laurel and Hardy, Abbott and Costello, others, had his own series of short films at Columbia with Gus Schilling. Best known as Inspector Farraday in the *Boston Blackie* pictures. Died in 1982.

Chester Lauk. Lum to Norris Goff's Abner on radio and in the film *Dreaming Out Loud*. Died in 1980.

Janet Leigh. Famous actress, once married to Tony Curtis, mother of Jamie Lee Curtis. Appeared with Jerry Lewis in *Living It Up* and *Three on a Couch*.

Jack "Tiny" Lipson. Comic heavy in many films, most notably with the Stooges. Died in 1947.

Lucien Littlefield. Mad scientist in Laurel and Hardy's *Dirty Work*, Joe E. Brown's *The Gladiator*, appeared in many films. Died in 1960.

Carole Lombard. Famous screen actress of the thirties. Appeared in silent comedies at Roach, Sennett, and Christie, and with Jack Benny in *To Be or Not To Be*, which was her last film. Died in 1942.

Walter Long. Comic heavy in Roach pictures, also did *Three Little Pigskins* with the Stooges and Lucille Ball. Died in 1950.

Peter Lorre. Famous character actor. Appeared with Jerry Lewis in *The Sad Sack* and *The Patsy*, with Bob Hope in *My Favorite Brunette*. Died in 1964.

Diana Lynn. Actress who appeared with Martin and Lewis in *My Friend Irma* and *You're Never Too Young*. Died in 1971.

Sharon Lynne. Saloon girl in Laurel and Hardy's *Way Out West* (the one that battles Stan for the gold mining deed). Died in 1963.

Eddie Lyons. Christie comic teamed in silents with Lee Moran. Died in 1926.

Donald MacBride. Comic foil (a cop, sergeant in the army, whatever) in wonderful performances with Jerry Lewis, the Bowery Boys, many others. Died in 1957.

Kenneth MacDonald. Wily comic villain in Stooges films like *Hold That Lion, Vagabond Loafers*. Died in 1972.

Matt McHugh. "Claude" in the Stooges comedy *Pardon My Clutch* and its remake, *Wham! Bam! Slam!*. Brother of Warner actor Frank McHugh. Died in 1971.

Christine McIntyre. Actress in Columbia shorts with Three Stooges, Harry Langdon, Andy Clyde, others. Died in 1984.

Hank Mann. Last of the original Keystone Cops. Remained active through the sixties. Died in 1971.

Charles Middleton. Remembered as Ming the Merciless in Flash Gordon serials, also did work as comic villain in Laurel and Hardy films like *Pack Up Your Troubles, Flying Deuces*. Died in 1949.

Geneva Mitchell. Actress in many Columbia short comedies of the thirties with the Three Stooges, Andy Clyde, Buster Keaton, Leon Errol, others. Died in 1949.

Bull Montana. Heavy in Harold Lloyd silents, other films. Died in 1950.

Lee Moran. In Christie comedies with Eddie Lyons. Died in 1961.

Patsy Moran. Film and radio comedienne. Appeared with Laurel and Hardy in *Blockheads*, other films. Died in 1968.

Polly Moran. Comedienne in Christie silents and early talkies. Often appeared opposite Marie Dressler. Died in 1952.

Milburn Morante. Silent screen comic. Died in 1964.

Mantan Moreland. Black comic in films like *King of the Zombies*. Also did Charlie Chan series at Monogram as chauffeur Birmingham Brown and starred in his own very popular all-black comedy vehicles during the 40s. Died in 1973.

James C. Morton. Comic heavy in many films at Christie, Roach, Columbia, elsewhere. Best known as irate father in Stooges' *The Sitter Downers*. Died in 1942.

Eddie Murphy. "Saturday Night Live" alumnus, appeared in films like *48 Hours* with Nick Nolte, *Trading Places* with Dan Aykroyd, and *Best Defense* with Dudley Moore. Proved a major talent with *Beverly Hills Cop* (1984).

Charlie Murray. Keystone player (one of the original cops). Also did work at Christie, and in Kelly's and Cohen's series at Universal. Died in 1941.

John T. Murray. Comic supporter in films at Columbia with Charley Chase, Stooges, etc. Died in 1957.

Burt Mustin. Old man in many comedies of the fifties and sixties, did much television work as well. Best remembered as the kindly fireman Gus on TV's "Leave It To Beaver." Died in 1977.

Tommy Noonan. One half of comedy team Noonan and Marshall (with Peter Marshall). Also did bits in films with Jayne Mansfield, others. Usually comic jester in fifties-era sex farces. Died in 1968.

Jack Norton. Comic drunk in many films from the late thirties through the fifties. Appeared with Laurel and Hardy, Abbott and Costello, others. Died in 1958.

Jack Oakie. Comic actor in many Hollywood films, appeared with W.C. Fields in *Million Dollar Legs*, and shone opposite Chaplin in *The Great Dictator*. Died in 1978.

Vivien Oakland. Appeared in many RKO comedies with Edgar Kennedy, Leon Errol, others. Died in 1958.

Dave O'Brien. Star of the Pete Smith Specialties. Also did work with East Side Kids, others. Died in 1970.

Edna May Oliver. Appeared at RKO with Wheeler and Whoolsey, Also appeared in comedy/mystery series as Miss Marple opposite James Gleason. Died in 1942.

Eugene Pallette. Gruff, bullfrog-voiced heavy in many features, including Abbott and Costello's *It Ain't Hay*, others. Died in 1954.

Franklin Pangborn. Fussy, fidgety, prissy spinster type in W.C Fields's *The Bank Dick* and *Never Give a Sucker an Even Break* as well as *The Horn Blows at Midnight* with Jack Benny, *Wild Poses* with Our Gang, others. Died in 1958.

Emory Parnell. With Stooges in *All the World's a Stooge*; many other films. Played the boss on TV's "The Life of Riley" with William Bendix. Died in 1979.

Paul Parrott (Jimmy Chase). Brother of Charley Chase, also wrote and directed under the name James Parrott. As Paul he appeared in many amusing but unremarkable one-reelers for Roach. Directed classics like Laurel and Hardy's *The Music Box* and Chase's *Girl Grief*. Died in 1939.

Blanche Payson. Mean old lady in Roach films featuring Charley Chase, Laurel and Hardy, Our Gang, others. Died in 1964.

Alice Pearce. Nosy lady type in many films with Jerry Lewis, others. Died in 1966.

Nat Pendelton. Comic heavy in Abbott and Costello's *Buck Privates* and its sequel, *Buck Privates Come Home*. Also played the cab driver in Universal's *Dr. Kildare* film series with Lew Ayers. Died in 1967.

Al Pierce. Comedian in films of the forties and fifties at Republic studios. Died in 1961.

ZaSu Pitts. Comedienne in films like *Ruggles of Red Gap* and *Sing and Like It*. Also appeared opposite Thelma Todd in a short subject series at Roach during the early thirties. Died in 1963.

Daphne Pollard. Short, chubby woman in many films at Sennett, Christie, and finally Roach. Appeared with Laurel and Hardy in *Thicker Than Water* and *Our Relations*, both times as Mrs. Hardy. Died in 1978.

Marie Prevost. Actress in silent comedies. Died in 1937.

Edna Purviance. Ingenue in Chaplin's Essanay and Mutual comedies. Died in 1958.

Gilda Radner. "Saturday Night Live" alumnus, appeared opposite Gene Wilder in *Hanky Panky*, and *The Woman in Red*.

Rags Ragland. Popular character comic. Did nightclubs with Phil Silvers, appeared in films with Red Skelton, Abbott and Costello, others. Died in 1946.

Harold Ramis. Comedian in films like *Stripes* with Bill Murray and *Ghostbusters* with Murray and Dan Aykroyd, having penned the latter with Aykroyd.

Anders Randolf. Silent actor who did some work in Roach comedies with Charley Chase, others. Died in 1930.

Alan Reed. Did character roles in films, but mostly radio. Also noted as voice of cartoon character Fred Flintstone. Died in 1977.

Charles Reisner. Actor and director of many Chaplin Keystones. Did other films. Died in 1962.

Burt Reynolds. Famous film star. Did many popular comedies during the seventies, all rather unremarkable.

Jack Rice. Pesty, lazy brother-in-law in Edgar Kennedy series, and unscrupulous office rival for Dagwood in the Blondie series. Very good in both roles, also did other films, television shows. Died in 1968.

Billy Ritchie. Comedian in early silents who bore an uncanny resemblance to Chaplin in style and appearance. Ritchie claimed that Chaplin stole his tramp idea, which is a silly accusation, because Ritchie wasn't funny. Chaplin was. Died in 1921.

Bert Roach. Comic actor in many silents. Died in 1971.

Lyda Roberti. Blonde, fiery actress with Fields in *Million Dollar Legs*, Laurel and Hardy in *Pick a Star* (aka *Movie Struck*), and opposite Patsy Kelly in two short films as a replacement for Thelma Todd. Died in 1938.

Tony Roberts. Woody Allen's buddy who lends a shoulder to cry on and gives meaningful advice in many of the comedian's films.

May Robson. Old lady who could play a crab or a kindly type. Died in 1942.

Mickey Rooney. Major screen, TV, and stage actor since early childhood, did virtually every type of role from heavy drama to lighthearted fare. Appeared in many comedies, including *The Atomic Kid, A Slight Case of Larceny, Nice Little Bank That Should Be Robbed, Everything's Ducky*, many others. Has won Emmys, Oscars, Tonys, and several other awards. One of America's finest actors and entertainers.

Maxie Rosenbloom. Former prizefighter. Usually played dumb thug in films with Jerry Lewis, Abbott and Costello, others. Also did drama, and had his own series of short subjects at Columbia with Max Baer, Sr., during the mid- to late forties and early fifties. Died in 1975.

Gene Roth. Heavy in many Three Stooges comedies. Was hit by a car and killed in 1976.

Charlie Ruggles. Top actor in comedies like *Six of a Kind, If I Had a Million*, both of which also featured W.C. Fields. Active until his death in 1970.

Sig Ruman. Heavy for Marx Brothers in *A Night at the Opera, A Day at The Races*, and *A Night in Casablanca*. Performed similar service for the Bowery Boys, Jerry Lewis, Danny Kaye, others. Died in 1967.

Margaret Rutherford. British actress in many English comedies. Died in 1972.

Irene Ryan. Remembered as Granny on TV's "Beverly Hillbillies," Miss Ryan also appeared in Monogram and RKO comedies with her husband, Tim. Died in 1973.

Sheila Ryan. Ingenue in a couple of later Laurel and Hardy comedies at Fox. Died in 1975.

Tim Ryan. Actor in comedies as well as writer of many Bowery Boys features. Husband of Irene Ryan. Died in 1956.

Al St. John. Keystone player who also did westerns as Fuzzy St. John (Fuzzy Q. Jones) opposite Lash La Rue, Buster Crabbe, others. Died in 1963.

Chic Sale. MGM comedian in shorts and features during the early thirties. Died in 1936.

Ralph Sanford. Heavy in comedies like Laurel and Hardy's *The Bullfighters*. Died in 1963.

Tiny Sanford. Heavy for Chaplin, Laurel and Hardy, Chase, many others. Died in 1961.

Gus Schilling. Comic relief, former burlesque comic. Appeared in series of short films at Columbia with Richard Lane (as Schilling and Lane). Died in 1957.

Sybil Seely. The wife/girlfriend in many Buster Keaton silents.

George Sidney. Character actor in comedies at Universal during the thirties. Died in 1945.

Phil Silvers. Top banana in burlesque, Tony Award winner on Broadway, Emmy winner on TV's classic "Sgt. Bilko" series, actor in several films. Died in 1985.

Emil Sitka. Character actor in films featuring Three Stooges, Andy Clyde, Billie Burke, Hugh Herbert, Schilling and Lane, Arthur Lake, William Bendix, Lucille Ball, dozens of others. Appeared in over 400 roles in a career spanning some 40 years. One of the favorites in Character Land.

Alison Skipworth. With W.C. Fields in *If I Had a Million, Tillie and Gus* (as Tillie), and other films with many leading players. Died in 1952.

Walter Slezak. Heavy (German) for Danny Kaye, Abbott and Costello, others. Committed suicide in 1983.

Pete Smith. Produced many humorous short films for MGM. Committed suicide in 1979.

Ned Sparks. Crabby-voiced character comic in RKO films. Died in 1957.

Robert Strauss. Character actor for Jerry Lewis in many films, for Mickey Rooney in *The Atomic Kid*, and performer in several movies. Died in 1975.

Frank Sully. Character actor in Columbia comedies of mid- to late forties and fifties. Died in 1976.

Slim Summerville. Original Keystone Cop, character actor in silents and talkies. Died in 1946.

Mack Swain. Foil in Chaplin's Keystones and Essanays, as well as later features like *The Gold Rush*. Appeared in Sennett's *Ambrose* series, among others. Died in 1935.

Thelma Todd. Actress in Roach comedies with Laurel and Hardy, Charley Chase, and her own series opposite Zasu Pitts and later Patsy Kelly. Found murdered in 1935.

Emerson Treacy. Character actor at Roach. Died in 1967.

John Tyrell. Character actor in Columbia comedies. Died in 1949.

Elvia Ullman. Comic foil for Abbott and Costello on radio and in many films. Did extensive TV work and also did movies with Jerry Lewis, Danny Kaye, others. Another favorite.

Vera Vague (Barbara Jo Allen). Star of comedy short subject series at Columbia. Died in 1974.

Dick Van Dyke. Predominantly a TV comic, but did some movies.

Phil Van Zandt. Character actor at Columbia from thirties through fifties. Did TV also. Committed suicide in 1958.

Lupe Velez. Fiery Mexican actress. Appeared with Laurel and Hardy and Jimmy Durante in *MGM's Hollywood Party*, also starred in *Mexican Spitfire* series at RKO with Leon Errol. Committed suicide while pregnant in 1944.

Harry Von Zell. TV and radio announcer. Did some screen work at Columbia. Died in 1982.

Doodles Weaver. Character in many films, member of Spike Jones Band. Committed suicide in 1983.

Billy West. Chaplin imitator for Christie studios. Died in 1975.

Robin Williams. Standup comic, "Mork" on TV's "Mork and Mindy" show. Did some minor screen work, succeeding better in dramatic roles (e.g. *Moscow on the Hudson*).

Leo Willis. Tough heavy in Roach films. Also did silent drama. Died in 1952.

Ed Wynn. Favorite character actor in hundreds of films. Died in 1966.

Keenan Wynn. Son of Ed, did many movies and television shows, both comedy and drama.

Rudy "Duke" York. Heavy in some Columbia comedies. Committed suicide in 1952.

Tammany Young. W.C. Fields' sidekick in many Paramount films. Died: 1936.

Appendix B
Bibliography

Anobile, Richard J. *The Marx Brothers Scrapbook*. New York: Darien House, 1973.

Barr, Charles. *Laurel & Hardy*. London, England: Movie Magazine Limited, 1967.

Durgnat, Raymond. *The Crazy Mirror*. New York: Dell, 1969.

Everson, William K. *American Silent Screen*. New York: Oxford University Press, 1980.

Everson, William K. *The Art of W.C. Fields*. New York: Bobbs-Merrill, 1967.

Everson, William K. *The Films of Laurel & Hardy*. Secaucus, NJ: Citadel, 1967.

Forrester Jeffrey. *The Stooge Chronicles*. Chicago: Triumvirate, 1981.

Howard, Moe. *Moe Howard and the Three Stooges*. Secaucus, NJ: Citadel, 1977.

Lahue, Karlton and Samuel Gill. *Clown Princes & Court Jesters*. Cranbury, NJ: A.S. Barnes, 1970.

Lenburg, Jeff, Greg Lenburg, Joan Howard Maurer. *The Three Stooges Scrapbook*. Secaucus, NJ: Citadel, 1982.

Maddock, Brent. *The Films of Jacques Tati*. Metuchen, NJ: Scarecrow, 1973.

Maltin, Leonard. *The Great Movie Comedians*. New York: Crown, 1978.

Maltin, Leonard. *The Great Movie Shorts*. New York: Crown, 1972.

Mast, Gerald. *The Comic Mind*. New York: Bobbs-Merrill, 1973.

McCabe, John. *Mr. Laurel and Mr. Hardy*. New York: Doubleday, 1961.

McCaffery, Donald. *The Golden Age of Sound Comedy*. New York: A.S. Barnes, 1973.

Mulholland, Jim. *The Abbott & Costello Book*. New York: Popular Library, 1975.

Thomas, Bob. *Bud & Lou*. New York: J.B. Lippincott, 1977.

Index

239